DENMAN C

CONTEMPORARY COOKERY

Victor Ceserani

Ronald Kinton

David Foskett

CONTEMPORARY COOKERY

Victor Ceserani
MBE, MBA, FHCIMA
*Formerly Head of
The School of Hotel Keeping and Catering,
Ealing College of Higher Education*

Ronald Kinton
BEd (Hons), FHCIMA
*Formerly of
Garnett College, College of Education for Teachers
in Further and Higher Education*

David Foskett
BEd (Hons), MHCIMA
*Principal Lecturer,
The School of Hotel Keeping and Catering,
Ealing College of Higher Education*

Edward Arnold
A division of Hodder & Stoughton
LONDON   BALTIMORE   MELBOURNE   AUCKLAND

© 1988 Victor Ceserani, Ronald Kinton and David Foskett

First published in Great Britain 1988

British Library Cataloguing in Publication Data

Ceserani, Victor
  Contemporary cookery.
  1. Food – Recipes
  I. Title II. Kinton, Ronald III. Foskett, David
  641.5

  ISBN 0–7131–7752–7

Typeset in 11/12pt Plantin
Printed and bound in Great Britain for Edward Arnold, the educational,
academic and medical publishing division of Hodder & Stoughton
Limited, 41 Bedford Square, London WC1B 3DQ by
Richard Clay Ltd, Bungay, Suffolk

Contents

Introduction

The aim of this book is to extend the repertoire of catering students, using the fundamental knowledge, experience and skills acquired from using *Practical Cookery* or other basic cookery books. The book will also assist those who cook in the industry and in the home.

This aim should be achieved by:

a) developing individual ability
b) using a wider variety of ingredients
c) developing imagination and creativity
d) producing original and adapted dishes
e) broadening awareness of classical, traditional, ethnic and vegetarian recipes
f) considering original recipes of respected British chefs.

When this is achieved the breadth of knowledge of contemporary cookery practice will be increased and the ability to construct more varied and interesting menus should follow.

Where appropriate we suggest variations for recipes, with the intention of stimulating further ways of adapting and creating different dishes.

One important skill for a good chef or cook is adaptability. This is essential when producing dishes which at first glance appear impractical and expensive. By using common sense and with practical application almost all recipes can be adapted to meet budgetary or any other restrictions.

Many Continental chefs have developed fresh culinary trends and we would recommend the following books: *The New Cuisine* Paul Bocuse, *Cuisine of the Sun* Roger Vergé, *French Regional Cookery* Anne William, *Nouvelle Cuisine* Troisgros Brothers, *New Classic Cuisine* Roux Brothers, *Cuisine Gourmande* Michel Guèrand, *Master Chefs of France Book*.

We consider that students taking all courses which include practical cookery or gastronomy will find this book helpful after acquiring the basic culinary knowledge and skills. The content is not restricted to a specific examination syllabus but could be used by those taking intermediate or advanced City and Guilds courses 706/2, 706/3; BTEC Certificate and Diploma and Higher Certificate and Higher Diploma; and the examinations of the Hotel, Catering and Institutional Management Association. We suggest the book could be useful for those involved in Open Learning, Caterbase and the NCVQ (National Council for Vocational Qualifications).

Over the past two decades a number of British chefs have emerged who have developed individual styles of cooking and serving food. Their success has led to many now being in charge of their own kitchens, having established enviable reputations not only for their food but as personalities within the community. It is to mark this achievement that we include a chapter of British dishes, the recipes for which were all willingly contributed by more than thirty of the top chefs in the UK.

We hope that these examples may stimulate young men and women in training, either at college or in industry, to emulate these men who make such a sound contribution to the prestige and respect of the British chef.

Healthy eating

For those wishing to reduce fat and cholesterol levels in the diet the following suggestions may be useful.

Consideration where suitable can be given to using:

a) polyunsaturated fats and oils in place of animal fats
b) the minimum of salt or low-sodium salt
c) wholemeal flour in place of, or partly in place of, white flour
d) natural yoghurt, quark, crème frais or fromage frais (all low fat) in place of cream
e) skimmed milk, or semi-skimmed, instead of full cream milk
f) minimum use of sugar and use of unrefined sugar in place of white sugar or, in some cases, reduced calorie sweeteners
g) low-fat cheese instead of full-fat cheese.

Many of the recipes in this book have been adjusted, incorporating some of these principles as alternatives to be used as and when required. Where we state oil, sunflower oil is recommended other than for fierce heat, when olive oil is more suitable. When yoghurt is stated we mean natural yoghurt with a low-fat content.

The following table is an example of how traditional recipe ingredients may be replaced by healthier ones.

Instead of	Choose
Whole milk	Skimmed milk (or semi-skimmed)
Butter or hard margarine	Polyunsaturated margarine
Lard, hard vegetable fats	Pure vegetable oils, e.g. corn oil, sunflower oil
Full-fat cheeses e.g. cheddar	Low-fat cheeses, e.g. low-fat cheddar has half the fat
Fatty meats	Lean meat (smaller portion) or chicken or fish
Cream	Plain yoghurt, quark

A number of non-dairy creamers are available now. Some are produced specifically for pastry work and — being sweetened — are unsuitable for savoury recipes. However, there are also various unsweetened products which may be used in place of fresh cream for soups, sauces etc. It is important to determine the heat stability of these products before use, i.e. by testing whether they will withstand boiling without detriment to the product.

The following chart indicates which cooking oils, fats and margarines are healthiest, i.e. those with the smallest percentage of saturated fats.

Oil/fat	Saturated	Mono-unsaturated	Poly-unsaturated
	%	%	%
Coconut oil	85	7	2
Butter	60	32	3
Palm oil	45	42	8
Lard	43	42	9
Beef dripping	40	49	4
Margarine, hard (vegetable oil only)	37	47	12
Margarine, hard (mixed oils)	37	43	17
Margarine, soft	32	42	22
Margarine, soft (mixed oils)	30	45	19
Low-fat spread	27	38	30
Margarine, polyunsaturated	24	22	54
Ground nut oil	19	48	28
Maize oil	16	29	49
Wheatgerm oil	14	11	45
Soya bean oil	14	24	57
Olive oil	14	70	11
Sunflower seed oil	13	32	50
Safflower seed oil	10	13	72
Rape seed oil	7	64	32

Measurement tables and oven temperatures

Approximate equivalents of weights and measures

Imperial weight	Metric weight	Imperial measure	Metric measure
¼ oz	5 g		5 ml
½ oz	10 g		10 ml
1 oz	25 g	1 fl oz	25 ml
2 oz	50 g	2 fl oz	50 ml
2½ oz	60 g	2½ fl oz (⅛ pt)	60 ml
3 oz	75 g	3 fl oz	75 ml
4 oz (¼ lb)	100 g	4 fl oz	100 ml
5 oz	125 g	5 fl oz (¼ pt)	125 ml
6 oz	150 g	6 fl oz	150 ml
7 oz	175 g	7 fl oz	175 ml
8 oz (½ lb)	200 g	8 fl oz	200 ml
9 oz	225 g	9 fl oz	225 ml
10 oz	250 g	10 fl oz (½ pt)	250 ml (¼ litre)
11 oz	275 g	11 fl oz	275 ml
12 oz	300 g	12 fl oz	300 ml
13 oz	325 g	13 fl oz	325 ml
14 oz	350 g	14 fl oz	350 ml
15 oz	375 g	15 fl oz (¾ pt)	375 ml
16 oz (1 lb)	400 g	16 fl oz	400 ml
		20 fl oz (1 pt)	500 ml (½ litre)
		2 pt (1 qt)	1000 ml (1 litre)

Imperial	Metric	Imperial	Metric
¼ in	½ cm	4 in	10 cm
½ in	1 cm	5 in	12 cm
1 in	2 cm	6 in	15 cm
1½ in	4 cm	6½ in	16 cm
2 in	5 cm	7 in	18 cm
2½ in	6 cm	12 in	30 cm
3 in	8 cm	18 in	45 cm

Oven temperatures

	Celsius	Regulo	Fahrenheit
Cool	110	¼	225
	130	½	250
	140	1	275
	150	2	300
	160	3	325
Moderate	180	4	350
	190	5	375
	200	6	400
Hot	220	7	425
	230	8	450
Very hot	250	9	500

1

Hors-d'oeuvre and salads

See Also Chapter 10 British dishes
  Chapter 11 Ethnic recipes

As almost any item of food can be used, the ingenuity and creativity of the
chef will ensure that their culinary and artistic skills are exploited to the
full in the making of hors-d'oeuvre and salads.

Ingredients

The following are just some of the ingredients which can be used.

Leaves

round lettuce
cos (romaine) lettuce
iceberg lettuce
oak leaf lettuce
radicchio
curly endive
chicory
cress
watercress

corn salad (lamb's lettuce)
sorrel
dandelion
escarole (broad-leafed endive,
  Batavian lettuce)
nasturtium
red cabbage
white cabbage
spinach
Chinese leaves

Vegetables (raw)

celery
carrots
onions
spring onions
pimentos

radishes
tomatoes
mushrooms
cucumber

Vegetables (cooked)

sweetcorn
baby sweetcorn
beetroot
potatoes
carrots
turnips

peas
beans–French, broad, runner
artichokes
Jerusalem artichokes
asparagus
broccoli

Herbs

chives
parsley
basil
mint
coriander leaves
fennel leaves
dill

thyme
lovage
sweet cicely
marjoram
tarragon
bay leaves
chervil

Pulses

black-eyed beans

chick peas

flageolets
borlotti beans
haricot beans

mung beans
red kidney beans

Pasta
macaroni, spaghetti etc.

noodles

Fruits
grapefruit
orange
apples
grapes
dates
mango
avocado

guava
kiwi
bananas
melon
pineapples
cherries

Nuts
walnuts
hazelnuts
almonds

peanuts
Brazil nuts

Miscellaneous
hard-boiled eggs
cheese
rice
poppyseeds
sunflower seeds
seasame seeds

olives
gherkins
capers
mung bean sprouts
bamboo shoots
water chestnuts

Meats
cooked meats–beef/lamb/pork
sausages
chicken
turkey

duck
ham
bacon
tongue

Fish
anchovies
tuna
salmon
sardines
white fish
mackerel
herring

crab
lobster
shrimps
prawns
mussels
cockles

Salad dressings

Vinaigrette and mayonnaise are used extensively for salads, but sour cream, tofu and yoghurt may also be used (see overleaf).

Oils	*Vinegars*	*Vinaigrettes*
olive	cider	With the addition of:
corn	red wine	garlic
sunflower	white wine	capers
peanut	malt	curry paste
seasame	herb	eggs
safflower	lemon	blue cheese etc.
walnut	raspberry etc.	

Seasonings	*Herbs*	*Mayonnaise*
English mustard	chervil	with the addition of:
French mustard	tarragon	tomato ketchup
Dijon mustard	thyme	horseradish
German mustard	mint	lemon juice
salt	basil	herbs
pepper	marjoram	capers
spices etc.	coriander	gherkins
	fennel	curry powder etc.
	dill etc.	

Also
fresh cream with	smetana
lemon or lime juice	crème frais
tofu	quark
yoghurt	

1   Garlic-flavoured mayonnaise   *4 portions*

2 egg yolks
2 teaspns vinegar or lemon or lime juice
salt, ground white pepper
⅛ teaspn English mustard
2 cloves of garlic (juice or chopped)
250 ml   ½ pt   olive oil or vegetable oil
1 teaspn boiling water

1 Place the yolks, vinegar, seasoning and garlic in a bowl and mix well.
2 Gradually pour on the oil very slowly, whisking continuously.
3 Add the boiling water, whisking well.
4 Correct the seasoning.

Other suggested additions:
a)   tomato ketchup (to taste)
b)   anchovy essence (to taste)
c)   tomato and anchovy essence
d)   horseradish, finely grated

2 Tofu salad dressing

This soya bean curd can be used as a salad dressing. As tofu is tasteless it can be flavoured with garlic, lemon, mint etc. Tofu has to be mixed to a creamy consistency before use with skimmed milk, lemon juice etc.
Quark, crème frais, fromage frais and yoghurt may also be used.

3 Smoked salmon, avocado and walnut salad   *4 portions*

100 g	4 oz	smoked salmon
		2 avocado pears
50 g	2 oz	walnuts
		fennel or parsley
		vinaigrette
		radicchio
		curly endive

1 Cut the smoked salmon in strips and neatly dice the peeled avocado.
2 Carefully mix together with the walnuts, chopped fennel or parsley and vinaigrette.
3 Neatly pile on a base of radicchio and curly endive leaves.

Note Flaked cooked fresh salmon or flaked smoked mackerel can be used to create a variation of this salad.

4 Herring and citrus salad   *4 portions*

		4 herring fillets
		2 limes
		1 lemon
200 g	8 oz	potato
		vinaigrette (using lime and lemon juice)
		chopped dill
		lamb's lettuce
		4 gherkins

1 Cut the filleted and skinned herring into strips and marinade in the juice of the limes and lemon for approx. 2 hours.
2 Mix with the diced cooked potato and vinaigrette.
3 Arrange on a bed of lamb's lettuce, sprinkle with chopped dill and decorate with fans of gherkin.

Note In place of raw herring, rollmops or soused herring (using lime and lemon in place of vinegar) can be used. If lamb's lettuce is not available other lettuce can be substituted.

5   **Marina salad**   *4 portions*

100 g	4 oz	prawns } cooked and peeled
100 g	3 oz	shrimps } cooked and peeled
		dry white wine
		4 eggs, hard boiled
		4 tomatoes, skinned
		½ cucumber, diced
		yoghurt
		1 bunch watercress
		1 punnet mustard and cress
		parsley, chervil or chives

1 Marinade the prawns and shrimps in the wine for approx. 2 hours.
2 Retain 2 eggs and 2 tomatoes for garnish.
3 Lightly mix the cucumber, 2 diced tomatoes and 2 diced hard-boiled eggs with the shellfish.
4 Season and bind with yoghurt.
5 Arrange on a bed of watercress and mustard and cress, and decorate with quarters of hard-boiled eggs and skinned tomatoes cut in quarters.
6 Finish with chopped parsley.

Note Any shellfish or flaked cooked white fish could be used, and cider vinegar or wine vinegar in place of white wine. Mayonnaise or vinaigrette are alternatives to yoghurt.

6   **Herring, apple and potato salad**   *Hareng Livonienne*

4 portions

		2 smoked herrings
100 g	4 oz	cooked potato
100 g	4 oz	eating apple
		chopped parsley, chervil and fennel
		vinaigrette

1 Fillet and skin the herrings and cut the flesh into dice.
2 Mix with the diced potato and diced apple.
3 Add the herbs and vinaigrette. Correct seasoning.

Note As a variation smoked mackerel, eel or trout could be used.

7   **Salmon and tomato salad**   *4 portions*

200 g	8 oz	salmon or other very fresh white fish
		juice of 1 lemon or lime
50 g	2 oz	shallots
		chopped basil, chervil or parsley
25 g	1 oz	tofu
		seasoning
		8 skinned tomatoes, deseeded and lids removed

1 Remove the bones and skin from the fish.
2 Chop the fish and mix with half the lemon juice and allow to stand for 20 minutes.
3 Finely chop the shallots, mix with the rest of the lemon juice, the herbs and the tofu, and beat well.
4 Add the drained fish, season and use to fill the tomato shells.

Note The fish must be very fresh as it is eaten raw. However, as an alternative, the fish may be cooked.

8   Smoked fish platter   *4 portions*

		2 fillets of smoked mackerel
		1 fillet of smoked trout
200 g	8 oz	smoked eel
100 g	4 oz	smoked salmon
		1 lemon
60 ml	⅛ pt	mayonnaise with horseradish

1 Carefully remove the skin from the mackerel, trout and eel fillets, and divide into four pieces.
2 Arrange with a cornet of salmon on each plate.
3 Garnish with quarter of lemon.
4 Serve separately, mayonnaise sauce containing finely grated horseradish.

9   Shellfish platter

A selection of shellfish, e.g. lobster, crab, prawns and shrimps, neatly arranged and garnished with heart of lettuce, tomato quarters, and quarters of hard-boiled eggs; served with mayonnaise sauce separately.

10   Beef salad with peas and carrots   *4 portions*

200 g	8 oz	cooked beef
125 ml	¼ pt	cider vinegar
		salt, pepper
200 g	8 oz	mange-tout (cooked or raw)
200 g	8 oz	carrots (cooked or raw)
		olive oil
50 g	2 oz	chives

1 Cut the lean beef in julienne and marinate in sufficient cider vinegar to just cover for 2 hours. Drain off the vinegar.
2 Season, and prior to serving add the julienne of mange-tout and carrots.
3 Mix lightly together with a little oil and chopped chives.

Note Any cooked meat or poultry can be used in place of beef.

11   Chicken, ham, tongue and cheese salad   *4 portions*

200 g	8 oz	cooked chicken
100 g	4 oz	cooked ham
100 g	4 oz	cooked tongue
100 g	4 oz	cheese (emmental or gruyèrè)
		1 lettuce
		2 tomatoes (skinned if desired)
		2 hard-boiled eggs
125 ml	¼ pt	salad dressing

1 Cut the chicken, ham, tongue and cheese in julienne.
2 Arrange neatly on the bed of lettuce garnished with quarters of tomato and egg.   .
3 Serve a salad dressing or mayonnaise separately.

Note As a variation, the meat and cheese can be mixed with salad dressing and garnished with, for example, olives, capers, gherkins chopped parsley, watercress.
   Instead of using chicken, salami or other similar sausage could be used.

12   Salad of chicken curry   *4 portions*

200 g	8 oz	cooked chicken
50 g	2 oz	finely chopped onion
		1 eating apple, diced (peeled if required)
100 g	4 oz	celery, diced
50 g	2 oz	walnut pieces
125 ml	¼ pt	mayonnaise blended with curry paste to taste

1 Cut the chicken into neat dice and mix with the onion, apple, celery and walnuts.
2 Bind with the curried mayonnaise.

Note Turkey can be used in place of chicken and garnished with lemon segments, desiccated coconut and sultanas. Left-over curried chicken is ideal for this dish.
   In place of curry paste, curry sauce can also be used.

13   Avocado stuffed with cream cheese, walnuts and chives   *4 portions*

		2 avocados
		1 lemon
100 g	4 oz	cream cheese
		mayonnaise
50 g	2 oz	chives
50 g	2 oz	walnuts

1 Halve and remove the stone from the avocados.
2 Scoop out some of the flesh to slightly enlarge the cavity and sprinkle with lemon juice.
3 Mix this pulp with the cream cheese, mayonnaise, chopped chives and nuts, and season.
4 Use to fill the avocado halves and dress on lettuce leaves.

Note Fillings can include shellfish, cheese and ham, tuna fish etc.

14   Avocado with kiwi fruit   *4 portions*

2 avocados
2 kiwi fruits
radicchio
salad dressing

1 Peel, halve and remove the stones from the avocados.
2 Peel the kiwi fruit and cut in slices crosswise.
3 Slice the avocado crosswise and arrange with the kiwi fruit on a bed of radicchio.
4 Serve a salad dressing as desired, e.g. lemon vinaigrette, sour cream or mayonnaise.

Note Avocado pears must be ripe and need to be handled with care. When diced they may be lightly mixed with single or mixed items such as grapes, apples, nuts, prawns, cauliflower, ham, cheese, chicken etc.

15   Avocado mousse   *4 portions*

		1 large avocado
		juice of 1 lemon
		seasoning
60 ml	⅛ pt	mayonnaise
60 ml	⅛ pt	aspic jelly *or*
		1 or 2 sheets gelatine
60 ml	⅛ pt	double cream or unsweetened vegetable creamer
		salad vegetables for garnish

1 Cut the avocado in half, remove the stone and peel.
2 Pass through a sieve or liquidise in a food processor.
3 Add the lemon juice and seasoning and place in a bowl.
4 Stir in the mayonnaise and aspic jelly or the soaked, melted gelatine.
5 Place on ice and stir until setting point, then carefully fold in the beaten cream.
6 Pour into individual china serving dishes or dariole moulds.
7 When set, unmould the darioles onto plates and decorate with lettuce, tomatoes, radish and cucumber.

16   Red and white coleslaw

4 portions

400 g	8 oz	red cabbage
200 g	4 oz	white cabbage
		seasoning
		yoghurt

1 Finely shred the red and white cabbage; wash and drain.
2 Season and bind with yoghurt.

Note Variations can include the addition of shredded onion, julienne of pimento, shredded carrots, chopped chives or apple etc.
   Mayonnaise or vinaigrette can be used in place of yoghurt.

17   Chinese cabbage salad

4 portions

		1 Chinese cabbage
200 g	4 oz	onion
		soy sauce, 1 part ⎫
		oil, 8 parts ⎬ vinaigrette
		vinegar, 2 parts ⎭

1 Shred the cabbage and onion; season slightly.
2 Mix with the vinaigrette.

Note Additions can include celery, cucumber, water chestnuts, bamboo shoots. Sesame seeds and poppy seeds also give variety to this salad.

18   Pickled red cabbage

4 portions

400 g	1 lb	red cabbage
		vinegar
10 g	½ oz	castor sugar
100 g	4 oz	eating apple
		salt and pepper

1 Finely shred the cabbage, just cover with vinegar and sugar and allow to stand for approx. 4 hours.
2 Drain the cabbage and add a julienne of apples, salt and pepper.

Note Firm apples such as russets or coxes are suitable; soft eating apples break up. The apples may be peeled if required.

19   Minted carrot salad   *4 portions*

400 g   1 lb   carrots
                mint
                1 lemon
                1–2 tablespoons oil
                seasoning

1 Finely shred or grate the carrots.
2 Mix with the lemon juice, oil and chopped mint and season.

Note Cooked small carrots with a sprig of mint can be used in place of
raw carrots, and orange juice can be used instead of lemon juice.

20   Bean sprout salad   *4 portions*

400 g   1 lb   fresh bean sprouts
                ¼ teaspoon chilli powder
                2 tablespns cider vinegar
                1 tablespn soy sauce
                ½ tablespn freshly chopped coriander
                1 clove garlic, chopped or juiced
                salt

1 Trim both ends of the sprouts.
2 Mix well with the remaining ingredients.
3 Leave for approx. 2 hours, turning occasionally.
4 Drain off the liquid and serve.

21   Palm hearts salad   *4 portions*

400 g   1 lb   tinned palm hearts
                1 dessertspn lime or lemon juice ⎫
                1 tspn French mustard   ⎬ dressing
                salt and mill pepper   ⎪
                4 dessertspns oil   ⎭

1 Drain palm hearts thoroughly and cut into even-shaped pieces.
2 Mix dressing ingredients, pour over palm hearts, toss well and serve.

22   Fennel, Greek style

Fenouil à la grecque   *4 portions*

		2 fennel bulbs	
250 ml	½ pt	water	
60 ml	⅛ pt	olive oil	
		juice of 1 lemon	
		½ bayleaf	
		sprig of thyme	cooking liquid
		6 peppercorns	
		6 coriander seeds	
		salt	

1 Trim and cut each fennel bulb into six or eight pieces.
2 Add the fennel to the cooking liquid; simmer until just cooked and slightly crisp.
3 Correct the seasoning and serve cold with the unstrained liquid.

23   Rice salad with apples

4 portions

100 g	4 oz	rice, cooked	
100 g	4 oz	apples, diced	
60 ml	⅛ pt	cream	mixed together
		seasoning	
		lemon juice	

Note In place of cream, yoghurt or vinaigrette may be used. Pineapple, pimento, onions or chives, cucumber, tomatoes, peas, carrots, chicken, tunny fish, eggs etc. can be used in place of, or as well as, apples.

24   Rice, tomato and pepper salad   *Salade andalousian*

4 portions

50 g	2 oz	tomatoes, skinned, deseeded and diced
50 g	2 oz	red peppers in julienne
100 g	4 oz	cooked rice
		1 clove garlic, crushed and chopped
25 g	1 oz	chopped onion
		chopped basil, tarragon or parsley
		vinaigrette

Mix all the ingredients together lightly. If required, more garlic can be added.

25   Watercress and potato salad

4 portions

100 g	8 oz	potatoes, cooked
60 ml	⅛ pt	vinaigrette
		1 bunch watercress
		2 eggs, hard boiled
		chopped parsley, mint or chervil

1 Slice the cooked potatoes (preferably new potatoes) whilst still warm and add vinaigrette; correct seasoning.
2 When cold, mix lightly and place on the bed of watercress.
3 Sprinkle chopped hard-boiled egg and parsley onto the potatoes.

26   Rice, chicken and pimento salad   *4 portions*

50 g	2 oz	cooked chicken
50 g	2 oz	pimento
25 g	1 oz	peas, cooked
100 g	4 oz	rice, cooked
		vinaigrette ⎱
		tarragon ⎰ mixed together
		1 teaspn French mustard

1 Cut the chicken and pimento into paysanne or dice.
2 Mix together and add the tarragon vinaigrette; correct seasoning.

27   Rice, anchovy and vegetable salad   *4 portions*

50 g	2 oz	tomatoes, skinned, deseeded and diced
50 g	2 oz	red and green pimentos, diced
50 g	2 oz	French beans, cooked and diced
100 g	4 oz	cooked rice
		1 clove garlic, chopped and crushed
		4 anchovy fillets, diced
		vinaigrette

Mix all ingredients together and correct seasoning.

28   Fruit and nut salad   *4 portions*

		4 red eating apples
5 oz	2 oz	banana, diced
50 g	2 oz	pineapple, diced
25 g	1 oz	walnuts
		I lemon
		salt
60 ml	⅛ pt	cream or natural yoghurt
		1 lettuce

1 Slice off the stalk end of the top of each apple to act as a lid.
2 With a parisienne cutter remove the centre, leaving only a thin layer by the skin. Rub the inside with lemon juice.
3 Mix the neatly diced apple flesh, banana, pineapple and walnuts together with lemon juice.
4 Add a little salt and cream to bind, refill the apples and replace the lid.

5 Serve with the heart of lettuce cut into quarters.

Note Variations can include fruits such as redcurrants, grapes etc. and peeled almonds or mixed nuts.

29   Tropical salad   *4 portions*

½ melon (depending on type and size)
1 avocado, skinned, stoned and diced
1 kiwi fruit, peeled and sliced
juice of 1 lemon
2 tablespns olive or vegetable oil
salt and pepper
mint
Chinese leaves

1 Remove the skin and seeds from the melon and dice.
2 Place with the avocado and kiwi fruit.
3 Add the lemon juice and carefully mix with the oil, seasoning and chopped mint.
4 Dress on a bed of Chinese leaves.

Note Other fruits, such as fresh figs and paw paw, can also be used. In place of oil, bind with tofu, natural yoghurt or mayonnaise. If tofu is used it must be mixed to a creamy consistency with skimmed milk or lemon juice.

30   Salami and vegetable salad   *4 portions*

50 g	2 oz	celeriac
50 g	2 oz	carrots
25 g	1 oz	salami, diced
25 g	1 oz	peas, cooked
60 ml	⅛ pt	mayonnaise
		salt and pepper
		8 slices salami
		4 anchovy fillets

1 Cut the raw celeriac and carrots into fine julienne.
2 Mix with the diced salami, peas and mayonnaise.
3 Season and decorate with the slices of salami and anchovy fillets.

31 Lamb's lettuce, beetroot and celery salad *Salade Lorette*

4 portions

100 g	4 oz	cooked beetroot in batons
100 g	4 oz	raw celery or celeriac in julienne
		lamb's lettuce
		vinaigrette

Dress the three ingredients separately and serve vinaigrette.

32 Egg and vegetable salad

4 portions

		1 cos lettuce
50 g	2 oz	peas, cooked
50 g	2 oz	French beans, cooked
		2 hard-boiled eggs
100 g	4 oz	tomatoes
60 ml	⅛ pt	mayonnaise with Worcester sauce

1 Shred the lettuce.
2 Arrange the peas and beans neatly on the lettuce.
3 Decorate with quarters of egg and tomato. Serve the mayonnaise separately.

Note As a variation, bind the vegetables and egg with the mayonnaise and serve on the cos lettuce leaves.

33 Apple, banana and celery salad

4 portions

		4 apples, diced
		2 bananas, sliced
200 g	8 oz	celery, diced
		mayonnaise
		few drops of lemon juice

Mix all the ingredients together. Serve on a bed of lettuce, curly endive or radicchio.

34 Salmon marinaded in dill

Gravlax *8 portions*

1½ kg	3 lb	middle-cut, fresh, descaled salmon
		1 bunch dill, washed and chopped
50 g	2 oz	castor sugar
50 g	2 oz	salt
		2 tablespns peppercorns, crushed

1 Cut the salmon lengthwise and remove all the bones.
2 Place one half, skin-side down, in a deep dish.
3 Add the dill, sugar, salt and peppercorns.
4 Cover with the other piece of salmon, skin-side up.
5 Cover with foil and lay a tray or dish on top, or try and evenly
   distribute weights on the foil.
6 Refrigerate for 48 hours, turning the fish every 12 hours and basting
   with the liquid produced by the ingredients. Separate the halves of
   salmon and baste between them also.
7 Replace the foil, tray and weights between basting.
8 Lift the fish from the marinade, remove the dill and seasoning.
9 Place the halves of salmon on a board, skin-side down.
10 Slice thinly, detaching the slice from the skin.
11 Garnish gravlax with lemon and serve with mustard and dill sauce.

Mustard and dill sauce

125 ml	¾ pt	mayonnaise
60 ml	⅛ pt	white wine
12 g	½ oz	castor sugar
		1 dessertspn coarse mustard
		½ teaspn fresh chopped dill
		salt and pepper

1 Mix into the mayonnaise the rest of the ingredients; correct the
   seasoning with salt and pepper.

Note There are many variations to this recipe: 60 ml (⅛ pt) double cream
or natural yoghurt may be added; alternatively a French dressing base may
be used in place of mayonnaise.

35   Tomatoes stuffed with tunny fish, egg and herbs
Tomate monégasque   *4 portions*

		4 or 8 tomatoes, depending on size (skinned if required)
		salt and pepper
100 g	4 oz	tunny fish
		2 eggs, hard-boiled
25 g	1 oz	onion, diced
		chopped parsley, tarragon, and chervil
		mayonnaise

1 Slice the tops of the tomatoes to form a lid.
2 Remove the seeds from the inside, season.
3 Fill with a mixture of tunny fish, chopped hard-boiled egg, onion and
   herbs, bound with mayonnaise.
4 Replace the lid.

Note A variety of fillings can be used, for example: white fish with capers and gherkins; smoked salmon and avocado; mixed vegetables in vinaigrette; chicken and ham in sour cream; mushrooms and peas in yoghurt; sweetcorn, rice and flageolet beans etc.

Cucumber can also be stuffed with such fillings. The cucumber should be cut in 5 cm (2 in.) lengths, the centres removed with a parisienne cutter, the shells blanched if required and then stuffed with the required filling.

Cold preparations and buffet items

See also Chapter 10 British dishes

1 Notes on the use of aspic jelly and chaudfroid

Aspic jelly is produced from meat stock with the addition of gelatine. Vegetarian aspic jelly is produced from vegetable stock with the addition of agar-agar as a setting agent.

Great care must be taken when using aspic jelly as it is an ideal medium for the growth of micro-organisms. Therefore the following procedures should be observed:

1 Always use fresh aspic, *bring to the boil* and simmer for 10 mins. Cool quickly and use sparingly.
2 Avoid using warm aspic, especially over long periods.
3 Do not store aspic for long periods at room temperature.
4 If required for further use, chill rapidly and store in the refrigerator.
5 If stored in refrigerator, simmer for 10 mins before further use. Discard after 24 hours storage.
6 Once a dish has been glazed with aspic, keep refrigerated and consume within 8 hours.
7 It is advisable, if possible, to make only the quantity required for use and so avoid storage. Where possible, display in refrigerated units.

Uses
• As a glaze for cold preparations
• To prevent food from losing moisture
• As a garnish for certain dishes
• To aid presentation and appearance

2 Points to observe when using aspic jelly or chaudfroid

1 Always work with one basin of aspic at coating consistency and another of hot jelly, so that when the jelly being used becomes too thick a little hot may be added to bring it back to coating consistency. The same applies when using fairly large quantities of chaudfroid.
2 It is best to let jelly set naturally. It remains at coating consistency much longer than when 'forced' on ice because the container is the temperature of the jelly, whereas if it has been on ice it will continue to reduce the temperature of the jelly.

3 Always work with two trays: one to glaze on and one for any surplus jelly or sauce to drip on while your work is setting in the fridge.

4 Use plenty of sauce or jelly so that the object to be coated may be completely covered in one steady sweep of the ladle. For larger objects, such as galantines or tongues, aim first at the top of the curve nearest to you so that the sauce or jelly runs both forwards and backwards. This should be followed immediately by two or more ladles in quick succession, so that a smooth surface completely free of ridges is formed. When saucing whole poultry, start by coating the tail end under the legs, from the rear, then coat the rest of the bird from the front. Two or even three coats of chaudfroid will be needed and each coat should be allowed to set in the fridge before applying the next, unless you are already working in a very cold temperature.

5 All decorations should be fastened in place with a little jelly so that they are not washed off when the final glaze of jelly is applied.

6 To chemise or glaze a dish it is best to use hot jelly. This reduces the risk of forming bubbles, which should be avoided at all times as they detract from the appearance of the dish. Allow to set on a level surface, preferably in a refrigerator. If the dish is such that it is necessary to apply the jelly after it has been dressed, the jelly must be applied carefully and quickly – almost at setting point.

7 When the weather is warm, or if the jelly is likely to be in a warm room for some time, it should have extra gelatine added. Jelly for chopping or cutting should also be firmer.

3   Materials which may be used for decorating

The decoration of various cold dishes provides great scope for the chef's artistic talents, and a wide variety of materials may be used. The designs should be neat and accurately cut; a good effect may be obtained not only by fine intricate designs but also by bold, uncomplicated ideas. In these days, when speed is so important, bold effective designs which can be produced quickly are very necessary; but when the occasion arises, and time permits, a great impression may be made by fine decoration. It is appreciated by the customer if the decoration of a buffet takes its theme from something topical or from the occasion of the party.

Among the materials suitable for decoration, the following are used most often: tomato flesh, with or without skin, pimento, cucumber skin (scraped clean of any adhering flesh), green of leek (blanched), white of egg (which may also be tinted to give a two-tone effect), radishes, carrots, truffle, black and green olives, mint leaves (for lamb), watercress and cressonette, chervil, parsley, and celery leaves.

Materials which have a shiny surface, such as tomato skin or cucumber peel should always be put on shiny side down. All pieces should be dipped in cool jelly before placing in position.

To make pimento easier to work with, and to economise with truffles, make a purée of them, add a little strong jelly and run out thinly on to plates or trays to allow to set.

4   Methods of cutting decorations

The principal tool used is a small sharp knife, preferably with a fine sharp point. If the design is to be floral, care must be taken to make it look natural. It is not necessary to copy exactly a particular type of flower, but take care to avoid obvious faults. Do not mix natural and geometrical designs of flowers, but designs of flowers may have geometrical borders etc. or patterns may be made entirely of geometrical shapes.

Leaves and petals should be natural leaf shape.

Petals may be cut from tomatoes or eggs by cutting round a selected point and continuing all round, thus forming the points for a second line of petals. By cutting in the same way, but with a sawing movement, egg or coloured chaudfroid may be formed into carnation-type petals. Flowers may also be formed by fluting carrots or radishes down the four quarters and then cutting in thin slices.

Squares and triangles or diamonds are cut with a small knife also and may be 'mass produced' by cutting several parallel lines at once. Circles or dots may be cut by using the appropriate sized plain tubes. Fancy cutters of all shapes and sizes are used to form parts of decorative schemes. Large ones make pieces which may be cut into smaller ones.

5   Decoration of whole hams

When the ham is cooked and cold remove the rind and all the brown flesh from the underside. Remove surplus fat from the upperside and scrape the surface with a knife until it is smooth. Place in the refrigerator to get thoroughly cold and firm.

Place on a wire tray and coat with aspic jelly which is almost at setting point. Decorate. Glaze with aspic jelly.

Allow to set thoroughly and place on a ham stand with a paper frill around the bone.

Hams may be coated wtih chaudfroid before decorating.

Two simple methods of preparation where decoration is required are as follows:
1 The ham is trimmed as above then coated in brown breadcrumbs.
2 The ham is parboiled, skinned, studded with cloves, dusted with brown sugar, baked and glazed.

6   Cold ox tongue   *Langue de boeuf a l'écarlate*

Tongues for cold buffet use should be soaked in brine for 8 to 10 days
before cooking, but this is usually done by the supplier. The tongue is
then placed in plenty of cold water, brought to the boil and simmered for
2½ to 3 hours according to size. When cooked it should be easy to remove
the skin. This should be done while hot, the small bones and gristle
removed and the underneath trimmed. The tongues should be pressed in a
specially constructed box, giving them a 'slipper' shape, and covered with
a damp cloth.

When cold and set, the tongue is coated with a strong red-brown aspic.
If a number of tongues are to be coated they may be dipped in the jelly,
drained on a wire tray and the jelly ladled over, taking care to coat
smoothly. When cold, trim off any 'tears' of jelly and dress on an oval dish
with bunches of watercress under the arch of the tongue.

7   The serving of cold cooked meats

Cold cooked meat should be sliced and arranged neatly on a dish with
finely diced or chopped aspic around the edge and decorated with a bunch
of picked watercress.

A dish or plate of slices of assorted cooked meats is known as *Assiette
anglaise*.

Whole joints, particularly ribs of beef, are often placed on a buffet table.
They should be trimmed if necessary, strings removed and, after glazing
with aspic jelly or brushing with oil, dressed on a dish garnished with
watercress; lettuce leaves and fancy-cut pieces of tomato may also be used
to garnish the dish.

8   The serving of cold roast chicken

If the chicken is to be displayed whole at a buffet it should be brushed
with aspic, or oil. It is then dressed on a suitably-sized oval dish with
watercress and a little diced aspic jelly.

When serving individual portions it is usual to serve either a whole wing
of chicken neatly trimmed, or a half chicken. If a half is served, the leg is
removed, the wing trimmed, and the surplus bone removed from the leg,
which is then placed in the wing (1½ kg/3 lb chickens). Larger chickens
may be cut into four portions, the wings in two lengthwise and the legs in
two joints. Sometimes the chicken may be requested sliced; it is usual to
slice the breast only and then reform it on the dish in its original shape.

9   The serving of cold duck

Use the same methods as for chicken.

10   The serving of cold turkey or goose

For display, cold turkey or goose is brushed with jelly or oil, but otherwise it is normally served sliced, with dark meat under the white, chopped jelly and watercress.

11   The serving of cold game

Larger birds, such as pheasant, are served in halves or quarters; small birds, whole or in halves. The birds are served with watercress and game chips. Most of the smaller birds are served on a fried bread croûton spread with a little of the corresponding paté, farce au gratin, or pâté maison.

12   Preparation of chicken in cold white sauce   *Poularde en chaudfroid*

Select a large well-shaped chicken (poularde); it must not be damaged at all, particularly the legs. Remove all the toes except the longest one on each foot, from these just clip off the claws. In order for the chicken to have a good shape it should be cleaned entirely through the neck. Truss the chicken firmly, as for roasting, so that the wings and back are as flat as possible.

Poach the chicken, taking care not to damage the legs, which may be loosely tied together to prevent splaying. When cooked, remove from the stock and allow to cool. If the legs have pulled down towards the tail during cooking, hang the feet over some suitable object so that the weight of the chicken gradually drops – pulling the legs back into an almost upright position.

When the chicken is cold, carefully remove the suprêmes and pull out the breast bone. The breast is replaced by the required mousse (foie gras, ham, tomato, etc.) and moulded nicely to a rounded shape. Allow to cool thoroughly in a cold room. Meanwhile cut the suprêmes into two or three neat pieces each, maintaining the original shape as much as possible. When dealing with large numbers, whole suprêmes from smaller chickens are often used.

When thoroughly cooled, coat the poularde and suprêmes with chaudfroid, taking care that all is covered completely and smoothly, leaving no 'tears' around the tail of the poularde. Decorate, glaze and dress with the appropriate garnish.

Note For reforming the breast of a poularde a little more gelatine may be required.

13   Cold poached chicken with tomato mousse   *Poularde Rose de Mai*

Poach the chicken prepared as in previous recipe. When cold, skin and remove the suprêmes and breastbone. Reform the breast with a tomato mousse, refrigerate until set and chaudfroid the rest of the carcass. Decorate. The pattern may include truffle and, if possible, roses of tomato or egg. Cut the suprêmes into escalopes and chaudfroid. Decorate to match the poularde and glaze with aspic.
   There are two methods of garnishing:
1 Dress the escalopes on small pastry barquettes filled with tomato mousse.
2 Pipe a little mousse part way or right round each escalope. Dress on a glazed dish, with the poularde on a socle of rice or stearine or semolina (p. 25).

14   Cold poached chicken with ham mousse   *Poularde Rose Marie*

Prepare the poulardes as for Rose de Mai, but use a ham mousse.
   Cover the suprêmes with white chaudfroid. Mould all barquettes or pads of ham mousse to fit each piece of chicken. Mask the poularde with pale pink chaudfroid, decorate and glaze with aspic. (The breast may also be left unsauced for Rose Marie.)
   Dress the poularde on a socle on a glazed dish with the decorated suprêmes on the pads of mousse. Decorate the edge of the dish with croûtons of jelly.

15   Pale pink chaudfroid

This is normal chaudfroid to which a little sweated paprika has been added to give a pale pink colour.

16   Cold wild duck with cherries   *Canard sauvage Montmorency*

The duck is roasted, but kept well underdone. When it is cold remove the breasts and take out the breast bone. Reform the breast with a mousse made from the debris of the flesh, the liver of the duck and foie gras (proceed as for chicken liver mousse, p. 28). Slice the breasts thinly. Arrange a few slices to cover the mousse and arrange the rest neatly on the dish on which the duck is to be served. A border of the mousse may be piped all round the slices and decorated with stoned cherries (tinned or fresh, poached in bordeaux wine). Glaze the dish and the duck with port wine or red wine jelly.

When set, place a croûton of fried bread or a socle on the dish and dress the duck on top. Decorate with tiny points of parsley. Alternatively, the duck may be cut in aiguillettes and coated with brown chaudfroid before reforming on the mousse. The cherries may then be served set in small darioles of aspic.

17   Cold duck with orange   *Caneton a l'orange en aspic*

This may be made using either Aylesbury or wild duck. Prepare the duck in the same way as for Montmorency, a little of the mousse being piped around the slices of meat on the breast only. The remaining slices are arranged neatly on the dish.

Glaze with aspic jelly containing a little Curaçao and fine julienne of blanched orange peel. Decorate the dish with glazed segments of orange, or fancy cut slices, or small darioles of orange. Place a line of chopped jelly around the sliced duck on the dish, and place a bunch of picked watercress at either side of the duck's tail.

18   Brown chaudfroid

This is demi-glace with the addition of gelatine; use 25 g (1 oz) to 500 ml (1 pt) of sauce.

19   Socles

Socles are bases, usually of rice, wax (stearine) or semolina, on which decorated chickens etc. are mounted. Stearine has the advantage that once it has been moulded and carved it can be used many times without deterioration. It may also be remoulded. Stearine with the addition of mutton fat and bee's wax may be worked by hand to make flowers, animals etc. Socles are also made from ice for certain dishes.

The simplest method of making a socle is to make a very thick semolina pudding from milk and semolina with the addition of soaked gelatine, pour into a lightly oiled dish and allow to set in the refrigerator. For example, 500 ml (1 pt) milk, 150 g (6 oz) semolina, 50 g (2 oz) gelatine.

20   Cold suprêmes of chicken in white sauce with foie gras or liver pâté   *Suprême de volaille Jeanette*

Use cooked poached chickens, allow to cool and remove the skin. Cut off the suprêmes and carefully trim. Cut into two or leave whole.

Cover each suprême with purée of foie gras or liver pâté, approx ¼ cm (⅛ in.) thick. Cover with chaudfroid sauce. Decorate with blanched tarragon leaves and finish with aspic jelly.

Serve in a base of aspic flavoured with tarragon. Garnish with small bouquets of asparagus tips which have been glazed. Finish with chopped jelly around the base of the suprêmes.

21   Cold salmon   *Saumon froid*

Clean, scale and remove the fins from the salmon, and wash it. Prepare a court bouillon, cook it for 15 minutes and allow to cool completely. Place in the whole salmon, bring to the boil, and poach gently on the side of the stove for about 30 minutes, according to size. Allow to stand in the liquor until cold and then remove all the skin.

Garnish with overlapping slices of hard-boiled egg and peeled tomatoes round the sides, alternately with lettuce quarters. Serve mayonnaise separately.

22   Decorated cold salmon   *Saumon froid à la russe*

Cook as for above and remove the skin. Decorate with prawns from which the tail has been removed, leaving the carapace. The prawns are placed along the middle of the salmon with the points into the fish. Place a trellis of blanched tarragon leaves on each side of the prawns, and glaze with a clean fish jelly.

Dress on a dish with a jelly base and garnish with boats of cucumber, which have been blanched and stuffed with prawns, bound with mayonnaise and flavoured with horseradish.

23   Poached cold salmon trout   *Truite saumonée norvégienne*

Open the salmon trout out flat, leaving it joined along its stomach, removing all the bone. Poach carefully in a court bouillon. When cold, place the fish on the bottom of an upturned tray and remove the skin. Decorate. (The decoration should include tails of prawns.) Glaze.

When set, dress on a glazed dish and garnish with small 2 cm (1 in.) pieces of blanched cucumber filled with a purée of smoked salmon, halves of stuffed eggs and small decorated tomatoes. Serve a green sauce separately.

24 Cold mousses

A mousse is basically a purée of the bulk ingredient from which it takes its name, with the addition of a suitable non-dairy or cream sauce, cream and aspic jelly. The result should be a light creamy mixture, just sufficiently set to stand when removed from a mould.

Care must be taken when mixing not to curdle the mixture, which will produce a 'bitty' appearance with small white grains of cream showing. The cream should only be half whipped as a rubbery texture will otherwise be obtained; also, if fresh cream is over-whipped the mixture will curdle.

Various types of mousse are used as part of other dishes as well as dishes on their own. A mould of a particular substance may be filled with a mousse of the same basic ingredient. Whole decorated chickens may have the breast reformed with a mousse such as ham, tomato or foie gras. Mousse may be piped to fill cornets of ham, borders for chicken suprêmes or cold egg dishes.

Although most recipes quote a lined mould for the mousse to be placed in when being served as an individual dish, mousses may often be poured into a glass bowl (or even smaller dishes for individual portions) to be decorated on top when set, then glazed. Although truffle is frequently quoted, garnishing paste or other materials are now used.

Note Convenience aspic jelly granules may be used for all mousse recipes.

25 **Tomato mousse** *Mousse de tomates* *4 portions*

50 g	2 oz	finely chopped onion
50 g	2 oz	butter or margarine
500 ml	1 pt	white stock or consommé
250 g	10 oz	tomatoes, skinned, deseeded and diced
25 g	1 oz	tomato purée
		salt and pepper
		pinch of paprika
125 ml	¼ pt	velouté
125 ml	¼ pt	aspic jelly
125 ml	¼ pt	whipping cream, half beaten

1 Sweat the onion in the butter or margarine without colour.
2 Moisten with the stock or consommé, reduce by half.
3 Add the tomatoes and tomato purée. Simmer for approx 20 mins, season and add paprika.
4 Add the velouté and aspic, simmer for 2 mins, then liquidise.
5 Place in a basin on ice, stir till setting point, and fold in the half-whipped cream.
6 Use as required: either place in individual moulds, allow to set, turn out on to individual plates, decorate and serve as a first course; or use as part of a cold dish.

26   **Chicken liver pâté mousse**   *Mousse de foie de volaille*

4 portions

100 g	4 oz	chicken liver pâté
125 ml	¼ pt	aspic jelly
125 ml	¼ pt	velouté
		2 sheets of soaked gelatine
		salt and pepper
125 ml	¼ pt	whipping cream, half beaten

1 Cream the liver pâté well; add the hot aspic and velouté, mix well.
2 Pass through a sieve or liquidise.
3 Add the gelatine, place in a basin on ice and season.
4 Allow to cool until setting point.
5 Fold in the half-whipped cream.
6 Place in individual moulds to use as a starter or use as required as part of a cold dish.   .

Note The mousse may also be turned out on to individual plates, decorated with salad items and served.

27   **Ham mousse**   *Mousse de jambon*

4 portions

400 g	1 lb	minced cooked ham
125 ml	¼ pt	velouté
125 ml	¼ pt	aspic jelly
		salt and pepper
250 ml	½ pt	whipping cream

1 Place the minced ham into a basin, add the velouté and aspic jelly. Season with salt and pepper.
2 Place into a saucepan and boil out for approx 2 mins.
3 Purée in a food processor, then pour into a basin over ice.
4 Stir until setting point and fold in the half-whipped cream. Use as required.

Note 25 g (1 oz) finely chopped onion sweated in 10 g (½ oz) butter or margarine with 10 g (½ oz) paprika may be added at stage 2 if desired.

28   **Chicken mousse**   *Mousse de volaille ou poulet*

4 portions

As above, using minced cooked chicken, omitting any paprika.

29 Salmon mousse *Mousse de saumon*   *4 portions*

400 g	1 lb	cooked salmon
125 ml	¼ pt	velouté
125 ml	¼ pt	fish aspic jelly
		little sweated paprika if desired
		salt and pepper
250 ml	½ pt	whipping cream

1 Purée the salmon, place in a saucepan with the velouté and aspic and boil for 2 mins.
2 Pass through a sieve, add a little sweated paprika if desired, and mix well. Season.
3 Place in a basin over a bowl of ice, stir until setting point, then fold in the half-whipped cream.
4 Pour into a glass bowl or individual moulds. Decorate and use as required.

30 Smoked eel flan Bendien   *4 portions*

150 g	6 oz	short pastry
100 g	4 oz	smoked eel slices
25 g	1 oz	finely chopped shallots
25 g	1 oz	butter or margarine
		salt and pepper
		lime or lemon juice
		2 eggs
125 ml	¼ pt	milk
25 g	1 oz	stuffed olives

1 Bake an 18 cm (7 in.) flan case blind for approx 10–15 mins at 200°C (400°F, Reg. 6).
2 Cut the eel slices into uniform pieces.
3 Sweat the shallots in butter or margarine and sprinkle on the base of the flan.
4 Cover with overlapping slices of eel, reserving a few for decoration.
5 Season with salt and pepper, sprinkle with lime or lemon juice.
6 Beat the eggs and milk together well, season and pour over the eel pieces.
7 Bake in oven at approx 200°C (400°F, Reg. 6) until the custard sets.
8 Allow to cool and decorate with sliced stuffed olives, slivers of smoked eel and serve.

31 Cold hake with pickled walnut sauce   *4 portions*

600 g–1 kg	1½–2 lbs	cold poached hake
		lettuce
		10 pickled walnuts
		salt, pepper, nutmeg

(Contd.)

125 ml	¼ pt	natural yoghurt
250 ml	½ pt	mayonnaise
		1 lemon
		8 slices cucumber
		2 blanched tomatoes

1 Arrange the hake on a bed of crisp lettuce.
2 Grind the walnuts in a food processor. Add seasoning, nutmeg, yoghurt and mayonnaise.
3 Mask fish with this sauce; garnish with lemon wedges and slices of cucumber and tomato.

Note Other types of white fish may also be used, e.g. cod, halibut, turbot, lemon sole, Dover sole.
 For a first course, allow 100–150 g (4–6 oz) per portion. Cut the hake into portions before serving.

32   Terrine of eel with white wine and watercress sauce

4 portions

200 g	8 oz	filleted eel	
125 ml	¼ pt	dry white wine	
		1 tablespn each of chopped tarragon, chervil and chives	marinade
		salt and pepper	
25 g	1 oz	butter or margarine	
12 g	½ oz	chopped shallot	deuxelle
150 g	6 oz	chopped mushrooms	
		freshly chopped parsley	
150 g	6 oz	filleted salmon, whiting or lemon sole	
		2 eggs	
75 g	3 oz	soft butter or margarine	
		1 teaspn chopped chervil	
		1 teaspn chopped chives	forcemeat
		cayenne/pepper	
		pinch of saffron	
		salt, peppermill	

1 Soak the eel fillets in the marinade overnight.
2 Place the eels and marinade in a suitable pan, bring gently to the boil, simmer until cooked.
3 Allow to cool in the marinade.
4 Melt the 25 g (1 oz) butter in a suitable pan and sweat the shallot for approx 5 mins.
5 Add the mushrooms and parsley, season, and sweat for a further 2 mins.
6 Allow to cool.
7 Place the fish fillets into a food processor, season and purée to a smooth paste. Blend in the eggs gently.
8 Add the soft butter and herbs, cayenne and saffron. Mix well.

9 Place into a bowl and add the cold mushrooms.
10 Take a suitable small terrine, approx 8 cm (6 in.) long × 5 cm (2 in.) wide, spread the inside of the terrine with forcemeat to a depth of 1 cm (½ in.).
11 Lay alternative layers of eel fillets, drained from the marinade, and forcemeat, finishing with a layer of forcemeat.
12 Cover with aluminium foil and cook in a bain-marie for approx 1½ to 2 hours at 180°C (350°F, Reg. 4).
13 When cooked, allow to cool and refrigerate for 24 hours.
14 Turn out, cut into slices, and serve on individual plates with watercress sauce (see below).

Watercress sauce

25 g	1 oz	chopped shallot
25 g	1 oz	butter
		1 bunch watercress, washed
		1 tablespn chopped tarragon
		1 clove of crushed and chopped garlic
60 ml	⅛ pt	dry white wine
375 ml	¾ pt	whipping cream
		salt and pepper
25 g	1 oz	gelatine, soaked in water (optional)
		lemon juice

1 Sweat the shallot in the butter.
2 Add the watercress, tarragon, garlic and white wine, cover and cook for 1 min.
3 Add 125 ml (¼ pt) of cream, season and reduce for 10 mins.
4 Remove from heat, add the soaked gelatine. Stir well.
5 Liquidise, add a squeeze of lemon juice, place into a basin and chill in the refrigerator.
6 Half whip the remaining cream and add to the chilled watercress purée, stirring gently.
7 Correct seasoning and use as required.

33 Red mullet with tomatoes, garlic and saffron
Rouget à l'orientale   *4 portions*

4 × 150 g	6 oz	red mullet
		salt and pepper
125 ml	¼ pt	dry white wine
60 ml	⅛ pt	vegetable oil
150 g	6 oz	tomatoes, skinned, deseeded and diced
		1 clove of garlic (crushed)
		spring of thyme, bayleaf
		pinch of saffron
		4 slices of peeled lemon

1 Clean and prepare the fish. Dry them.
2 Place in a suitable oiled dish. Season with salt and pepper.
3 Add the white wine, oil, tomatoes, garlic, herbs and saffron.
4 Cover with aluminium foil and bake in the oven at 220°C (425°F, Reg. 7) for approx. 10 mins. Allow to cool in dish.
5 Serve on individual plates with a little of the cooking liquor, garnished with a slice of peeled lemon.

34   Vegetable and chicken terrine   *4 portions*

200 g	8 oz	raw chicken breast, diced
		2 egg whites
		salt
250 ml	½ pt	double cream
400 g	1 lb	leeks
100 g	4 oz	thin French beans (optional)
100 g	4 oz	carrot
100 g	4 oz	courgettes
100 g	4 oz	large open mushrooms

1 Liquidise the chicken with the egg whites and salt until smooth.
2 Chill thoroughly on ice or in a refrigerator.
3 Keeping the mixture on ice gradually beat in the cream. Test the texture by poaching a teaspoonful in simmering water, it must not be too soft.
4 Blanch and refresh the light green of leek and drain on a cloth.
5 Top and tail beans, cook for 5 mins and refresh.
6 Peel and cut carrot into strips the same thickness as the beans, cook for 5 mins and refresh.
7 With a small knife lightly scrape and blanch the courgettes. Cut into strips.
8 Peel and wash the mushrooms and cut into strips, keep raw.
9 Line a suitable sized terrine with leeks.
10 Pipe on a layer of one-third of the chicken farce.
11 Neatly add a row of beans and mushrooms, alternating.
12 Pipe on a second third of the chicken farce.
13 Neatly add the courgettes and carrots.
14 Pipe on remainder of the chicken farce.
15 Completely cover with the remaining leeks.
16 Cook in a bain-marie in the oven at 180°C (350°F, Reg. 4) for approx. 45 mins.
17 Leave to set when cooked; then turn out carefully and cut one thick slice per portion.
18 Serve warm with a butter-type sauce e.g. hollandaise, or cold with a fresh tomato sauce (see opposite).

Note Half the chicken farce can be mixed with spinach purée to give colour variation. Variations to vegetable terrine can include: ham instead of chicken farce, coarse duxelle, asparagus, artichokes, courgettes etc.

35 Fresh tomato sauce (raw) *Coulis de tomates* *4 portions*

400 g	1 lb	tomatoes, skinned and pips removed
		½ tablespn vinegar
		3 tablespns oil
		salt and mill pepper
		1 tablespn chopped parsley and tarragon

1 Squeeze the tomatoes to remove excess juice and liquidise the flesh.
2 Place in a bowl and gradually whisk in the vinegar and oil.
3 Season and mix in the herbs.

Note A recipe for a cooked tomato sauce can be found on p. 64.

36 White chaudfroid

50 g	2 oz	leaf gelatine
1 litre	2 pt	béchamel or velouté
125 ml	¼ pt	cream (if necessary to improve the colour of the sauce)

1 Soak the gelatine in cold water.
2 Bring the sauce to the boil.
3 Remove from the heat.
4 Add the well-squeezed gelatine and stir until dissolved, and correct the seasoning.
5 Pass through a tammy cloth.
6 When the sauce is half cooled mix in the cream.

Reception snacks and hot hors-d'oeuvre

See also Chapter 11 Ethnic recipes

1   Anchovy sticks   *Allumettes d'anchois*

150 g   6 oz   puff pastry
100 g   4 oz   anchovy fillets
               egg wash

1 Roll out half the puff pastry in a rectangle 7 cm × 12 cm (3 in. × 5 in.).
2 Place onto a lightly greased baking sheet.
3 Lay on the anchovy fillets; egg wash the edges.
4 Roll out remaining puff pastry slightly larger than the first half.
5 Cover the anchovies with this pastry, seal down the edges well.
6 Egg wash all over, mark edges with the back of a small knife. Cut into sticks ½ cm (¼ in.) wide.
7 Bake in a moderate oven (220°C, 425°F, Reg. 7) for approx 10 mins until golden brown.
8 May be served hot or cold.

2 Spinach and cheese sticks *Allumettes florentine*

As for Anchovy sticks; in place of anchovies use chopped, cooked spinach bound with béchamel and sprinkled with grated parmesan cheese.

3 Garlic and pimento sticks *Allumettes à la éspagnole*

Proceed as for Anchovy sticks; in place of the anchovies, spread the pastry with a mixture of garlic butter, finely chopped red pimento and ham.

4 Haddock sticks *Allumettes à l'ecossaise*

As above, using a purée of creamed cooked smoked haddock.

5 Dartois

These savoury puff pastry slices are similar to allumettes, made and cooked in a long strip, then cut after cooking.

Fillings include:

smoked haddock	tuna	chicken and mushroom
anchovies	chicken	ratatouille
sardines	mushroom	

6 Attereaux

These are small pieces of cooked food, which are coated with a thick sauce, allowed to cool, passed through flour, egg and breadcrumbs and then deep fried. They are served on cocktail sticks.

Meat
chicken – coated with suprême sauce
pork – coated with tomato sauce
veal – coated with a mustard sauce
beef – coated with a red wine sauce

Fish
scampi ⎫
mussels ⎬ white wine,
goujons of plaice or sole ⎭ curry or tomato sauce

Vegetables
cauliflower ⎫
courgettes ⎬ curry, cream or tomato sauce
broccoli ⎭

7   Brioches

Small bite-sized brioches may be made for appetisers using the recipe on
p. 289. The centre is scooped out and various fillings may be used, for
example:

Fish – Creamed smoked haddock
– Lobster in lobster sauce
– Prawns in curry sauce
– Mussels in cream or curry sauce etc.

Meat – Diced cooked beef or lamb in red wine or tomato sauce
– Diced cooked chicken or veal in cream or white wine sauce

Vegetables – Finely diced ratatouille
– Mushrooms in cream sauce
– Courgettes in tomato sauce

8   Deep-fried savoury pancakes   *Craquelins*

These are very small pancakes which may be stuffed with a variety of
fillings, as for brioche, folded over or rolled. They are passed through
flour, egg and breadcrumbs and deep fried.

9   Savoury fritters   *Fritots*

These are small pieces of marinaded meat, fish or vegetables, which are
dipped in batter, deep fried and served on cocktail sticks.

10   Cassolettes

These are individual dishes, e.g. ramekins, in which small hors-d'oeuvre are served.

The dishes may be filled with any purée or sliced ingredients, with appropriate sauces, sprinkled with breadcrumbs or grated cheese, and browned in the oven before serving.

Cassolettes can be made with a border of duchess potato or an edging and a lid of puff pastry. A little duchess potato may be piped over the top of the filling, which is brushed with egg and browned in the oven. For cocktail appetisers or hot hors-d'oeuvre, small short pastry tartlets or bouchées can be used in place of ramekins.

11   Game ramekins   *Cassolettes St Hubert*

Fill cooked short pastry tartlets with game purée, cover with duchess potato and glaze in the oven.

12   Chicken liver and mushroom ramekins   *Cassolettes ambassadrice*

Fill cooked short pastry tartlets with a cooked dice of chicken livers and mushrooms bound with madeira sauce, top with duchess potato and brown in the oven.

13   Asparagus and French bean ramekins   *Cassolettes vert pré*

Line tartlette moulds with short pastry, fill with a purée of asparagus and French beans, bound with a little cream sauce, and cover with puff pastry. Egg wash and bake in a moderately hot oven (190°C, 375°F, Reg. 5) for approx 15 mins.

14   Mixed vegetable ramekins   *Cassolettes bouquetière*

Fill cooked short pastry tartlets with small tips of asparagus, florets of broccoli or cauliflower, peas and cooked dice of carrots, bound with natural yoghurt or cream sauce.

Using a small star tube, pipe a border of duchess potato around the edge of each tartlet, glaze in the oven or under the salamander.

15   **Macaroni and mushroom ramekins**   *Cassolettes à l'italienne*

Fill cooked short pastry tartlets with diced macaroni and mushrooms bound with a cream sauce or natural yoghurt, sprinkle with fried breadcrumbs and parmesan cheese, and glaze under the salamander.

16   **Chicken and celery ramekins**   *Cassolettes à la regence*

Fill cooked short pastry tartlets with a mixture of diced cooked chicken and celery bound with suprême sauce. Using a piping bag and star tube pipe a border of duchess potato around the edge of each tartlet and glaze under the salamander. Finish with small tips of asparagus and brush with butter or margarine.

17   **Deep-fried noodle paste with gruyère cheese**
Beurrecks à la turque   *4 portions*

150 g	6 oz	noodle paste
100 g	4 oz	finely diced gruyère cheese
60 ml	⅛ pt	béchamel (cold)
		salt, cayenne, pepper
		flour, egg, breadcrumbs

1 Roll out noodle paste thinly, cut into 3 cm (1½ in.) discs.
2 Mix the gruyère cheese with the cold béchamel. Season.
3 Place a little cheese mixture on each of the discs. Egg wash the edges.
4 Fold over like a turnover. Pass lightly through flour, egg and breadcrumbs.
5 Deep fry in hot oil 190°C (375°F) until golden brown. Serve on a flat dish on dish paper.

Note Beurrecks may also be made cigar shaped.

18   **Mussel pastry boats**   *Barquettes de moules*   *4 portions*

100 g	4 oz	short pastry
375 ml	¾ pt	fresh mussels
10 g	½ oz	chopped shallot
60 ml	⅛ pt	white wine
		¼ lemon, juiced
60 ml	⅛ pt	fish stock
		salt and pepper
10 g	½ oz	butter or margarine } beurre manié
10 g	½ oz	flour
60 ml	⅛ pt	single cream
		chopped parsley

1 Line small barquette moulds with short pastry and bake blind.
2 Clean the mussels; place in a suitable pan with the chopped shallot, white wine, lemon juice and fish stock.
3 Place over a fierce heat until the mussels open, remove from heat.
4 Remove mussels and shells, clean off the tongue, weed and beard from the mussels.
5 Strain the cooking liquor place into a clean pan, season with salt and pepper.
6 Bring to boil and lightly thicken with the beurre manié.
7 Finish with cream; add the mussels.
8 Fill the barquettes with the mussels. Finish with a little chopped parsley. (Alternatively sprinkle with breadcrumbs and brown in the oven or under the salamander, then sprinkle with chopped parsley.)
9 Serve in a hot dish on dish paper.

Note Instead of barquettes small tartlets or bouchées may be used. A mixture of prawns and mussels and other seafood may also be used, e.g. lobster, crab, shrimps, cockles etc. Additional or alternative flavours which enhance this appetizer include curry, paprika, pepper, saffron etc.

19 Hungarian soufflé fritters *Beignets soufflés à l'hongroise*
4 portions

125 ml	¼ pt	choux pastry (p. 275)
25 g	1 oz	finely chopped sweated onion
		¼ teaspn paprika
		1 teaspn grated parmesan

1 Prepare choux paste as on p. 275 (omit the sugar); mix in onion and paprika.
2 Mould into small quenelles onto oiled greaseproof paper. Allow to set.
3 Deep fry at approx 190° C (375° F) until well risen and golden brown; drain well onto kitchen paper and sprinkle with parmesan.
4 Serve on a flat dish on a dish paper with a sauceboat of Hongroise sauce separately.

20 Hungarian sauce *Sauce hongroise*
4 portions

25 g	1 oz	butter or margarine
50 g	2 oz	finely chopped onion
25 g	1 oz	paprika
60 ml	⅛ pt	white wine
250 ml	½ pt	chicken velouté
60 ml	⅛ pt	single cream
		salt and pepper

1 Melt the butter or margarine and sweat the onions.
2 Add the paprika and cook for 2 mins.

3 Moisten with white wine and reduce by two-thirds.
4 Add the chicken velouté, boil out, strain and finish with cream. Correct seasoning.

21   Lamb, peach and cashew bitoks   *4 portions*

100 g	4 oz	dried peaches
450 g	1 lb	minced lamb
		1 clove of garlic, crushed and chopped
		salt and pepper
		1 egg
50 g	2 oz	breadcrumbs
50 g	2 oz	cashew nuts

1 Reconstitute the peaches in boiling water for 5 mins.; drain well. Chop finely and add to the lamb.
2 Add the garlic and season. Bind with egg and breadcrumbs.
3 Form into small cocktail pieces, insert a cashew nut into each and mould into balls. Flatten slightly.
4 Fry the bitoks in a shallow pan in vegetable oil, drain.
5 Place on a dish with a cocktail stick in each. Serve a yoghurt and cucumber dressing separately (see below).

Note Pine kernels may be used in place of cashew nuts and beef used in place of lamb.

22   Yoghurt and cucumber dressing   *4 portions*

100 g	4 oz	cucumber
125 ml	¼ pt	natural yoghurt
		salt/pepper
		¼ teaspn chopped mint

1 Peel the cucumber, blanch in boiling water for 5 mins, refresh and drain.
2 Purée the cucumber in a food processor.
3 Add the cucumber to the natural yoghurt, season and finish with freshly chopped mint.

23   Potato nests with chicken and mushroom   *Mazagrins*
4 portions

200 g	8 oz	duchess potato mixture
		flour, egg, breadcrumbs
50 g	2 oz	finely diced chicken
50 g	2 oz	finely diced mushrooms
60 ml	⅛ pt	chicken velouté

1 Mould small pieces of duchess mixture into oval cakes 5 cm (2 in.) diameter.
2 Pass through flour, egg and breadcrumbs twice.
3 Mark top with a 2.5 cm (1 in.) plain cutter; deep fry in hot oil 190° C (375° F) until golden brown, drain.
4 When cool, remove the marked top and scoop out centre.
5 Fill with a mixture of finely diced cooked chicken and mushrooms bound with chicken velouté; replace lid.
6 Serve on a flat dish on dish paper garnished with fried parsley.

Note This filling can also be used in tartlets, barquettes, bouchées etc.

24 Puff pastry slice with spinach *Jalousie florentine*

4 portions

200 g	8 oz	chopped spinach
25 g	1 oz	butter or margarine
125 ml	¼ pt	Mornay sauce
10 g	½ oz	parmesan
		salt, pepper, nutmeg
150 g	6 oz	puff pastry

1 Prepare the filling by sweating the spinach in the butter or margarine, mix with a little Mornay sauce, add the parmesan and season, then allow to cool.
2 Roll out pastry into a rectangle 15 cm × 24 cm (6 in. × 10 in.) long.
3 Cut into half lengthwise, slightly off centre.
4 Lay narrower half onto a lightly greased baking sheet.
5 Spread spinach over the band of pastry, egg wash the edges.
6 Fold the remaining half of pastry into half lengthwise and, with a sharp knife, cut slits across the fold about ½ cm (¾ in.) apart to within approx 1 cm (½ in.) up the edge.
7 Lay this over the spinach, seal the edges with egg wash.
8 Brush all over with egg wash and bake at 220°C (425°F, Reg. 7) for approx 10 mins.
9 When cooked cut into fingers 1½ to 2 cm (¾ in. to 1 in.) wide.
10 Serve on a flat dish on dish paper.

Note Low-fat natural yoghurt or fromage frais may be used in place of Mornay sauce.

25 Spinach, egg and smoked salmon slice

4 portions

150 g	6 oz	short pastry
100 g	4 oz	puff pastry
150 g	6 oz	cooked leaf spinach

25 g	1 oz	butter or margarine
		salt and pepper
		2 hard-boiled eggs
125 ml	¼ pt	Mornay sauce
100 g	4 oz	smoked salmon trimmings
25 g	1 oz	parmesan cheese

1 Roll out short pastry into a rectangle 15 × 24 cm (6 × 10 in.).
2 Place onto a lightly greased baking sheet. Dock* the base, egg wash the edges.
3 Roll out 2 strips of puff pastry 24 cm (10 in.) long, 2 cm (1 in.) wide. Lay these strips on top of the short pastry to form two edges.
4 Press down firmly, with the back of a small knife, scallop the edge. Egg wash lightly.
5 Bake in a moderately hot oven (220°C, 425°F, Reg. 7) for approx 10 mins.
6 Reheat the spinach in butter or margarine, season. Spread the spinach on the pastry base.
7 Dice the hard-boiled eggs, bind with Mornay sauce. Add the chopped smoked salmon trimmings.
8 Lay the mixture over the spinach and sprinkle with grated parmesan cheese.
9 Glaze under the salamander or in the oven.
10 Cut into fingers approx 2 cm (1 in.) wide, and serve on a dish garnished with picked parsley.

*Dock: to perforate pastry with numerous small holes.

26   Smoked haddock pouches   *Talmousse d'aiglefin*   *4 portions*

150 g	6 oz	puff pastry
100 g	4 oz	cooked smoked haddock
60 ml	⅛ pt	cream sauce
25 g	1 oz	finely diced gruyère cheese

1 Roll out the pastry and cut out discs 8 cm (3 in.) in diameter.
2 Bind the smoked haddock with the cream sauce; add the finely diced gruyère cheese.
3 Place some mixture in the centre of the discs and egg wash the edges.
4 Seal edges up into the form of a tricorn hat with three points.
5 Place on lightly greased baking sheets, relax for 10 mins, and bake in a moderately hot oven (220°C, 425°F, Reg. 7) for approx 10 to 15 mins.
6 Serve on suitable dish on dish paper, garnished with picked parsley.

27 Spring rolls

	2	eggs	
125 ml	¼ pt	milk	batter
50 g	2 oz	flour	
		salt	
50 g	2 oz	butter or margarine	
25 g	1 oz	finely chopped onion	
50 g	2 oz	sliced bamboo shoots	
50 g	2 oz	cooked diced pork	filling
25 g	1 oz	finely diced celery	
		1 tablespn ground nut oil	
		½ tablespn ve-tsin*	
100 g	4 oz	peeled shrimps	

1 Make the batter by, first, beating the eggs and milk together.
2 Gradually add the flour, season and strain.
3 Lightly oil a small shallow pan, diameter approx 8 cm (3 in.). Heat over a fierce heat.
4 Gently pour in a thin layer of batter. Cook for 1 min on one side only. Turn out and allow to cool.
5 Prepare the filling: heat the butter or margarine in a suitable pan, add the finely chopped onion, sweat without colour for 2 mins.
6 Add all other ingredients except the shrimps, mix well. Simmer for 3 mins.
7 Turn out into a clean basin and leave to cool. Add the shrimps.
8 Put a small spoonful of filling on to the cooked side of each pancake, roll up, tucking in and sealing the edges with egg wash. Place on a tray and chill well for 20 mins approx.
9 Deep fry in hot oil approx 190° C (375° F) until golden brown; drain well and serve immediately on a dish on dish paper.

*Ve-tsin is a flavour enhancer, similar to monosodium glutamate.

28 Tuna fish and water chestnut pouches

25 g	1 oz	butter or margarine
25 g	1 oz	chopped green pimento
25 g	1 oz	finely chopped red pimento
		1 clove garlic, finely chopped
125 ml	¼ pt	jus-lié
		salt and pepper
100 g	4 oz	tuna fish
100 g	4 oz	water chestnuts
150 g	6 oz	puff pastry or short pastry

1 Melt the butter or margarine in a suitable pan, add the pimento and garlic, sweat for 2 mins.

2 Add the jus-lié, bring to boil, season.
3 Remove from heat, add the flaked tuna fish and chopped water chestnuts. Mix well. Allow to cool.
4 Roll out pastry; cut out discs 8 cm (3 in.) in diameter. Place on a little cold filling in the centre of each and egg wash edges.
5 Seal edges up to form tricorn hats with three points. Place on lightly greased baking sheets, allow to relax for approx 10 mins.
6 Bake in a moderate over (200°C, 400°F, Reg. 6) for approx 10 to 15 mins.
7 Serve on a suitable dish on dish paper, garnished with picked parsley.

Note Other fish may also be used, such as salmon, haddock, cod etc.

4

Soups

See also Chapter 10 British dishes
Chapter 11 Ethnic Recipes

Introduction

In keeping with healthy eating practices these points can be considered
when making soup:

1 Purée soups may be thickened by vegetables and require no flour;
2 Wholemeal flour can be used for thickened soups;
3 Cream and velouté soups may be made with skimmed milk and finished
with non-dairy cream, low-fat natural yoghurt, quark or fromage frais;
4 Velouté soups may be finished with non-dairy cream, natural yoghurt or
fromage frais.

Variations can be created, for example by:

a) Combining finished soups, e.g. adding a watercress soup to a tomato
soup;
b) Using the main ingredients together, e.g. tomatoes and watercress in
the initial preparation;
c) Careful use of different herbs to introduce a subtle flavour, e.g. basil,
rosemary, chervil;
d) Using a garnish which is varied, e.g. blanched watercress leaves,
chopped chives and tomato concassée and finishing with non-dairy
cream or yoghurt.

The following are some examples of 'combination' soups:

watercress with lettuce	tomato with courgette
watercress and spinach	potato and spinach
watercress and courgettes	tomato and mushroom
leek and onion	tomato and celery
leek and broccoli	tomato and cauliflower
leek and tomato	tomato and cucumber
leek and cucumber	chicken and mushroom
potato and endive	chicken and leek

An essential ingredient for soup is the liquid and only the best quality stock of the appropriate flavour should be used to enhance the soup. Care should be taken, however, to preserve the flavour of the main ingredient, for example, mushroom, lettuce etc. should not be overpowered.

The following table indicates the variety of stocks, finishes, accompaniments and garnishes which can be used in the making and serving of soups.

Stocks	Finishes	Accompaniments	Garnishes	
bacon	cream	toasted flutes	julienne or brunoise of:	
ham	milk	bread sticks	beetroot	celery
chicken	yolks	melba toast	celeriac	peppers
beef	yoghurt	toast spread with paté	carrots	beans
veal	quark	cheese straws	turnips	leeks
game	fromage frais	grated cheese	mushrooms	game
mutton	non-dairy cream	profiteroles	poultry	meat
vegetable	port	croûtons	also savoury pancakes	
fish	madeira white wine		meat balls, quenelles	
			chopped or leaves of:	
			parsley	mint
			sorrel	chervil etc.

1 Clear soup *Consommé* *4 portions*

200 g	8 oz	minced beef
		1–2 egg whites
		salt
l litre	1 qt	white or brown beef stock
100 g	4 oz	mixed vegetables (onion celery, leek, carrot)
		bouquet garni
		3–4 peppercorns

1 Mix the beef, egg white and salt with 250 ml (½ pt) cold stock in a thick-bottomed pan.
2 Add the finely chopped vegetables, remainder of the stock, bouquet garni and peppercorns.
3 Bring slowly to the boil, stirring frequently.
4 Boil rapidly for 5–10 seconds, give a final stir.
5 Simmer very gently for 1½ to 2 hours without stirring.
6 Strain through a double muslin, removing all fat.
7 Correct the seasoning and colour.

2   Clear veal soup

Use minced veal and veal stock in place of minced beef and beef stock and follow recipe above.

3   Clear chicken or game soup   *Consommé de volaille ou gibier*

Proceed as for beef clear soup, using brown chicken or game stock in place of beef stock and add chopped giblets with the minced beef.

4   Tomato, mushroom or celery flavoured clear soup

Proceed as for recipe 1; when adding the vegetables, add 300–400 g (12 oz–1 lb) of chopped tomato, mushroom or celery.

5   Clear chicken soup with quenelles

Garnish the clear chicken soup with piped, pea-sized quenelles (p. 122), gently poached in clear soup.

6   Clear tarragon-flavoured soup

Proceed as for beef clear soup; for the final 15 minutes simmering, infuse the soup with a sprig of tarragon.

7   Clear chicken soup with toasted cheese   *Consommé aux diablotins*

Accompany a chicken clear soup with ½ cm (¼ in.) slices of French flutes, covered with cheese and gratinated.

8   Clear soup with tomatoes and peppers   *Consommé Carmen*

Tomato-flavoured clear soup, garnished with tomato concassée and julienne of red pepper, cooked in a little clear soup and cooked rice.

9   Clear soup with tomatoes, beans and potatoes   *Consommé niçoise*

Tomato-flavoured clear soup, garnished with tomato concassée, diamonds of cooked French beans and small-diced cooked potato.

10   Clear soup with celery and savoury custard   *Consommé Grimaldi*

Tomato-flavoured clear soup, garnished with julienne of celery cooked in clear soup and the savoury custard cut in neat dice.

Purée soups *(purée based)*

As well as the pulses listed, others such as borlotti beans, red kidney beans, black beans, pinto beans, chick peas, green lentils, etc. may also be used.

The following soups can be made by using the named pulse in the basic pulse soup recipe below.

11	**Red lentil soup**	*Purée Conti*
12	**Brown lentil soup**	*Purée Esaü*
13	**Red kidney bean soup**	*Purée Condé*
14	**Flageolet bean soup**	*Purée musard*
15	**Flageolet and haricot bean soup**	*Purée tourangelle*

16   Basic pulse soup recipe   *4 portions*

200 g	8 oz	pulse
1½ litres	3 pts	white stock or water
50 g	2 oz	carrot
50 g	2 oz	onion
50 g	2 oz	knuckle of ham or bacon
		bouquet garni
		salt, pepper
		1 slice stale bread } croûtons
50 g	2 oz	butter

1 Pick over and wash the pulses, then place in a thick-bottomed pan with stock or water.
2 Bring to the boil, skim and add all other ingredients except salt (which will toughen the pulse).
3 Simmer until the pulse is very soft, skim and season with salt.
4 Remove the bouquet garni (and the carro* if making flageolet bean soup) and the ham.
5 Pass through a sieve and fine strainer or liquidise.
6 Correct the seasoning and consistency.
7 Serve with fried or toasted croûtons separately.

Note Combinations of beans, lentils or peas can be considered and, instead of frying the croûtons in butter, use bacon fat or vegetable oil.

17 Chicken soup with mushrooms and tongue
Velouté Agnès Sorel   *4 portions*

1 litre	2 pts	chicken velouté
200 g	8 oz	mushroom trimmings
125 ml	¼ pt	2 yolks of egg / cream } liaison
		salt and pepper
25 g	1 oz	mushrooms
25 g	1 oz	chicken } garnish
25 g	1 oz	tongue

1 Prepare a chicken velouté, adding the chopped mushroom trimmings at the initial stage.
2 Liquidise and add the liaison by adding some soup to the liaison of yolks and cream and returning all to pan.
3 Bring almost to the boil, stirring continuously, then strain into a clean pan.
4 Correct the seasoning and consistency, add the garnish and serve.

Note 100 g (4 oz) raw minced chicken may be cooked in the velouté then liquidised with the soup to give a stronger chicken flavour.

18 Chicken and barley soup with macaroni
Velouté Marie Louise   *4 portions*

300 g	12 oz	pearl barley
250 g	½ pt	chicken stock
500 ml	1 pt	chicken velouté
		salt and pepper
125 ml	¼ pt	2 yolks of egg / cream } liaison
25 g	1 oz	macaroni, cooked, cut in small dice

1 Simmer the barley in the chicken stock until cooked.
2 Strain the stock onto the velouté and bring to the boil.
3 Correct the seasoning and consistency.
4 Add the liaison as in the previous recipe and strain.
5 Garnish with the macaroni, some of the barley and serve.

19   Chicken and barley soup with vegetables
Velouté Marie Stuart   *4 portions*

1 Prepare as for Velouté Marie Louise.
2 Garnish with 50 g (2 oz) cooked brunoise of vegetables and 25 g (1 oz)
   pearl barley cooked in chicken stock.

20   Cream of green pea soup with rice, sorrel and lettuce
Crème Ambassadeur   *4 portions*

400 g	1 lb	shelled peas
		sprig of mint
25 g	1 oz	onion
		bouquet garni
500 ml	1 pt	thin béchamel
60 ml	⅛ pt	cream
		¼ lettuce
25 g	1 oz	sorrel
50 g	2 oz	rice, cooked

1 Cook the peas in water with a little salt, mint, onion and bouquet garni.
2 Remove the mint, onion and bouquet garni.
3 Purée the peas in a food processor or liquidiser and add to the
   béchamel.
4 Bring to the boil and simmer for 5 minutes.
5 Correct the seasoning; pass through a medium strainer.
6 Correct the consistency and add the cream.
7 Garnish with shredded lettuce, sorrel, cooked in butter, and cooked
   rice, and serve.

21   Cream of green pea soup with vegetables and chervil
Crème Faubonne   *4 portions*

1 Proceed as for Crème Ambassadeur.
2 Garnish with 50 g (2 oz) julienne of vegetables and a few chervil leaves.

22   Cream of tomato and potato soup with spinach   *Crème Malakoff*

1 Combine equal quantities of tomato soup and potato soup.

2 Alternatively, prepare a tomato soup, adding 200 g (8 oz) potatoes to the stock, which is liquidised after cooking.
3 For both methods: correct the seasoning and consistency and finish with cream.
4 Garnish with 25 g (1 oz) julienne of lightly cooked spinach.

Note If finished with a liaison, the soup is classically named Velouté Malakoff.

23 Cream of carrot and pea soup *Crème Médicis*

1 Proceed as for carrot soup, using half the amount of carrots with an equal amount of shelled or frozen peas.
2 Correct the seasoning and consistency.
3 Finish with cream and garnish with leaves of chervil.

Note This soup is known as Velouté Médicis when finished with a liaison.

24 Cream of tomato with rice and pimento
Crème andalouse   *4 portions*

1 Prepare 1 litre (2 pts) finished cream of tomato soup.
2 Garnish with 50 g (2 oz) cooked rice and 50 g (2 oz) red pepper, cut into julienne and cooked in butter.

25 Chicken soup thickened with yolks and cream, garnished with sorrel and chervil *Potage Germiny* *4 portions*

75 g	3 oz	sorrel
75 g	3 oz	butter
750 ml	1½ pt	chicken or veal consommé
		6 egg yolks } liaison
125 ml	¼ pt	cream
		salt and pepper
		chervil leaves

1 Finely shred the sorrel and sweat in 25 g (1 oz) butter.
2 Bring consommé to the boil in a thick-bottomed pan.
3 Very carefully add half the boiling consommé to the liaison, whisking all the time.
4 Return to the pan containing the remainder of the consommé and stir continuously until the consistency of the soup coats the back of a wooden spoon.
5 Immediately remove from the heat and strain through a fine strainer.
6 Add the remainder of the butter and sorrel.
7 Correct the seasoning and garnish with chervil leaves.

Note Cheese straws or croûtes may be served separately.

26   Cream of asparagus soup   *Crème d'asperges*   *4 portions*

50 g	2 oz	onions or white of leek
50 g	2 oz	celery
50 g	2 oz	butter
50 g	2 oz	flour
1 litre	2 pts	chicken stock
400 g	1 lb	asparagus trimmings
		bouquet garni
		salt and pepper
250 ml	½ pt	milk *or*
125 ml	¼ pt	cream

1 Sweat the sliced onion and celery in the butter without colour.
2 Remove from heat, add flour, return to heat and cook for a few minutes without colour.
3 Cool, gradually add the hot stock, stir to the boil.
4 Add the washed asparagus trimmings, the bouquet garni and season.
5 Simmer for 30 to 40 minutes. Remove bouquet garni.
6 Pass through a sieve and fine strainer or liquidise.
7 Return to a clean pan, reboil, add the milk or cream.
8 Correct the seasoning and consistency and serve.

27   Asparagus and mint soup

Proceed as for recipe 26, adding 25 g (1 oz) sprigs of mint with the asparagus.
   Garnish with blanched mint leaves, using 2 or 3 per portion.

28   Asparagus and avocado soup

As for recipe 26, with the addition of the flesh of 1½ avocado pears added with the asparagus trimmings. The remaining half of avocado pear is neatly diced and used as garnish.

29   Asparagus and mushroom soup

Proceed as for recipe 26, using 200 g (8 oz) asparagus trimmings and 200 g (8 oz) mushrooms. Slice 150 g (6 oz) mushrooms and sweat them with the onion and celery.
   Garnish with the remaining 50 g (2 oz) sliced mushrooms cooked in a little butter.

30   Cream of celery and cheese soup   *4 portions*

200 g	8 oz	celery ⎫
50 g	2 oz	onions ⎬ chopped
50 g	2 oz	leeks ⎭
50 g	2 oz	butter or margarine
50 g	2 oz	flour
750 ml	1½ pts	white stock
		bouquet garni
		salt and pepper
100 g	4 oz	cheese (stilton or strong cheddar), grated
250 ml	½ pt	milk *or*
125 ml	¼ pt	cream

1 Sweat the vegetables in the fat without colour.
2 Mix in the flour, cook for a few minutes and cool.
3 Gradually add the hot stock, stir to the boil.
4 Add the bouquet garni, season and simmer for approx. 45 mins.
5 Skim, remove the bouquet garni and pass or liquidise.
6 Return to a clean pan, bring to the boil, add the cheese and stir until incorporated into the soup.
7 Correct the seasoning and consistency, add the milk or cream and serve.

31   Leek and mange-tout soup   *4 portions*

400 g	1 lb	leeks
600 g	1½ lb	mange-tout
50 g	2 oz	butter or margarine
1 litre	2 pts	chicken stock
		bouquet garni
		salt and pepper
125 ml	¼ pt	cream

1 Shred the leeks (reserving some white of leek for garnish) and mange-tout and sweat in the butter.
2 Add the stock and bouquet garni, season and simmer for approx. 45 mins.
3 Liquidise, bring back to the boil, correct the seasoning and consistency and finish with cream.
4 Garnish with julienne of white of leek cooked in butter.

32   Leek and onion soup   *4 portions*

200 g	8 oz	onions
50 g	2 oz	butter or margarine
200 g	8 oz	leek
1 litre	(2 pts)	brown stock or consommé
		salt and pepper

1 Sweat the finely shredded onions in butter for a few mins.
2 Add the shredded leek and cook for a further few minutes without colour.
3 Add the stock, season and simmer for approx. 15 mins.
4 Correct the seasoning and serve with bread croûtes, as for onion soup, or grated cheese.

Note Alternatively, white stock can be used and the vegetables sweated without colour. A thickening agent of 25 g (1 oz) flour may be added after stage 2.

33 Okra or gumbo soup   *4 portions*

50 g	2 oz	butter, oil or margarine
200 g	8 oz	okra
100 g	4 oz	leek, in brunoise
750 ml	1 ½ pts	chicken stock
25 g	1 oz	lean ham
25 g	1 oz	cooked chicken
		salt and pepper
50 g	2 oz	diced tomato, peeled, deseeded and diced
25 g	1 oz	cooked rice

1 Heat the fat or oil and sweat the sliced okra in a thick-bottomed pan, covered with a lid, until nearly cooked.
2 Add the leeks and cook until soft.
3 Add the stock, diced ham and chicken and simmer for 5 mins.
4 Correct the seasoning, add the rice and tomato, bring to the boil and serve.

34 Bamboo and spinach soup   *4 portions*

750 ml	1 ½ pts	chicken stock
50 g	2 oz	trimmed bamboo shoots, drained, washed and sliced
50 g	2 oz	spinach
100 g	4 oz	lean ham
50 g	2 oz	button mushrooms, sliced
		salt
		½ teaspn sesame seed oil

1 Bring the stock to the boil; add the bamboo shoots and spinach cut in 2 cm (1 in.) pieces.
2 Simmer for 3 to 5 mins.
3 Add the ham cut in ½ cm (¼ in.) dice and the mushrooms.
4 Simmer for 5 mins., season with salt.
5 Add the oil and serve.

35   Sweet potato soup   *4 portions*

300 g	12 oz	white sweet potatoes
100 g	4 oz	leek or onion
25 g	1 oz	butter, margarine or oil
200 g	8 oz	tomatoes
500 ml	1 pt	chicken stock
		salt and pepper
		chopped parsley or fresh coriander

1 Peel, wash and cut the sweet potatoes into even pieces.
2 Cover with water, season with salt, cook till tender, approx. 20 minutes, and drain thoroughly.
3 Sweat the onions or leeks in the butter or oil and add the skinned tomatoes.
4 Cook for a few minutes, add the potatoes and liquidise into a purée.
5 Return to a clean pan, add the stock, bring to the boil and stir until smooth.
6 Correct the seasoning and serve, garnished with herbs.

36   Pumpkin soup   *Potage potiron*   *4 portions*

100 g	4 oz	chopped onion
800 g	2 lb	pumpkin, peeled, seeded, chopped
100 g	4 oz	butter or margarine
500 ml	1 pt	white stock
50 g	2 oz	flour
500 ml	1 pt	milk
		salt and pepper
125 ml	¼ pt	cream
50 g	2 oz	grated cheese
		chopped parsley

1 Sweat the onion and pumpkin in half of the butter for a few minutes.
2 Add the stock and simmer until cooked.
3 Make a white sauce with the remaining butter, flour and milk.
4 Add to the pumpkin, blend and pass or liquidise.
5 Season, bring to the boil and finish with cream, cheese and parsley.

37   Chive, potato and cucumber soup with cream   *4 portions*

50 g	2 oz	onions ⎞
50 g	2 oz	spring onions ⎬ chopped
50 g	2 oz	celery ⎠
50 g	2 oz	butter
375 ml	1 ½ pts	chicken stock
400 g	1 lb	potatoes, diced
		1 large cucumber, diced
		salt and pepper

125 ml	¼ pt	cream
		chopped parsley
		chopped chives

1 Sweat the onions and celery without colour in the butter.
2 Add the stock, potatoes and cucumber; season and simmer until soft.
3 Liquidise and cool. Correct the seasoning and consistency.
4 Finish with cream, parsley and chives.
5 Chill and serve.

Note This soup is usually served chilled but may be served hot.

38 Chilled tomato, pimento and garlic soup *Gazpacho*

4 portions

This Spanish soup has many regional variations. It is served chilled and has a predominant flavour of cucumber, tomato and garlic.

500 ml	1 pt	tomato juice
100 g	4 oz	tomatoes, skinned, deseeded and diced
100 g	4 oz	cucumber, peeled and diced
50 g	2 oz	green pepper, diced
50 g	2 oz	onion chopped
		1 tablespn mayonnaise
		1 tablespn vinegar
		seasoning
		1 clove garlic

1 Mix all the ingredients together.
2 Season and add crushed chopped garlic to taste.
3 Stand in a cool place for an hour.
4 Correct the consistency with iced water and serve chilled.

Note Instead of serving with all the ingredients finely chopped, the soup can be liquidised and garnished with chopped tomato, cucumber and pepper. The soup may also be finished with chopped herbs.

Sometimes a tray of garnishes may accompany the soup, e.g. chopped red and green pepper, chopped onion, tomato, cucumber and croûtons etc.

39 Carrot and orange soup

4 portions

400 g	1 lb	carrots, sliced
50 g	2 oz	white of leek
50 g	2 oz	onion
25 g	1 oz	butter or margarine
25 g	1 oz	flour
		1 teaspn tomato purée

1 litre	2 pts	white stock
		zest and juice of 2 oranges
		bouquet garni
		salt and pepper
125 ml	¼ pt	natural yoghurt

1 Gently sweat the sliced vegetables in the butter or margarine without colour, until soft. Mix in the flour.
2 Cook over a gentle heat without colouring.
3 Mix in the tomato purée.
4 Gradually add the boiling stock. Stir well.
5 Prepare a fine julienne from the zest of the oranges, blanch and refresh.
6 Add the orange juice to the soup.
7 Add bouquet garni, salt and pepper.
8 Simmer gently for approx. 45 mins.
9 Remove bouquet garni, liquidise and pass through a coarse strainer.
10 Return to a clean pan, re-boil, correct the seasoning and consistency, finish with yoghurt. Garnish with the julienne of orange zest.

Note Alternatively, the soup may be finished with cream or fromage frais.

40   Cream of tomato and orange soup

Prepare a cream of tomato soup. Prior to straining, add thinly peeled strips of orange zest and simmer for a few minutes. The juice of one orange may be added and a blanched julienne of orange zest used for garnish to every 500 ml (1 pt) of soup. Serve hot.

Fruit soups

Soups with a fruit base are served hot or cold and may be served for breakfast as well as lunch or dinner.

41   Fruit soup   *4 portions*

50 g	2 oz	raisins, seedless
50 g	2 oz	currants
50 g	2 oz	dried apples, diced
50 g	2 oz	dried appricots, diced
50 g	2 oz	prunes (stoned), diced
500 ml	1 pt	water
		1 orange, in segments
		1 lemon, in segments
500 ml	1 pt	pineapple juice

1 Soak the dried fruit overnight in the water or a mixture water and wine.
2 Drain, cover the dried fruit with water and cook for 10 mins.
3 Add the diced orange and lemon segments, free from pith, and the pineapple juice and simmer for a few minutes. Serve hot or cold.

Note This soup may also be finished with 125 ml (¼ pt) Madeira, port or dry sherry.

42   Mussel soup   *4 portions*

400 g	1 lb	mussels
1 litre	2 pts	fish stock
50 g	2 oz	shallots or onions ⎫
50 g	2 oz	celery ⎬ chopped
50 g	2 oz	leek ⎭
		parsley
		salt and pepper
60 ml	⅛ pt	white wine
125 ml	¼ pt	cream
		1 egg yolk

1 Scrape and thoroughly clean the mussels.
2 Place in a pan with the stock, chopped vegetables and herbs and season.
3 Cover with a lid and simmer for 5 mins.
4 Extract the mussels from the shells and remove the beards.
5 Strain the liquid and bring to the boil, add the wine.
6 Correct the seasoning, finish with a liaison and garnish with the mussels and chopped parsley.

Note Variations for this soup include: scallops in place of mussels, fennel and dill in place of parsley.
   A further variation is to prepare a potato soup using fish stock, garnish with mussels and finish with cream.

43   Fish soup   *4 portions*

50 g	2 oz	onions or shallots, chopped
		1 clove garlic
50 g	2 oz	butter, margarine or oil
400 g	1 lb	monk fish or any white fish
100 g	4 oz	potato
100 g	4 oz	tomato
1 litre	2 pts	fish stock
		bouquet garni
		salt and pepper
		parsley

1 Sweat the onion and garlic in the butter without colour.

2 Add the fish, free from skin and bone, cook for 2 to 3 mins.
3 Add the remainder of the ingredients, season.
4 Simmer for 20 mins.
5 Remove the bouquet garni and liquidise.
6 Correct the seasoning and consistency.
7 Finish with chopped parsley.

Note Variations to this soup include the addition of wine, cream or yoghurt or fromage frais, saffron, curry powder, tomato purée, rice, shrimps, or mushrooms.

44   Stilton soup   *4 portions*

50 g	2 oz	butter or margarine
50 g	2 oz	white of leek ⎫ finely sliced
50 g	2 oz	celery ⎭
35 g	1½ oz	flour
750 ml	1½ pts	chicken or veal stock
250 ml	½ pt	milk
200 g	8 oz	grated or crumbled stilton cheese
		salt, pepper
60 ml	⅛ pt	cream

1 Melt the butter and gently sweat the vegetables without colour.
2 Stir in the flour and cook out for 1–2 mins. without colour.
3 Remove from heat, mix in the stock and milk.
4 Return to heat, stir to the boil and simmer for 30 mins.
5 Mix in the cheese, correct the seasoning and bring to the boil.
6 Pass through a sieve or strainer, or liquidise.
7 Add the cream, reheat and serve.

5

Egg dishes

1   Poached eggs in potato nest with mushrooms and horseradish sauce   *Oeufs pochés duchesse*   *4 portions*

		4 eggs
200 g	8 oz	duchess potato
100 g	4 oz	finely chopped onion
50 g	2 oz	butter or margarine
		½ teaspn paprika
100 g	4 oz	finely chopped mushrooms
250 ml	½ pt	horseradish sauce

1 Poach the eggs, keep in ice cold water until required.
2 On a lightly greased and floured baking sheet, pipe a nest of duchess potato to hold each egg. Egg wash. Lightly brown in a moderate oven (180°C, 350°F, Reg. 4).
3 Sweat the finely chopped onion in the butter without colour; add the paprika, sweat together for 2 mins.
4 Add the mushrooms, cook out for a further 2 to 3 mins.
5 Reheat the poached eggs in boiling salted water, drain and dry well on a cloth.
6 Place the potato nests onto a suitable plate, arrange a spoonful of the mushroom mixture on the bottom of each and carefully place an egg on the top. Coat with horseradish sauce (see below) and serve immediately.

Horseradish sauce

125 ml	¼ pt	chicken velouté or natural yoghurt
125 ml	¼ pt	single cream
		1 tablespn freshly grated horseradish
		lemon juice

1 Boil out the velouté, season with salt and pepper, add the cream.
2 Continue to cook until correct consistency and then strain. Add horseradish and a squeeze of lemon juice.

2   Poached eggs with prawns, sherry and French mustard   *Oeufs pochés Mariette*   *4 portions*

		4 eggs
		4 medium-sized tomatoes, peeled and sliced
100 g	4 oz	prawns
25 g	1 oz	butter or margarine
		2 tablespns of sherry
250 ml	½ pt	Mornay sauce
		½ teaspn French mustard
50 g	2 oz	grated parmesan cheese

1 Poach the eggs, reserve in a basin of cold water.
2 Divide the tomatoes into 4 individual dishes, e.g. egg dishes, season

lightly with salt and pepper. Place on a baking sheet in a moderate oven for approx. 5 mins.
3 Warm the prawns in the butter and sherry.
4 Reheat the Mornay sauce and flavour with the French mustard.
5 Reheat the eggs, drain well. Place on top of the slices of cooked tomato.
6 Sprinkle the prawns over the eggs.
7 Coat with Mornay sauce and sprinkle with parmeasn cheese.
8 Glaze under the salamander. Serve immediately.

3 Poached eggs with chicken and tomato and cream sauces *Oeufs pochés Halévy* 4 portions

		4 eggs
100 g	4 oz	short pastry
50 g	2 oz	diced cooked chicken
50 g	2 oz	tomatoes, peeled, deseeded and diced
50 g	2 oz	butter or margarine
125 ml	¼ pt	chicken velouté
		1 tablespn double cream
125 ml	¼ pt	tomato sauce
		meat glaze

1 Poach the eggs, retain in cold water.
2 Line 4 tartlet moulds with short pastry, bake blind.
3 Reheat the diced chicken and tomatoes in the butter or margarine.
4 Place the chicken and tomato in the bottom of the tartlet cases.
5 Reheat the eggs in boiling salted water; drain well. Arrange the eggs on top of the chicken and tomato.
6 Boil the chicken velouté, add the cream and strain.
7 Mask each egg with the two sauces: tomato sauce on one half and suprême sauce on the other.
8 Separate the two sauces with a thin line of warm meat glaze and serve.

4 Poached eggs on a muffin with hollandaise sauce
Oeufs pochés Benedictine 4 portions

		4 eggs
		4 muffins
		4 slices of tongue or ham
250 ml	½ pt	hollandaise sauce

1 Poach the eggs, reserve in cold water.
2 Toast the muffins cut out with a round plain cutter, the size of the eggs.
3 Cut a slice of ham or tongue the same size; warm gently by brushing with a little butter and placing in a moderate oven.

4 Place the buttered muffin on a suitable plate, with the ham or tongue on top and the reheated, well-drained poached eggs on the ham or tongue.
5 Coat with hollandaise sauce and serve immediately.

5   Deep-fried stuffed eggs with bacon and herbs
Oeufs durs Phoebe   *4 portions*

50 g	2 oz	streaky bacon
25 g	1 oz	butter or margarine
		4 eggs, hard-boiled
		1 tablespn mixed herbs (parsley, chervil, thyme, chives)
		1 raw egg yolk
		seasoned flour, white or wholemeal
		beaten egg
		breadcrumbs (white or wholemeal)

1 Finely dice the bacon, quickly fry in the butter and place in a basin.
2 Cut the hard-boiled eggs into two lengthwise, remove the yolks and sieve.
3 Add the sieved yolks to the bacon with the herbs and yolk. Cream well, season with salt and pepper.
4 Use this mixture to fill the whites. Sandwich together to form a whole egg, allow plenty of filling so that the two halves are slightly apart.
5 Pass through flour, egg and breadcrumbs.
6 Fry in deep fat, 185°C (370°F), until golden brown. Serve with a fresh tomato sauce or cullis (see below).

6   Fresh tomato sauce or cullis

1 kg	2 lb	tomatoes
50 g	2 oz	onion
		1 clove garlic
	1 oz	butter
		salt and pepper
		pinch of sugar

1 Skin, halve, remove the seeds and chop the tomatoes.
2 Sweat the chopped onion and garlic in the butter.
3 Add the tomatoes and season.
4 Simmer for 15 minutes.
5 Purée in a liquidiser or food processor.
6 Bring to the boil and correct the seasoning.

Note Herbs, such as rosemary, thyme or bay leaf, may be added and shallots used in place of onion.
   Fully, ripe, well-flavoured tomatoes are needed for a good fresh tomato sauce. Italian plum tomatoes are also suitable and it is sometimes advisable

to use tinned plum tomatoes if the fresh tomatoes which are available lack flavour and colour.

7   Eggs on the dish with sliced onion, bacon and potatoes
Oeufs sur le plat bonne femme   *4 portions*

50 g	2 oz	shredded onion
60 ml	⅛ pt	oil
		2 small potatoes, peeled and sliced
100 g	4 oz	lardons of bacon
50 g	2 oz	butter
		4 eggs
		salt and pepper
		4 tablespns cream
		chopped parsley

1 Sauté the onions in oil until they are lightly coloured.
2 Separately fry the potatoes in oil until cooked and golden brown; drain.
3 Add the onions to the potatoes.
4 Blanch the lardons; quickly fry in the butter, do not drain.
5 Divide the potatoes, onions and lardons into 4 egg dishes.
6 Break in the eggs, season with salt and pepper and mask with cream. Cook in a moderate oven until the eggs are set.
7 Sprinkle with chopped parsley and serve immediately.

8   Eggs on the dish with chicken livers and mushrooms in Madeira sauce   *Oeufs sur le plat chasseur*   *4 portions*

75 g	3 oz	butter or margarine
		4 eggs
100 g	2 oz	chicken livers
		1 tablespn oil
		salt and pepper
50 g	2 oz	sliced button mushrooms
125 ml	¼ pt	demi-glace
		2 tablespns Madeira wine
		parsley or chervil

1 Divide 50 g (2 oz) butter between 4 egg dishes and allow to melt.
2 Break in the eggs, season with salt and pepper, place on a baking sheet. Cook in a moderate oven until set.
3 Clean the chicken livers, neatly slice.
4 Sauté the chicken livers in the oil, keeping them undercooked. Drain and season with salt and pepper.
5 Sauté the sliced mushrooms in the remaining butter or margarine.
6 Boil the demi-glace with the Madeira wine, strain and add the mushrooms.

(Contd.)

7 Arrange a cordon of Madeira sauce and mushrooms around the eggs, garnish with chicken livers and a sprig of parsley or chervil and serve.

9   Eggs on the dish with grilled lamb's kidney and Madeira sauce   *Oeufs sur-le-plat Meyerbeer*   *4 portions*

		2 lamb's kidneys
		salt and pepper
		2 tablespns oil
50 g	2 oz	butter or margarine
		4 eggs
125 ml	¼ pt	demi-glace
		2 tablespns Madeira wine

1 Remove the membrane from the kidneys, cut in half and remove centre core.
2 Place on a suitable tray. Season and brush with oil; grill under salamander, leaving them slightly under cooked.
3 Divide the butter between 4 egg dishes, melt, break in the eggs and season with salt and pepper.
4 Place on a baking sheet and cook in a moderate oven until set.
5 Boil the demi-glace, add the Madeira wine and strain.
6 Serve the eggs with a cordon of Madeira sauce, garnished with half a grilled kidney and a sprig of parsley or chervil.

10   Soft-boiled eggs with mushroom duxelle
Oeufs mollets Volnay   *4 portions*

		4 eggs	
100 g	4 oz	short pastry	
25 g	1 oz	shallots	
100 g	4 oz	mushrooms	duxelle
50 g	2 oz	butter or margarine	
		salt and pepper	
125 ml	½ pt	Mornay sauce	
25 g	1 oz	grated parmesan cheese	

1 Soft boil the eggs for 5 to 6 mins. then remove and place in a basin of cold water to cool. Shell. Retain in cold water.
2 Line 4 tartlet moulds with short pastry and bake blind.
3 Prepare a mushroom duxelle from the shallots, mushrooms and butter or margarine. Season.
4 Place tartlet cases in individual serving dishes and fill with the duxelle.
5 Reheat the eggs in boiling salted water, drain. Place the reheated eggs in the tartlet cases.
6 Mask with Mornay sauce, sprinkle with grated parmesan cheese and gratinate. Serve immediately.

11　Soft-boiled eggs in pastry cases with watercress
Oeufs mollets en croustade cressonnière　　　　　　　　　　*4 portions*

		4 eggs
100 g	4 oz	short pastry
25 g	1 oz	butter or margarine
		1 bunch watercress, washed and finely shredded
		1 teaspn anchovy essence
		salt and pepper
250 ml	½ pt	Mornay sauce
25 g	1 oz	grated parmesan cheese

1　Soft boil the eggs for 5 to 6 mins., refresh in cold water, shell and retain in cold water until required.
2　Line 4 tartlet cases, bake blind.
3　Melt the butter in a suitable pan, add the watercress and allow to sweat for 2 to 3 mins. Add the anchovy essence and season lightly.
4　Divide the watercress between the tartlet cases.
5　Reheat the eggs in boiling water for approximately 1 minute. Drain well and arrange on top of the watercress.
6　Coat the eggs with Mornay sauce, sprinkle with grated parmesan cheese, and glaze under the salamander. Serve immediately.

12　Deep-fried eggs with tomatoes and bacon　*Oeufs frits americaine*

oil
4 eggs
4 round croûtons
salt and pepper
4 halves of grilled tomatoes
4 rashers of grilled bacon

1　Half fill an omelet pan with oil.
2　Heat oil until approx 180°–190°C (350°–375°F). Break the eggs into a saucer and slide them carefully into the oil.
3　With a wooden spoon fold the white to envelope the yolk. When cooked and nicely coloured, remove and drain on a cloth.
4　Serve on individual plates on a round fried bread croûton. Season and garnish with grilled tomato and bacon.

13　Omelet with creamed smoked haddock and cheese
Omelette Arnold Bennett　　　　　　　　　　　　　　　　*4 portions*

10 g	½ oz	butter or margarine
50 g	2 oz	cooked, flaked, smoked haddock

90 ml	3/16 pt	Mornay sauce
		1 × 3 egg flat omelet
10 g	½ oz	parmesan cheese

1 Melt the butter or margarine in a suitable pan, reheat the smoked haddock. Bind with a little of the Mornay sauce.
2 Prepare a flat omelet, place on to a plate.
3 Arrange the fish on top of the omelet, coat with the remainder of the sauce, sprinkle with parmesan cheese and glaze under the salamander. Serve immediately.

14   Omelet with mushrooms and chicken livers
Omelette chasseur   *4 portions*

100 g	4 oz	chicken livers
50 g	2 oz	butter or margarine
50 g	2 oz	sliced mushrooms
60 ml	⅛ pt	jus-lié
		salt and pepper
		4 × 2 egg omelets
		chopped tarragon

1 Trim the livers, cut into quarters, sauté quickly in half the butter or margarine, keeping slightly under-cooked.
2 Sauté the mushrooms in the remaining butter or margarine.
3 Add the mushrooms to the chicken livers, bind with jus-lié and season with salt and pepper.
4 Make the omelets and fold.
5 Serve the omelets on individual plates. Cut an incision in the tops, fill with mushrooms and chicken livers, and sprinkle with chopped tarragon. Serve a little sauce around the omelets.

15   Omelet with lamb and cream or yoghurt   *Omelette bergère*
4 portions

100 g	4 oz	diced cooked lamb
75 g	3 oz	butter or margarine
60 ml	⅛ pt	double cream or natural yoghurt
		salt and pepper
		4 × 2 egg omelets

1 Reheat the diced, cooked lamb in the butter or margarine, add the cream or natural yoghurt, bring to the boil and season with salt and pepper.
2 Prepare the omelets; fill with the lamb when folding.
3 Serve on individual plates.

16   Omelet with potatoes and gruyère cheese
Omelette savoyarde   *4 portions*

100 g	4 oz	potatoes
60 ml	⅛ pt	oil
		salt and pepper
		8 eggs
100 g	4 oz	gruyère cheese
100 g	4 oz	butter or margarine

1 Cut the potatoes into ¼ cm (⅛ in.) dice, fry in the oil until lightly brown, drain and season with salt.
2 Beat the eggs well, season, add the potatoes.
3 Cut the cheese in ¼ cm (⅛ in.) dice and add to the mixture.
4 Use the butter or margarine to make 4 flat omelets.
5 Serve on individual plates at once.

17   Light fluffy omelet   *Omelette Mére Poularde*

For each omelet
2 – 3   egg yolks
salt and pepper
2 – 3   egg whites
1 oz butter or margarine

1 Beat the yolks with salt and pepper.
2 Half beat the whites, fold the yolks into the whites.
3 Heat the butter or margarine in the omelet pan and pour in the mixture; cook, stirring with a fork, until nearly set.
4 Fold the omelet in half, finish cooking in the oven until set.
5 Serve on individual plates immediately.

18   Eggs in cocotte with tomato and orange sauce
Oeufs en cocotte bigarade   *4 portions*

250 ml	½ pt	tomato sauce
		1 orange
10 g	½ oz	sugar
		½ tablespn vinegar
		juice of ½ lemon
		1 tablespn Cointreau
50 g	2 oz	butter or margarine
		salt and pepper
		4 eggs

1 Boil the tomato sauce.
2 Segment the orange, retain the juice.

3 Boil the sugar and vinegar to a light caramel, add the orange and lemon juice. Boil out.
4 Add the tomato sauce, simmer for 2 mins. Pass through a strainer.
5 Finish with the Cointreau.
6 Butter and season 4 cocotte dishes. Place a half tablespoon of the sauce in each. Break in the eggs.
7 Place in a shallow tray containing 1 cm (½ in.) water. Cook in a moderate oven until the eggs are lightly set.
8 Serve with a little of the sauce around each egg, garnished with a segment of orange.

19   Eggs Flemish style   *Oeufs à la flamande*   *4 portions*

		4 soft-boiled eggs, peeled
10 g	½ oz	butter or margarine
		1 teaspn French mustard
		salt and pepper
125 ml	¼ pt	single cream
100 g	4 oz	prawns
		1 teaspn chopped parsley
25 g	1 oz	grated gruyère cheese

1 Coarsely chop the eggs in a basin.
2 Heat the butter in a suitable small pan; add the eggs, with the mustard.
3 Season with salt and pepper, add the cream, prawns and parsley.
4 Stir gently over a moderate heat for 2 to 3 mins., then divide into individual egg dishes or cocottes.
5 Sprinkle with cheese, gratinate under the salamander and serve at once.

6

Pasta

See also Chapter 11 Ethnic recipes

Purchasing and storage

There are over fifty different varieties and shapes of pasta, usually factory mass-produced and dried, to give indefinite keeping quality and sold in packets or by the kilo. However, freshly made pasta is increasingly more available from suppliers and, where time and staff allow, it can also be made as required in the kitchen.

If eggs are used in the making of fresh pasta, the fresher they are the longer the keeping quality of the pasta. When fresh pasta is correctly stored it will keep for up to 3 or 4 weeks. Flat types of fresh pasta, such as noodles, which are dried and transferred to a container or bowl, will keep for up to a month in a cool, dry store. Other shapes can be stored in the freezer. To make fresh egg pasta, see recipe on page 74.

Types and sauces

There are basically 4 types of pasta, each of which may be left plain or flavoured with spinach or tomato.

- dried durum wheat pasta
- egg pasta
- semolina pasta
- wholewheat pasta

Examples of sauces to go with pasta include:
* tomato sauce
* cream, butter or béchamel based
* rich meat sauce
* olive oil and garlic
* soft white or blue cheese

Cheeses

Examples of cheeses used in pasta include:
* *Parmesan*, the most popular hard cheese, ideal for grating. The flavour is best when it is freshly grated. If bought ready grated, or if it is grated and stored, the flavour deteriorates.
* *Pecorino*, a strong ewe's milk cheese, sometimes studded with peppercorns. Used for strongly flavoured dishes, it can be grated or thinly sliced.
* *Ricotta*, creamy-white in colour, made from the discarded whey of other cheeses. It is widely used in fillings for pasta, e.g. cannelloni, ravioli etc. and for sauces.
* *Mozzarella*, made from the milk of the water buffalo. It is pure white and creamy, with a mild but distinctive flavour, usually round or pear-shaped. It will only keep for a few days in a container half-filled with milk and water.
* *Gorgonzola* or *dolcelatte*, distinctive blue cheeses which can be used in sauces.

Ingredients

The following are some examples of ingredients that can be used in pasta dishes. The list is almost endless but can include:

smoked salmon	peppers	sage
shrimps	broad beans	tarragon
prawns	broccoli	fennel
mussels	sliced sausage	chives
scallops	salami	spring onions
lobster	ham	marjoram
tuna fish	bacon	pine nuts
crab	beef	walnuts
anchovies	chicken	stoned olives
cockles	duck	capers
avocado	tongue	cooked, dried beans
mushrooms	chicken livers	eggs
tomatoes	smoked ham	grated lemon zest
onions	mustard and cress	saffron
courgettes	parsley	grated nutmeg
peas	rosemary	sultanas
spinach	basil	

Stuffed pasta

Examples of stuffed pasta include the following:

- *Agnolini* small half-moon shapes usually filled with ham and cheese or minced meat.
- *Cannelloni* squares of pasta poached, refreshed, dried, stuffed with a variety of fillings and rolled, e.g. ricotta cheese and spinach, and finished with an appropriate sauce.
- *Cappelletti* shaped like little hats, usually filled as agnolini, and are available dried.
- *Ravioli* usually square with serrated edges. A wide variety of fillings can be used – fish, meat, vegetarian, cheese, etc.
- *Ravolini* or 'little ravioli' are made half the size of ravioli
- *Tortellini* a slightly larger version of cappelletti, also available in dried form
- *Tortelloni* double-sized version of tortellini

Pasta which is to be stuffed must be rolled as thinly as possible. The stuffing should be pleasant in taste and plentiful in quantity. The edges of the pasta must be thoroughly sealed otherwise the stuffing will seep out during poaching.

All stuffed pasta should be served in or coated with a suitable sauce, and depending on the type of recipe may be finished 'au gratin'.

Stuffings

Some examples of stuffing for pasta which follow are for 400 g (1 lb) pasta. The list is almost endless as every district in Italy has its own variations and with thought and experimentation many more can be produced.

200 g	8 oz	cooked minced chicken
100 g	4 oz	minced ham
25 g	1 oz	butter
		2 yolks or 1 egg
25 g	1 oz	grated cheese
		pinch of grated nutmeg
		salt and pepper
25 g	1 oz	fresh white breadcrumbs
200 g	8 oz	cooked dry spinach, puréed
200 g	8 oz	ricotta cheese
25 g	1 oz	butter
		nutmeg, salt and pepper
200 g	8 oz	cooked minced lean pork
200 g	8 oz	cooked minced lean veal
25 g	1 oz	butter
25 g	1 oz	grated cheese
		2 yolks or 1 egg
25 g	1 oz	fresh white breadcrumbs
		salt and pepper
		pinch of chopped marjoram

150 g	6 oz	ricotta cheese
75 g	3 oz	grated parmesan
		1 egg
		nutmeg, salt and pepper
200 g	8 oz	cooked minced turkey
50 g	2 oz	cooked minced pork
25 g	4 oz	grated cheese
		pinch of sage and rosemary
		nutmeg, salt and pepper
		1 egg
		grated zest of 2 lemons

1   Egg pasta dough   *4 portions*

400 g	1 lb	strong flour
		salt
		4 eggs, beaten
		oil, as required

1 Sieve flour and salt, shape into a well.
2 Pour the eggs into the well.
3 Gradually incorporate the flour and add oil if necessary to adjust the consistency.
4 Pull and knead the dough well until it is of a smooth, elastic consistency.
5 Cover the dough with a dampened cloth and allow to rest and relax for half an hour in a cool place.
6 Roll out the dough on a well floured surface (or dust surface with fine semolina) until ¼ cm (⅛ in.) thick.
7 Trim the sides and cut the dough as required using a large knife.

Note There are pasta rolling machines available which considerably speed up the rolling out process.
   The amount of oil used in making the dough may vary according to the type of flour and the size of the eggs.

2   Butterfly pasta with crab   *Farfalle con il granchio*   *4 portions*

400 g	1 lb	pasta
200–300 g	8–12 oz	flaked white crabmeat
50 g	2 oz	butter
		2 tablespns brandy or white wine
125 ml	¼ pt	double cream
		salt and cayenne pepper
25 g	1 oz	chopped parsley

1 Cook pasta in boiling salted water and drain.
2 Gently heat the crabmeat in the butter.
3 Add brandy or wine; raise heat to evaporate the alcohol.

4 Mix in the cream, re-heat, correct seasoning, mix in parsley.
5 Serve pasta and coat with the sauce.

Note Any type of unfilled pasta can be used.
Any type of shellfish or combination of shellfish can be used.

3 Penne and mange-tout *6 portions* (Maddalena Bonino)

400 g	1 lb	penne or macaroni
150 g	6 oz	cream cheese
75 g	3 oz	gorgonzola
		2–3 tablespns single cream
400 g	1 lb	mange-tout
50 g	2 oz	butter
		salt and black mill pepper

1 Cook the pasta in plenty of boiling salted water.
2 Blend the cream cheese, gorgonzola and cream in a pan over a low heat, to a smooth sauce. If the sauce is too thick, thin with a little water from the pasta.
3 Cook the mange-tout in boiling salted water for 1–2 minutes, keeping them slightly firm.
4 Drain the pasta, add the butter, then the sauce and finally the mange-tout.
5 Finish with freshly ground black pepper. If desired, a few thin red strips of red pepper may be added for decoration.

Note A winning recipe from a national competition.
Penne is pronounced *pennay*. Macaroni may be used in place of penne.

4 Spaghetti with bacon and tomatoes *Spaghetti al guanciale* *4 portions*

400 g	1 lb	spaghetti
		2 tablespns oil
150 g	6 oz	diced bacon
100 g	4 oz	finely chopped onion
400 g	1 lb	tomatoes, peeled, deseeded and diced
5 g	¼ oz	marjoram
		salt and pepper
50 g	2 oz	grated cheese

1 Cook spaghetti in boiling salted water and drain.
2 Heat oil in a pan and gently cook bacon for 1–2 mins.
3 Add onion and continue cooking gently until soft.
4 Add tomatoes, marjoram and salt and pepper, and cook briskly for 10 mins.

5 Serve spaghetti coated with sauce and sprinkled with cheese.

Note This sauce can be used with any pasta dish. Mushrooms may be added as one of many variations to this recipe.

5   Spaghetti with broccoli and tomatoes   *Spaghetti alla calabria*
4 portions

400 g	1 lb	spaghetti
		1 large head of broccoli
		1 tablespn oil
		1–2 crushed cloves of garlic
400 g	1 lb	tomatoes, peeled, deseeded and diced
		salt and pepper
50 g	2 oz	seedless raisins or sultanas
50 g	2 oz	pine nuts
50 g	2 oz	grated cheese

1 Cook spaghetti in boiling salted water; drain.
2 Remove broccoli stalks, cut broccoli into bite-sized pieces, cook 'al dente' and drain.
3 Lightly brown the garlic in the oil, then discard the garlic, add the tomatoes and salt and pepper; simmer for 15 mins.
4 Stir in raisins and pine nuts.
5 Serve spaghetti coated with sauce and topped with broccoli and cheese.

6   Noodles or spaghetti with eggs and bacon
Fettucine alla carbonara   *4 portions*

400 g	1 lb	noodles or spaghetti
		2 tablespns oil
100 g	4 oz	diced streaky bacon
		1 crushed clove of garlic
		3 eggs
		salt and pepper
50 g	2 oz	grated cheese

1 Cook pasta in salted water and drain.
2 Heat the oil and lightly brown the bacon and garlic.
3 Drain off the bacon, discard the garlic.
4 Beat the eggs with salt and pepper.
5 Place the drained pasta back in its pan, mix in the bacon and eggs and stir over a low heat for 2–3 mins. Serve immediately.

Note This recipe can be used with any type of unfilled pasta.
  Fettucine and tagliatelle are narrower-cut noodles.

7

Fish dishes

Introduction

More people are eating fish in preference to meat these days and customers should always be offered a reasonable choice. The dishes available should include simply prepared and cooked items. It is a mistake to include on the menu all rich and elaborate dishes as good fresh fish is often at its best when simply cooked.

The contemporary trend is for hot fish sauces to be lightly thickened, preferably without the use of a roux-based sauce. However, in large-scale cookery, when considerable quantities of fish sauces may be required, the use of fish velouté may be necessary.

The quality of fish stock must be of the highest level if good quality fish dishes are to be produced. Care must be taken at all times to use only fresh, clean, selected fish bones, then to sweat them in butter with onion, season lightly with herbs and where possible moisten with white wine. Never allow fish stock to cook for more than 20 minutes otherwise the flavour will be impaired.

1   Bouillabaise   *4 portions*

This is a thick, full-bodied fish stew for which there are many variations. When made in the south of France, a selection of Meditteranean fish is used. If made in the north of France the following recipe could be typical.

1½ kg	3 lb	assorted prepared fish, e.g. red mullet, whiting, sole, gurnard, small conger eel, John Dory, crawfish tail
500 ml	1 pt	mussels (optional)
75 g	3 oz	chopped onion or white of leek
10 g	½ oz	crushed garlic
125 ml	¼ pt	white wine
500 ml	1 pt	water
100 g	4 oz	tomatoes, skinned, deseeded, diced
		or
25 g	1 oz	tomato purée
		pinch of saffron
		bouquet garni (fennel, aniseed, parsley, celery)
125 ml	¼ pt	olive oil
5 g	¼ oz	chopped parsley
		salt and pepper
25 g	1 oz	butter ⎱ beurre manié
10 g	½ oz	flour ⎰
		French bread

1 Clean, de-scale and wash the fish. Cut into 2 cm (1 in.) pieces on the bone, the heads may be removed. Clean the mussels.
2 Place the cut fish, with mussels and crawfish on top, in a clean pan.
3 Simmer the onion, garlic, wine, water, tomato, saffron and bouquet garni for 20 mins.
4 Pour onto the fish, add the oil and parsley, bring to the boil and simmer approx. 15 mins.
5 Correct seasoning, thicken with beurre manié.
6 The liquor may be served first as a soup, followed by the fish accompanied by French bread which has been toasted, left plain, or rubbed with garlic.

Note If using soft fish, e.g. whiting, add it 10 minutes after the other fish.

2   Cod poached in white wine, tomato, garlic and parsley
Cabillaud à la portugaise   *4 portions*

400 g	1 lb	cod fillet or 4 cod steaks (150 g/6 oz each)
		1 finely chopped shallot or small onion
		1 tablespn olive oil
300 g	12 oz	tomatoes, skinned, deseeded, diced
		1 small garlic clove, crushed
		chopped parsley
125 ml	¼ pt	white wine
125 ml	¼ pt	fish stock
		salt and pepper
50 g	2 oz	butter

1 Place the washed cod in a buttered ovenproof dish.
2 Cook the shallot in the oil without colour.
3 Add the tomatoes, garlic and parsley, and pour over the fish.
4 Add the wine, fish stock and season lightly with salt.
5 Cover with buttered paper and poach gently.
6 Remove the cod and drain.
7 Reduce the cooking liquor, mix in the butter, correct seasoning, and add a pinch of fresh chopped parsley.
8 Pour over the cod and serve.

Note This recipe can be used with any white fish, cooked on or off the bone. Always remove any bones or skin before coating with sauce. Filleted cod can be cooked in any of the other ways given for poached white fish, e.g. Dieppoise, Otéro, Suchet etc.

3   **Russian fish pie**   *Coulibiac de saumon*   *4 portions*

This dish can be made using brioche or puff paste

200 g	8 oz	brioche or puff paste
100 g	4 oz	coarse semolina or rice, cooked in good stock as for pilaff
400 g	1 lb	salmon, cut in small thick slices and very lightly fried in butter
50 g	2 oz	finely chopped onion ⎫
100 g	4 oz	chopped mushrooms ⎬ duxelle
		I tablespn chopped parsley ⎭
		1 hard-boiled egg, chopped
200 g	8 oz	fresh vesiga* (50 g/2 oz if dried), cooked and roughly chopped
		melted butter

1 Roll out the paste thinly into a rectangle approx. 30 × 18 cm (12 × 7 in.).
2 Place the ingredients in layers one on top of the other along the centre, alternating the layers, starting and finishing with the semolina or rice.

3 Egg wash the edges of the paste and fold over to enclose the filling completely.
4 Seal the ends and turn over onto a lightly greased baking sheet so that the sealed edges are underneath.
5 Allow to prove in a warm place for approx. 30 mins.
6 Brush all over with melted butter and cut two small holes neatly in the top to allow steam to escape.
7 Bake at 190°C (375°F, Reg. 5) for approx. 40 mins.
8 When removed from the oven, pour some melted butter into the two holes.
9 To serve, cut into thick slices and offer a butter-type sauce e.g. hollandaise, separately.

Notes
1 If using puff pastry, egg wash the completed dish before baking instead of brushing with butter.
2 Individual coulibiacs can be made using a 20 cm (8 in.) pastry cutter.
3* Vesiga is the spinal cord of the sturgeon obtained commercially in the shape of white, semi-transparent dry gelatinous ribbon. It must be soaked in cold water for 4 to 5 hours when it will swell to 4 to 5 times the size and the weight will increase six-fold. It is then gently simmered in white stock for 3½ to 4½ hours.
   If it is not possible to obtain vesiga, a layer of fish forcemeat may be substituted.
4 Coulibiac has been for many years a popular dish in high-class restaurants around the world. If the ingredients in this recipe are not available or are too expensive then other fish may be used to replace salmon, e.g. haddock. If vesiga is unobtainable then use more of all the other ingredients. With imagination many variations of this dish can be conceived.

Sole, plaice, turbot, halibut, hake, cod, fresh haddock, monkfish, whiting, or John Dory may be used for recipes numbered 4 to 12.

4 Fillets of fish on mushroom purée with cheese sauce
Filets de poisson Cubat   *4 portions*

200 g	8 oz	button mushrooms
400–600 g	1–1½ lb	fish fillets
50 g	2 oz	butter
250 ml	½ pt	Mornay sauce
		8 slices of truffle (see note overleaf)

1 Roughly slice the mushrooms and cook in a little fish stock.
2 Poach the fish in butter and the mushroom cooking liquor.
3 Drain the fish well, reduce the cooking liquor and add it to the Mornay sauce.

4 Thoroughly dry the mushrooms and chop, place in serving dish.
5 Place the fish on top of the mushroom purée and add 2 slices of truffle on each portion.
6 Correct seasoning and the consistency of the Mornay sauce.
7 Coat with the sauce, glaze and serve.

Note This is a simple classic dish with an excellent blend of flavours. Because truffles are so expensive it may not always be possible to use them, in which case the dish should be given an alternative name. Using the basic flavours of cheese sauce and mushroom there is scope for variation, e.g. asparagus tips, prawns or shrimps, turned mushrooms etc.

5   Fillets of fish in white wine sauce with shrimps, mussels and mushrooms   *Filets de poisson dieppoise*   4 *portions*

400–600 g	1–1½ lb	fish fillets
125 ml	¼ pt	white wine
125 ml	¼ pt	mussel cooking liquor
250 ml	½ pt	white wine sauce
250 ml	½ pt	mussels
250 ml	½ pt	shrimp tails
100 g	4 oz	small button mushrooms, cooked in butter and lemon juice

1 Poach the fish in a buttered dish with the white wine and mussel cooking liquor.
2 Drain, strain off the stock, reduce and add to the white wine sauce.
3 Gently re-heat the mussels, shrimps and mushrooms.
4 Dress the fish on a serving dish and surround with garnish.
5 Correct the seasoning and consistency of the white wine sauce.
6 Coat the fish and garnish and serve.

Note The white wine sauce can be made as follows:
a) mounted with butter from a straight reduction of the cooking liquors and fish stock.
b) as for (a) finished with 3–4 tablespns lightly whipped cream.
c) if an economical sauce is required, use fish velouté as the base, adding all the reduced cooking liquors and a little butter and cream as desired.

6   Fillets of fish marinière

Prepare as in previous recipe with the addition of chopped parsley in the sauce.

7 Shallow-fried fish with artichokes and potatoes *Filets de poisson Murat* *4 portions*

400–600 g	1–1 ½ lb	fish fillets
300 g	12 oz	potatoes, peeled
		2 artichoke bottoms, cooked in a blanc
100 g	4 oz	butter
60 ml	⅛ pt	oil
		juice of one lemon
		chopped parsley

1 Cut fish into goujons.
2 Cut potatoes into short batons – 1½ × ½ × ½ cm (¾ × ¼ × ¼ in.) and shallow fry in butter and oil and drain in a colander.
3 Cut artichokes into quarters or eighths, shallow fry and drain on top of the potatoes.
4 Flour the fish, shake off all surplus, and shallow fry quickly in oil and butter until golden brown. Place fish on serving dish.
5 Prepare 50 g (2 oz) noisette butter in a clean pan, add potatoes, artichokes and seasoning, toss carefully to mix.
6 Sprinkle with lemon juice, mask over the fish, finish with chopped parsley to serve.

Note If artichokes are unavailable, mushrooms (button or wild) can be used but the dish is not then called Murat.

8 Fillets of fish in a baked jacket potato with prawns and white wine and cheese sauce *Filets de poisson Otéro* *4 portions*

		2 large baked jacket potatoes
400–600 g	1–1 ½ lb	fish fillets
250 ml	½ pt	shelled prawns
125 ml	¼ pt	white wine sauce
250 ml	½ pt	Mornay sauce
50 g	2 oz	grated parmesan cheese

1 Bake the potatoes, cut into halves, scoop out half of the flesh.
2 Cut the fish into suitable sized pieces, poach in fish stock and drain.
3 Strain off the cooking liquor, reduce and use in the Mornay sauce.
4 Mix the prawns with the white wine sauce and place in the base of the potatoes.
5 Add the fish, coat with Mornay sauce, sprinkle with grated cheese, gratinate and serve.

Note Using the basic principle of this dish, a number of variations can be made using different combinations of ingredients and sauces e.g. a lobster, shrimp or white wine sauce in the bottom of the potato, then the fish, and finished with Mornay sauce.

9   Fillets of fish in a white wine and brandy sauce with tomatoes, mushrooms and tarragon   *Filets de poisson palace*

4 portions

25 g	1 oz	finely chopped shallots
400–600 g	1–1½ lb	fish fillets
5 g	¼ oz	chopped tarragon
		2 tablespns brandy
125 ml	¼ pt	white wine
125 ml	¼ pt	fish stock
250 ml	½ pt	white wine sauce
		4 tomatoes ⎫ 2 cm (1 in.) diameter
		4 button mushrooms ⎬
100 g	4 oz	butter
		2 egg yolks
60 ml	⅛ pt	lightly whipped cream

1 Half cook the shallots in a little butter without colour.
2 Place the fish on the shallots, season lightly and add tarragon. Poach in brandy, white wine and fish stock.
3 Remove fish, drain well, strain off cooking liquor, reduce and add to white wine sauce.
4 Peel and wash tomatoes and mushrooms, cut 8 neat slices from each.
5 Brush with melted butter and carefully cook without colouring.
6 Dress fish on serving dish; neatly arrange two slices of tomato and two slices of mushroom alternating on each portion.
7 Whisk in egg yolks to the boiling white wine sauce, remove from heat, strain, add cream, correct seasoning and consistency.
8 Completely mask the fish with the sauce, glaze and serve.

10   Fillets of fish in white wine sauce with onion and carrot
Filets de poisson à la russe   *4 portions*

100 g	4 oz	peeled carrots ⎫ 1 cm, ½ in. in diameter
100 g	4 oz	button onions ⎬
100 g	4 oz	butter
		small sprigs of fresh parsley
400–600 g	1–1½ lb	fish fillets
125 ml	¼ pt	white wine
125 ml	¼ pt	fish stock
		juice of half a lemon

1 Groove the carrots with a cannele knife and cut them and the onions into thin rings.
2 Cook gently without colour in a little butter in a covered pan.
3 Place onions, carrots and a few sprigs of parsley in a poaching dish; add fish, wine, stock, lemon juice, season lightly and cook gently.
4 Remove fish, place onion and carrot on top, drain well.

5 Strain off cooking liquid, reduce, whisk in remaining butter.
6 Correct seasoning and consistency, coat the fish and serve.

11   Fillets of fish with white wine sauce and fine vegetables   *Filets de poisson Suchet*

This is poached fish coated with a light white wine sauce, to which is added a julienne of cooked vegetables and truffles.

12   Fillets of fish, saffron sauce

This is poached fish coated with a light white wine sauce, gently flavoured with saffron, which has been steeped in boiling water.

13   Poached hake with cockles and prawns   *Colin basquaise*
4 portions

100 g	4 oz	finely chopped onion
		1 tablespn oil
250 ml	½ pt	fish stock
		1 tablespn chopped parsley
4 × 150 g	6 oz	hake steaks or fillets
		8–12 shelled cockles
		8–12 shelled prawns
		salt and pepper
		2 hard-boiled eggs, coarsely chopped
		chopped parsley

1 Lightly colour the onion in the oil, add fish stock and parsley and simmer 10–15 mins.
2 Place the fish in a shallow ovenproof dish, add cockles and prawns.
3 Pour on the fish stock and onion, season lightly.
4 Poach gently, remove any bones and skin from the fish.
5 If there is an excess of liquid, strain and reduce.
6 Serve coated with the unthickened cooking liquor, sprinkled with the egg and parsley.

14   Hake with shrimps, wild mushrooms and shrimp butter sauce

4 × 150 g	6 oz	hake slices on the bone or filleted	
250 ml	½ pt	white wine	
250 ml	½ pt	water	
50 g	2 oz	sliced onion	court bouillon
		bouquet garni with fennel	Simmer all ingredients for
		pinch of saffron soaked in	20 mins, strain
		boiling water	
		salt and peppercorns	
25 g	1 oz	butter	

		1 tablespn oil	
		1 small chopped garlic clove	
		1 chopped shallot	
200 g	8 oz	fresh ceps ⎫	
		or ⎬ sliced	
25 g	1 oz	dried ceps ⎭	
5 g	¼ oz	chopped parsley	
5 g	¼ oz	chopped tarragon	
50 g	2 oz	grated cheese	

1 Add the hake to the court bouillon and three-quarters cook.
2 Heat butter and the oil in a pan.
3 Add garlic, shallot, ceps, parsley, tarragon and cook gently for 10 mins; evaporate all moisture and season lightly.
4 Drain the fish, remove skin and bone.
5 Put the ceps in a shallow ovenproof dish. Lay the fish on top and sprinkle with grated cheese.
6 Bake in oven at 220°C (425°F, Reg. 7) until browned.
7 Serve a shrimp butter sauce separately (see below).

Shrimp butter sauce

125 ml	¼ pt	white wine ⎫	
30 ml	1/16 pt	wine vinegar ⎬ reduction	
		6 crushed peppercorns ⎭	
		4 tablespns court bouillon	
		2 egg yolks	
100 g	4 oz	butter, melted	
		salt and pepper	
125 ml	¾ pt	picked shrimps	
		chopped tarragon and parsley	

1 Make reduction, add court bouillon and reduce by a half, strain.
2 Add yolks and whisk over gentle heat to a sabayon.
3 Remove from heat, slowly whisk in butter, correct seasoning, strain.
4 Add shrimps, parsley and tarragon and serve.

15 Monkfish

Also known as angler fish (*lotte bandroie*), monkfish has firm, white flesh and is prepared by skinning, removing any dark patches, filleting and removing any gristle before cooking. It is suitable for adding to bouillabaisse and fish soups and can be prepared and cooked in a variety of ways, e.g. as for any of the cod or hake recipes.

16 Fried monkfish scallops

1 Cut the thick part of the monkfish into slices 1–1½ cm (½–¾ in.) thick, flatten slightly.
2 Pass through: (a) milk and flour, (b) a light batter, or (c) flour, egg and fresh breadcrumbs.
3 Deep fry, drain well and serve with quarters of lemon and a suitable sauce e.g. tartar, tomato.

17 Shallow-fried monkfish scallops

1 Prepare monkfish as in stage 1 of previous recipe.
2 Pass through a beaten egg mixed with a tablespoon of oil, salt and pepper and fine breadcrumbs.
3 Firm the coating with a palette knife, shake off surplus crumbs.
4 Shallow fry on both sides in butter and oil.
5 Serve with quarters of lemon and a suitable sauce.

18 Monkfish with a white wine herb sauce

400–600 g	1–1½ lb	prepared monkfish
		salt and pepper
10 g	½ oz	chopped parsley, tarragon and chives
125 ml	¼ pt	good fish stock
125 ml	¼ pt	dry white wine
100 g	4 oz	butter

1 Cut the monkfish into 8 or 12 pieces.
2 Place into a buttered dish, season and add half the herbs.
3 Add fish stock and white wine, cover with buttered greaseproof paper and poach gently.
4 Remove fish, drain well, keep warm.
5 Strain off cooking liquor, reduce to a glaze.
6 Incorporate the butter, correct seasoning and add remainder of the herbs.
7 Coat the fish and serve.

19 Mousse, mousseline, quenelle

These are all made from the same basic mixture known as forcemeat. Salmon, sole, trout, brill, turbot, halibut, whiting, pike and lobster can all be used for fish forcemeat in the preparation of mousse of sole, mousselines of salmon, quenelles of turbot, all of which would be served with a suitable sauce e.g. white wine, a butter sauce, lobster, shrimp, saffron, mushroom etc.

20   Fish forcemeat   *4 portions*

300 g	12 oz	fish, free from skin and bone
		salt, white pepper
		1–2 egg whites
250–500 ml	½–1 pt	double cream, ice cold

1 Process the fish and seasoning to a fine purée.
2 Continue processing, slowly adding the egg white(s) until thoroughly absorbed.
3 Pass mixture through a fine sieve and place into a shallow pan or bowl.
4 Leave on ice or in refrigerator until very cold.
5 Beating the mixture continuously, slowly incorporate the cream.

Notes When half the cream is incorporated test the consistency and seasoning by cooking a teaspoonful in a small pan of simmering water. If the mixture is very firm, a little more cream may be added, then test the mixture again and continue until the mixture is of a mousse consistency.

As mousses are cooked in buttered moulds in a bain-marie in the oven and turned out for service the mixture should not be made too soft otherwise they will break up.

Mousses are made in buttered moulds, usually one per portion but larger moulds for 2 to 4 can be made if required. It is sounder practice to use individual moulds because for large moulds the mousse needs to be of a firmer consistency to prevent them collapsing. They are cooked in a bain-marie in a moderate oven or in a low pressure steamer.

Mousselines are moulded using two tablespoons, dipping the spoons frequently into boiling water to prevent the mixture sticking. They are normally moulded into shallow buttered trays, covered with salted water, covered with buttered greaseproof paper and gently poached in the oven.

Quenelles are made in various shapes and sizes as required:

a) moulded with dessert or teaspoons
b) piped with a small plain tube

They are cooked in the same way as mousselines. When making lobster mousse, use raw lobster meat and ideally some raw lobster roe which gives authentic colour to the mousse when cooked. For scallop mousse use cooked scallops and the roe. In order to achieve sufficient bulk it is sometimes necessary to add a little other fish, e.g. whiting, sole, pike. Shellfish mousselines are best cooked in shallow individual moulds because of the looser texture.

21 Mussels with a butter and lemon sauce *Moules à la catalane*
4 portions

2 litres	2 quarts	large live mussels
100 g	4 oz	sliced onion
		parsley stalks
50 g	2 oz	finely chopped onion
75 oz	3 oz	butter
		juice of ¼ lemon
		salt and pepper

1 Scrape and thoroughly wash the mussels.
2 Place in a pan with sliced onion, parsley stalks and a little water.
3 Cover with tight fitting lid and cook rapidly until mussel shells open.
4 Drain off all cooking liquid, allow it to settle, then strain carefully – being careful of any sand or grit.
5 Cook the chopped onion without colour in a little butter.
6 Reduce the mussel cooking liquid and make into a lightly thickened fish sauce; incorporate the butter and lemon juice, and correct seasoning.
7 Remove mussels from shells, mix with the sauce, replace them and the sauce into the larger shells, glaze and serve.

Notes For the fish sauce see note following recipe 5 page 82.
   Mussels may be mixed with a fish sauce plus other ingredients if required, e.g. mushrooms, and served in a puff pastry case of any desired shape, see note page 90. They may also be served in the centre of a ring of pilaff rice which has been set in a savarin mould to give a neat presentation. In these ways they are suitable for serving either as a first, fish or main course.

22 Fried mussels *Moules frites*
4 portions

1 Select large mussels and cook them as for recipe 21.
2 Marinate for 20 mins. in lemon juice, olive or vegetable oil and chopped parsley.
3 Dip in a thin frying batter and deep fry in hot fat.
4 Drain well and serve with quarters of lemon or a tartare type sauce.

23 Oysters *Hûitres*

Oysters are most popular when freshly opened and eaten raw, together with their own natural juice which should be carefully retained in the deep shell.
   Oysters can also be cooked in a variety of ways. In all the following

recipes they are initially gently poached for a short time in their own juice and the beards removed (over-cooking will toughen them).

24   Oysters in cheese sauce   *Hûitres Mornay*

Warm the shells, add a little cheese sauce, place two oysters in each shell, coat with sauce, grated cheese, glaze and serve.

25   Oysters in cheese sauce with spinach   *Hûitres florentine*

As previous recipe, dressing the oysters on a bed of leaf spinach.

26   Gratinated oysters with lemon and breadcrumbs
Hûitres au gratin

Place one oyster on each shell, add a few drops of lemon, barely cover with breadcrumbs lightly fried in butter and gratinate under the salamander or in a very hot oven.

27   Deep fried oysters   *Hûitres frites*

Pass the well-dried oysters through a light batter, or flour, egg and crumb, deep fry and serve with quarters of lemon or lime.

28   Oysters with white wine sauce   *Hûitres au vin blanc*

Place two oysters in each shell, coat with white wine sauce, glaze and serve.

29   Oysters with champagne sauce   *Hûitres au champagne*

As previous recipe, using champagne in place of white wine.

Note Oysters can also be mixed with any of the poached fish sauces together with other ingredients if required, e.g. a few lightly poached bean sprouts, button or wild mushrooms and served in a bouchée, vol-au-vent, or any other shape of puff paste case – square, rectangular or diamond. They may then be served as a first course, fish course or main course, as required.

30 Paupiettes

These are fillets of suitable fish, e.g. sole, whiting, lightly flattened with a moistened meat bat or large knife to prevent shrinkage during cooking, coated with fish forcemeat (page 88) and rolled. They can be kept in a shape by: (a) tying with fine string, (b) placing in dariole moulds, or (c) placing them close together in the cooking pan.

Paupiettes are gently poached in fish stock and/or white wine in a well buttered pan and may be prepared and served as for any of the poached fish recipes.

Variations in the flavour of and/or additions to the forcemeat can give variety to a dish of paupiettes, e.g. paupiettes of sole stuffed with a lobster forcemeat and a lobster sauce, paupiettes of whiting stuffed with a forcemeat containing dice of wild mushrooms and a white wine sauce.

31 Red mullet *Rouget*

Sometimes known as the woodcock of the sea because, like the game bird, it has no gall bladder, red mullet can be cooked undrawn which enhances the flavour of the flesh. The gills are removed and the vent end must, however, be checked to ensure that it is clean. Red mullet is considered to be an essential constituent of bouillabaise.

32 Red mullet with red wine sauce *Rouget à la bordelaise*

1 Allow 1 × 200–300 g (8–12 oz) mullet per portion, clean as above.
2 Make 2–3 light incisions 2 mm (½ in.) deep on both sides of the fish.
3 Shallow fry in clarified butter or margarine.
4 Serve accompanied by bordelaise sauce.

Bordelaise sauce (Sauce bordelaise) ¼ litre(½ pt)   *4–6 portions*

50 g	2 oz	chopped shallots	⎫
125 ml	¼ pt	red wine	⎬ reduction
		pinch mignonette pepper	
		sprig of thyme	
		bay leaf	⎭
250 ml	½ pt	demi-glace	

1 Place reduction in a small sauteuse.
2 Allow to boil until reduced to a quarter.
3 Add the demi-glace. Simmer 20–30 min.
4 Correct the seasoning. Pass through a fine strainer.

33　**Grilled red mullet with anchovy butter**　*Rouget françillon*

1 Allow 1 × 200–300 g (8–12 oz) mullet per portion, clean and cut as in previous recipe.
2 Marinade in oil, lemon juice, salt and pepper for 20 mins., then grill.
3 Cut bread croûtons the shape of the fish, fry in butter and spread with anchovy butter.
4 Place a mullet on each croûton, garnish with fried parsley, straw potatoes and accompany with tomato sauce finished with 25–50 g (1–2 oz) anchovy butter.

34　**Red mullet in a paper bag**　*Rouget en papillotte*

1 Grill or fry the prepared red mullets.
2 Place 1–2 tablespns thick Italian sauce (below) on a large, oiled heart-shaped piece of greaseproof paper, or aluminium foil, allowing one for each fish.
3 Place the mullets on top of the sauce, surround with cooked tomato concassé and sliced cooked mushrooms.
4 Cover with a little more Italian sauce and sprinkle with brown breadcrumbs and melted butter.
5 Carefully fold and tightly pleat the paper so that the fish is completely enclosed.
6 Place on a tray in a hot oven (220°C, 425°F, Reg. 7) until the bag balloons up and lightly browns, then serve immediately in the bag.

Notes There are many other variations of fillings and sauces that can be added to red mullet when cooking 'en papillotte'.
　Sometimes only small mullet are available, in which case serve 2–3 per portion according to weight.

Italian sauce　*(Sauce italienne)*　¼ litre(½ pint)　　　*4–6 portions*

25 g	1 oz	margarine oil or butter	⎫
10 g	½ oz	chopped shallots	⎬ duxelle
50 g	2 oz	chopped mushrooms	⎭
250 ml	½ pt	demi-glace	
25 g	1 oz	chopped lean ham	
100 g	4 oz	tomatoes, skinned, deseeded, diced	
		chopped parsley, chervil and tarragon	

1 Melt the fat or oil in a small sauteuse.
2 Add the shallots and gently cook 2–3 min.
3 Add the mushrooms and gently cook 2–3 min.
4 Add the demi-glace, ham and tomatoes.
5 Simmer 5–10 min. Correct the seasoning.
6 Add the chopped herbs.

35 Slices of salmon with mustard and white wine sauce

4 portions

		2 finely chopped shallots
125 ml	¼ pt	dry white wine
125 ml	¼ pt	fish stock
200 g	8 oz	butter
		salt and pepper
4 × 100–150 g	4–6 oz	thin slices of salmon
		oil for frying the salmon
		1 tablespn French mustard

1 Gently reduce shallots and wine by two-thirds.
2 Whisk in the stock and butter, check seasoning, keep warm.
3 Gently fry the salmon on both sides in oil, drain well.
4 Reheat the sauce, whisk in the mustard.
5 Pour sauce onto the serving dish, place salmon on top and serve.

36 Salmon in red wine sauce *Darne de saumon chambord*

4 portions

4 × 150–200 g	6–8 oz	slices of salmon on the bone	for braising the salmon
100 g	4 oz	carrot, sliced	
100 g	4 oz	onion, sliced	
		sprig of thyme, bay leaf, parsley stalks	
125 ml	¼ pt	red wine	
60 ml	⅛ pt	fish stock	
50 g	2 oz	onion, sliced	Genevoise sauce
50 g	2 oz	carrot, sliced	
		thyme, parsley stalks	
50 g	2 oz	butter	
1 kg	2 lb	salmon head and bones	
125 ml	¼ pt	red wine	
60 ml	⅛ pt	fish stock	
100 g	4 oz	butter	
		salt and pepper	

1 To braise the salmon: place the fish on the vegetables and herbs. Add wine and fish stock to come two-thirds of the way up.
2 Cover and braise gently for 10 mins.
3 Remove lid, baste frequently and continue cooking until centre bones are easily removed from the salmon.
4 Remove all skin and bones, keep warm, strain off cooking liquor.
5 Make genevoise sauce by lightly browning onion, carrot and herbs in 50 g (2 oz) butter.
6 Add the salmon head, cook for 15 mins.
7 Add wine, stock and fish cooking liquid, simmer 10 mins.
8 Strain, reduce to a light glaze, incorporate butter and correct seasoning.

9 Dress salmon, mask lightly with sauce, garnish with fish quenelles (page 87), turned mushrooms, fried soft roes, cooked crayfish and slices of truffle.
10 Serve remainder of sauce separately.

Note The original classic recipe uses a fish espagnole as a base for the sauce.
The salmon may also be braised in one whole piece.

37   Salmon with white wine, leeks and tomato   *4 portions*

400–600 g	1–1½ lb	salmon fillet
		salt and pepper
200 g	8 oz	leeks, chopped
100 g	4 oz	butter
100 g	4 oz	tomatoes, skinned, deseeded, diced
125 ml	¼ pt	white wine
250 ml	½ pt	double cream

1 Cut salmon in 2 cm (1 in.) dice, season.
2 Sweat the leeks without colour in 50 g (2 oz) of butter.
3 Add the salmon and lightly brown.
4 Add tomatoes and wine, bring to boil and simmer 5–6 mins.
5 Strain off the cooking liquid, reduce if necessary.
6 Add cream and simmer until correct consistency is reached.
7 Incorporate remaining butter, correct seasoning, coat salmon with sauce and serve.

Note This dish is suitable for serving at a fork buffet with pilaff rice and noodles.

38   Fresh sardines with tomato sauce   *4 portions*

400–600 g	1–1½ lb	large fresh sardines
		oil for frying
150 g	6 oz	finely sliced onion
60 ml	⅛ pt	dry white wine
400 g	1 lb	tomatoes, skinned, deseeded, diced
		salt and pepper
		chopped parsley

1 Scale, gut, wash and dry the sardines.
2 Shallow fry rapidly in oil on both sides, remove from pan.
3 In the same oil gently cook the onions without colour.
4 Add wine, reduce by two-thirds, add tomatoes, season, reduce by half.
5 Pour the sauce into an ovenproof dish, place sardines on top.
6 Cook for 5–7 minutes in oven at 220°C (425°F, Reg. 7) and serve, sprinkled with parsley.

39 Deep-fried sardines with an egg, butter, tarragon and caper sauce   *Sardines à la basquaise*   *4 portions*

1 Remove heads and tails from sardines, gut and wash.
2 Flour, egg, crumb and deep fry.
3 Serve with a béarnaise sauce containing a few capers.

Béarnaise sauce   (Sauce béarnaise)

10 g	½ oz	chopped shallots
		6 crushed peppercorns
5 g	¼ oz	tarragon
		1 tablespn tarragon vinegar
		3 egg yolks
200 g	8 oz	butter
		sprig chopped chervil

1 Make a reduction with the shallots, peppercorns, tarragon stalks and vinegar.
2 Add 1 tablespn cold water and allow to cool.
3 Mix in the yolks with a whisk.
4 Return to a gentle heat and, whisking continuously, cook to a sabayon.
5 Remove from heat and cool slightly, then gradually whisk in the melted butter until thoroughly combined.
6 Correct the seasoning and pass through a muslin, tammy cloth or fine chinois.
7 Add chopped tarragon leaves and chervil.

40 Baked stuffed sardines

1 Slit the stomach openings of the sardines and gut.
2 From the same opening carefully cut along each side of the backbone and remove it by cutting through the end with fish scissors.
3 Scale, wash, dry and season the fish.
4 A variety of stuffings can be used, e.g.
   a) cooked chopped spinach seasoned with cooked chopped onion, garlic, nutmeg, salt, pepper
   b) fish forcemeat
   c) thick duxelle
5 Place the stuffed sardines in a greased ovenproof dish.
6 Sprinkle with breadcrumbs and oil.
7 Bake in hot oven (200°C, 400°F, Reg. 6) for approx. 10 mins. and serve.

Notes Herring, mackerel, sea-bass and trout can also be prepared and cooked in this way, and there is considerable scope for flair and imagination in the different stuffings and methods of cooking the fish.

Fresh sardines are also popular when plainly grilled and served with quarters of lemon.

41   Scallops   *Coquilles St Jacques*

Scallops can be served as a first, fish or main course.
1 Always use live scallops if possible, in order to ensure freshness, and open them at the last possible moment.
2 Slide the blade of a knife under the flat lid of the shell and cut through the muscle by which it is attached.
3 Carefully scoop out the scallop with a spoon, separate the coral, discard the frilly outer membranes and wash well.

Note Alternatively, place the shells on top of the stove in the oven for a few seconds; the shells will then open and the scallops can be cut away with a small knife.

42   Scallops with saffron, vermouth and cream sauce *4 portions*

		12–16 scallops, prepared and cleaned
10 g	½ oz	finely chopped shallot
25 g	1 oz	butter
		salt and pepper
125 ml	¼ pt	fish stock
60 ml	⅛ pt	dry vermouth
250 ml	½ pt	double cream
		a few threads of saffron

1 Halve the scallops horizontally.
2 Cook the shallots in the butter without colour.
3 Add scallops and roes, season lightly, add stock and wine, and simmer for 2 mins.
4 Remove scallops, keep warm.
5 Strain the stock, reduce, add cream and saffron and reduce to a light consistency.
6 Return scallops to the sauce, correct seasoning and serve.

Note For variation, a little dice of tomato, thinly sliced mushrooms, or chopped fennel or parsley may be added.

43   Scallops in white wine, butter and lemon sauce   *4 portions*

		12–16 scallops prepared, cleaned and halved.
125 ml	¼ pt	dry white wine
		few drops of lemon juice

10 g	½ oz	finely chopped shallot
100 g	4 oz	butter
		salt and pepper
		chopped chervil

1 Poach the seasoned scallops and roes in wine and lemon juice for 2 mins.
2 Remove scallops and keep warm.
3 Add shallot to the stock, reduce by half, strain.
4 Incorporate the butter and correct seasoning.
5 Add well-drained scallops, chopped chervil and serve.

Note Chervil can be replaced by fennel, parsley, chives or tarragon.

44 Scallops with cider   *4 portions*

10 g	½ oz	finely chopped shallot
25 g	1 oz	butter
		12–16 scallops, prepared, cleaned and halved
500 ml	1 pt	dry cider
		salt and pepper
250 ml	½ pt	double cream
		chopped parsley

1 Cook shallot in the butter without colour.
2 Add scallops and cider, season, and poach for 2 mins.
3 Remove scallops, keep warm.
4 Reduce liquid to 60 ml (⅛ pt) and strain.
5 Add cream, reboil, correct seasoning and consistency.
6 Add well-drained scallops, chopped parsley and serve.

Note 30 ml (1/16 pt) calvados can be added to the sauce if desired.

45 Grilled sea bass with fennel   *4 portions*

4 × 300–400 g	12 oz–1 lb	sea bass or two fish double the weight
		salt and pepper
50 g	2 oz	fennel sprigs
		oil for grilling

1 Scale, trim, gut and wash the fish.
2 Cut 3–4 incisions on either side and season.
3 Pack as much sprig fennel into the stomach cavity as possible.
4 Brush with oil and grill.
5 Serve sprinkled with chopped fennel and quarters of lemon.

Note 2–3 tablespns of an anise liquor, e.g. Pernod, may be flamed and poured over the fish.
   Sea bass or seawolf is known as *loup* or *loup de mer* in French.

46   Sea bass with lettuce   *4 portions*

4 × 300–400 g	12 oz–1 lb	sea bass, filleted and skinned
		1 tablespn oil
75 g	3 oz	butter
		2 cabbage lettuce
25 g	1 oz	finely chopped shallot
125 ml	¼ pt	white wine
		salt and pepper
		2 egg yolks
250 ml	½ pt	double cream

1 Pass the fish through flour and shallow fry quickly for a minute on both sides in the oil and a little butter.
2 Keeping the lettuce whole, separate the outer leaves and wash them with the hearts, blanch in boiling water, refresh and drain well.
3 Dry the outer leaves on absorbent paper and wrap them round the bass fillets.
4 Cut the lettuce hearts in quarters and flatten slightly.
5 Soften the shallot in a little butter and place in a buttered ovenproof dish.
6 Cover with the 8 flattened lettuce hearts.
7 Place the lettuce-wrapped fish on top.
8 Add white wine, season lightly and cook for 10–12 mins. in a moderate oven (180°C, 350°F, Reg. 4).
9 When cooked, thoroughly drain the fish and lettuce hearts and dress on serving dish.
10 Strain off the cooking liquid and reduce to about 60 ml (⅛ pt).
11 Mix egg yolks and cream, whisk into the boiling reduction and immediately remove from the stove, continuing to whisk.
12 Strain, incorporate the remaining butter, correct seasoning, pour over fish and serve.

47   Baked stuffed sea bass   *4 portions*

50 g	2 oz	finely chopped shallot
150 g	6 oz	butter
150 g	6 oz	chopped mushrooms
		salt and pepper
100 g	4 oz	tomato, skinned, deseeded, diced
		pinch of chopped marjoram
		1 beaten egg
		few drops of lemon juice
		fresh breadcrumbs
1 × 1 kg	2 lb	sea bass
60 ml	⅛ pt	white wine

1 Cook the shallots in 25–50 g (1–2 oz) butter without colour.
2 Add mushrooms, season and cook until dry.
3 Add tomato, marjoram, remove from heat, mix in the egg and lemon juice.

4 Bring to suitable consistency by adding breadcrumbs.
5 Clean, wash and stuff the fish. Place in buttered ovenproof dish and season.
6 Pour on the wine, sprinkle with breadcrumbs and remainder of butter in small thin pieces.
7 Bake at 200°C (400°F, Reg. 6), basting frequently until cooked and lightly browned, approx. 30–40 mins.

48 Skate *Raie*

Only the wings of the smaller common and thornback skate are used; they are usually purchased skinned and cleaned.

49 Skate with brown butter *Raie au beurre noisette* *4 portions*

4 × 150–200 g	6–8 oz	pieces of skate	
1 litre	2 pts	water	
50 g	2 oz	sliced onion	
50 g	2 oz	sliced carrot	cooking liquid
125 ml	¼ pt	vinegar	
10 g	½ oz	salt	
100 g	4 oz	butter	
		juice of 1 lemon	
		chopped parsley	
25 g	1 oz	capers (optional)	

1 Poach the skate in the cooking liquid, drain well.
2 Ensure the fish is quite dry, place in serving dish.
3 Heat butter to noisette stage, squeeze in the lemon juice.
4 Add the chopped parsley and capers, pour over the fish and serve.

Note For skate with black butter, heat the butter to just beyond the noisette stage.

50 Fried skate *Fritot de raie* *4 portions*

1 kg	2 lb	skate	
		juice of 2 lemons	
125 ml	¼ pt	oil	marinade
		thyme, bayleaf, salt, pepper, parsley stalks	

1 Cut skate into small slices and marinade for 2–3 hours.
2 Dip the skate pieces in a light batter and deep fry in hot fat.
3 Serve garnished with fried or sprig parsley and quarters of lemon.

51 Skate with mustard and lemon on spinach *4 portions*

4 × 150–200 g	6–8 oz	skate
1 kg	1½ lb	spinach, cooked
200 g	8 oz	butter
		juice of 1 lemon
		2–3 tablespns French mustard (according to taste)

1 Poach fish as in recipe 49, drain well.
2 Reheat spinach in half the butter, add a rub of nutmeg and season.
3 Boil the lemon juice and an equal amount of water and reduce.
4 Remove from heat, incorporate the remaining butter, then the mustard and correct seasoning.
5 Place the spinach on serving dish, add the skate.
6 Coat with sauce and serve.

Note The skate flesh may be removed from the bones if desired.

52   Fish soufflés

Haddock, sole, salmon, turbot, lobster, crab etc. can all be used for this dish.

300 g	10 oz	raw fish, free from skin and bone
50 g	2 oz	butter
250 ml	½ pt	thick béchamel
		3 eggs, separated
		salt and cayenne pepper

1 Cook the fish in the butter and process to a purée.
2 Mix with the béchamel, pass through a fine sieve and season well.
3 Warm the mixture and beat in the yolks.
4 Carefully fold in the stiffly beaten whites.
5 Place into 4 individual buttered and floured soufflé moulds.
6 Bake at 220°C (425°F, Reg. 7) approx. 14 mins.; serve immediately.

Notes If individual moulds are used, less cooking time is required. A suitable sauce may be offered, e.g. white wine, mushroom, shrimp, saffron, lobster etc.

   The use of an extra beaten egg white will increase the lightness of the soufflé.

53   Soufflés of sole or chicken turbot

These soufflés may be prepared by boning the whole fish and stuffing with a forcemeat, they are then poached, garnished and served whole with a suitable sauce.

Sole

1 Allow 1 × 300 g (12 oz) sole per person.
2 Remove black and white skins and the head.
3 Trim the edges of the fish lightly with scissors.
4 With a filleting knife cut along the backbone and loosen the fillets on both sides, stopping about 1½ cm (¾ in.) from the edge and leaving the same space at the head and tail end of the backbone.

5 Make a pocket in the sole by carefully cutting through the backbone and removing it.
6 Wash and dry the fish, season lightly.
7 Fill the pockets of the sole with fish forcemeat, page 88.
8 Draw the edges of the fish together leaving a gap of about 4 cm (1½ in.) in the middle and 1 cm (½ in.) at each end.
9 Smooth with a palette knife dipped in boiling water and wiped dry before use.
10 Place the fish into well buttered ovenproof dishes, covered with well buttered greaseproof paper.
11 Poach gently in fish stock and white wine for approx. 15 mins. The filling will expand during cooking.
12 When cooked, carefully remove the fish, strain off cooking liquid and reduce and make into the required fish sauce.
13 Dress the soles, garnish as required, coat with sauce and serve.

Notes There is considerable scope for variation in this dish. The forcemeat can be a contrasting fish, e.g. crab, scallop, lobster, and can also contain diced or flaked fish or shrimps, prawns, mushrooms or truffles. Any of the many variations of fish sauce may be used and the garnish may be simple, e.g. a prawn, or more lavish, e.g. mussel, oyster, turned mushrooms.

Chicken turbot   (Turbotin)

1 Allow 1 × 1½–2 kg (3–4 lb) chicken turbot for 4 portions.
2 Gut the turbot and clean the head, removing the gills and eyes.
3 Cut down backbone on black skin side and raise the fillets as in stage 4 for sole.
4 Proceed as for sole for preparation and cooking, allowing more cooking time.
5 Remove the black skin carefully, without damaging the flesh of the fish, before serving.

Note All the notes for sole apply equally to chicken turbot.

54   **Shallow-fried whiting**   *Merlan à l'anglaise*

1 Allow 1 × 250–300 g (10–12 oz) fish per person.
2 Cut on either side of the backbone and remove it.
3 Flour, egg and crumb the fish, leaving the fillets joined but flat and unseparated.
4 Shallow fry on both sides in oil and butter
5 Serve with parsley butter.

55   Whiting colbert   *Merlan colbert*

Prepare as in previous recipe, fill the centre with parsley butter and deep fry.

56   Whiting poached in white wine with shrimps, mussels and mushrooms   *Merlan dieppoise*

1 Cut fish on either side of the backbone and remove it.
2 Poach fish in white wine, mushroom cooking liquor and fish stock.
3 Strain off cooking liquor and make into a white wine sauce, strain.
4 Garnish fish with shrimps, mussels and mushrooms.
5 Add a little chopped parsley to the sauce, coat the fish and serve.

57   Whiting cooked in a brown mushroom and white wine sauce   *Merlan au gratin*

4 × 250–300 g	10–12 oz	whiting
50 g	2 oz	finely chopped shallot
200 ml	⅜ pt	white wine
125 ml	¼ pt	fish stock
200 g	8 oz	button mushrooms
250 ml	½ pt	thin demi-glace or jus-lié
		salt and pepper
		1 tablespn chopped parsley
		fresh white breadcrumbs
100 g	4 oz	butter or margarine
		juice of 1 lemon

1 Prepare fish as in previous recipe.
2 Make gratin sauce by reducing shallots, 125 ml (¼ pt) wine and fish stock by half.
3 Add 100 g (4 oz) chopped mushrooms and cook until dry.
4 Add demi-glace, simmer 5 mins., correct seasoning and add parsley.
5 Place a thin layer of sauce in a buttered ovenproof dish.
6 Place fish on top, season, surround with thinly sliced, overlapping raw mushrooms.
7 Place 3 turned mushrooms (cooked in a blanc) in the centre of each fish.
8 Add 60 ml (⅛ pt) wine and completely cover with gratin sauce.
9 Sprinkle with breadcrumbs, melted butter and cook in moderate oven (180°C, 350°F, Reg. 4), allowing sauce to reduce, fish to cook and crust to gratinate.
10 Finish with lemon juice and chopped parsley, and serve.

Note This recipe can also be used for whole sole (prepared as for Colbert) and to any filleted white fish.

8
Meat dishes

See also Chapter 2 Cold preparation and buffet items
   Chapter 10 British dishes
   Chapter 11 Ethnic recipes

Lamb

1   Best-end or rack of lamb with herbs and garlic   *4 portions*

		1 × 8 or 2 × 4 bone, best-end of lamb prepared for roasting
30 ml	1/16 pt	oil
		4 chopped cloves of garlic (optional)
5 g	¼ oz	chopped thyme
5 g	¼ oz	chopped rosemary
5 g	¼ oz	chopped savory
		salt and pepper

marinade }

1 Place meat in marinade for 30 mins, turning frequently.
2 Roast, keeping meat slightly pink, and serve with a herb butter.

Notes If dried herbs are used, halve the quantities. Other combinations of fresh herbs and spices may also be used. A well-browned boulangère potato makes a good accompaniment for this dish. Instead of marinading the meat, a coating of fresh breadcrumbs and rosemary (a herb particularly compatible with lamb) can be firmly pressed into the fat side of the meat half-way through cooking. Here again a range of herbs may be used as a variation, e.g. parsley, tarragon, basil etc.

   If 3 cutlets are being served per portion, then 3 bone racks of lamb can be prepared, cooked and served uncut.

2   Crumbed lamb cutlets with asparagus

Côtelettes d'agneau maréchale   *4 portions*

		8 prepared lamb cutlets, flour, egg and crumbed
50 g	2 oz	butter
		oil
		8 slices of truffle
		16–24 asparagus tips, according to size

1 Shallow fry cutlets in butter and oil on both sides.
2 Dress neatly, place slice of truffle on each.
3 Garnish with asparagus tips and serve.

Note If truffles are unobtainable, slices of cooked button mushroom may be used. Without the use of truffle this dish could retain its English title but would not be known as maréchale.

3   Crumbed lamb cutlets with artichokes, onions and mushrooms   *Côtelettes d'agneau Marie-Louise*   *4 portions*

		8 prepared lamb cutlets, flour, egg and crumbed
50 g	2 oz	butter
		oil
		4 cooked artichoke bottoms
200 g	8 oz	chopped mushrooms ⎫ cooked and combined
50 g	2 oz	chopped onion ⎭

1 Shallow fry cutlets in butter and oil on both sides.
2 Dress neatly, garnish with artichoke bottoms reheated in butter filled with mushroom and onion purée.

4   Noisettes of lamb in a cream herb sauce   *4 portions*

8 × 50 g	2 oz	noisettes
100 g	4 oz	butter
60 ml	⅛ pt	dry white vermouth
250 ml	½ pt	white chicken, lamb or veal stock
250 g	½ pt	double cream
10 g	½ oz	chopped fresh herbs, e.g. tarragon, chervil, basil, parsley
		salt and pepper

1 Sauté noisettes in a little of the butter, keeping them pink. Remove from pan and keep warm.
2 Pour off excess fat, add vermouth and reduce by three-quarters.
3 Add stock, reduce by half, then add cream.
4 Reduce to a light consistency. Strain, add herbs, and incorporate remainder of butter.
5 Correct seasoning and consistency, coat noisettes and serve.

Notes Two or three noisettes may be offered according to size and the prices charged.

White wine, sherry or port may be used in place of vermouth. One or a mixture of the herbs may be used. 100 g (4 oz) cultivated or wild mushrooms may be added.

5   Noisettes of lamb in cider, calvados and cream

Noisettes d'agneau à la normande   *4 portions*

8 × 50 g	2 oz	noisettes
50 g	2 oz	butter
250 ml	½ pt	white lamb, veal or chicken stock
125 ml	¼ pt	dry cider
30 ml	1/16 pt	calvados
250 ml	½ pt	double cream
		salt and pepper

1 Sauté noisettes in a little butter, keep warm.
2 Pour off excess fat, add stock and reduce by two-thirds.
3 Add cider, calvados and cream and reduce to a light consistency.
4 Strain, correct seasoning and consistency, pour over noisettes and serve.

Note This dish may be garnished with apples, e.g. cut in rings and fried, caramelised, baked in quarters etc.

6   Roast stuffed saddle of lamb

1 Select a short saddle, i.e. the chump-ends removed, and allow 150–200 g (6–8 oz) per portion.
2 Carefully remove the skin, starting from a breast flap at the head end.
3 Remove kidneys, excess fat and sinew.
4 Placing saddle fat down, carefully cut away the two fillets to expose the bones and bone-out.
5 Season the joint and insert a neat roll of stuffing in the space left by the bones, replace the fillets.
6 Thin out the breast flaps with a meat bat and trim so that they meet, forming a complete layer of fat around the saddle.
7 Turn the saddle over, lightly score the fat to form a pattern and tie securely with string at 2 cm (1 in.) intervals.

The saddle may be roasted and served with roast gravy and redcurrant jelly or pot-roasted, in which case it may be garnished in a variety of ways, for example:

Armenonville – quarters of artichoke bottoms, cocotte potatoes, tomatoes, French beans.

Brabançonne – tartlets garnished with Brussels sprouts and finished Mornay, potato croquettes.

Clamart – tartlets or artichoke bottoms filled with purée of peas, small château potatoes.

Renaissance – artichoke bottoms filled with carrots and turnips, French beans, peas, asparagus tips, cauliflower coated with hollandaise sauce, new potatoes.

With thought and imagination other garnishes making use of a wide variety of vegetables can be offered.

The stuffing can be varied in many ways, e.g.

- basic stuffing or forcemeat for lamb joints
- duxelle base thickened with fresh breadcrumbs and bound with egg
- diced lambs kidneys quickly sautéd in a little butter can be added
- diced or quartered cultivated or wild mushrooms can be added
- chicken forcemeat can be used as a base

Beef

7 Fillet of beef *Filet de boeuf*

Fillet of beef served as a joint may be roasted or pot-roasted. The joint can be larded with strips of pork fat in order to give an added flavour and succulence to the meat whilst cooking. There are numerous garnishes in the classical repertoire, for example:

Bréhan – artichoke bottoms filled with broad beans (whole or in purée), sprigs of cauliflower coated with sauce hollandaise, parsley potatoes.

Clamart – small tartlet cases filled with peas à la française or purée of peas and macaire potatoes.

Lorette – bouquets of buttered asparagus tips, Lorette potatoes.

A well flavoured roast gravy or a lightly thickened sauce made from the cooking juices should accompany this dish.

Attractive garnishes can also be made from the wide range of local and international vegetables available.

Do not over-elaborate when garnishing dishes, keep items to a minimum – simple, attractive and complementary to the meat.

8 Tournedos

Tournedos and sirloin steaks (also known as entrecôte steaks) may be cooked and served, in many ways according to the classical repertoire with classical sauces, e.g. bordelaise, marchand de vins; but with thought and ingenuity numerous appetising variations can be evolved.

1 Always trim steaks well, so that no sinew, gristle or excess fat remains on the meat.
2 Flavour is enhanced if steaks are cooked in butter, but margarine or oil can be used.
3 If chopped onion, shallots or mushrooms are added, cook them in the same fat in the same pan after removing the steaks.
4 Drain off all fat.
5 Always utilise cooking juices by deglazing the pan with stock, wine (red or white), a fortified wine (vermouth, port, sherry, madeira) or a spirit such as brandy, and use in making the accompanying sauce.
6 The sauce can be made in many ways, e.g.
   a) adding a thin demi-glace (plain or tomato flavoured), thickened gravy or a good, rich veal, beef or chicken stock.
   b) adding cream, yoghurt or a thin veal or chicken velouté:
Either sauce may have a little butter incorporated to enrich and enhance the shine and presentation.

For example:

Red wine sauce

100 g	4 oz	finely chopped onion
250 ml	½ pt	red wine
250 g	½ pt	beef or veal stock
		2 crushed cloves garlic (optional)
		1 sprig of thyme
150 g	6 oz	butter
		2 teaspns French mustard
		salt and pepper

1 After the steaks are cooked, drain off almost all the fat from the pan.
2 Add chopped onion and cook until soft.
3 Add wine, stock, garlic and thyme. Reduce by three-quarters and strain into a clean pan.
4 Incorporate the butter and mustard, season and pour over steaks.

Shallot sauce

100 g	4 oz	finely chopped shallots
250 ml	½ pt	dry white wine
250 ml	½ pt	beef or veal stock
150 g	6 oz	butter
		salt and pepper
5 g	¼ oz	chopped parsley

1 After steaks are cooked, drain off almost all the fat from the pan.
2 Add shallots and cook until soft. Add wine and stock, reduce by three-quarters and strain.
3 Incorporate butter, season, add parsley and pour over the steaks.

9   Fillet of beef Wellington   *8–10 portions*

1 kg	2 lb	even-shaped beef fillet
400 g	1 lb	chopped mushrooms
50 g	2 oz	chopped shallot or onion
125 ml	¼ pt	oil
5 g	¼ oz	chopped parsley
		salt and pepper
1 kg	2 lb	puff or brioche pastry (recipe p. 289)
		egg wash

duxelle (braces grouping chopped mushrooms, chopped shallot or onion, oil, chopped parsley, salt and pepper)

1 Trim off all sinew from the fillet, season and fry rapidly on all sides in very hot oil. Remove, drain and thoroughly cool.
2 Prepare the duxelle, keeping it fairly dry, and allow to cool.
3 Roll out the pastry 3 mm (⅛ in.) thick and with a large knife neatly cut a rectangle sufficiently wide to envelope the meat and long enough to seal the ends.
4 A layer of thin pancakes may now be added to help keep the pastry crisp.
5 Place half the duxelle in the centre, add the meat and cover with the other half.
6 Egg wash the edges of the paste and fold to make a neat roll, overlapping slightly, and neaten the ends to seal in the meat completely.
7 Place on to a greased baking sheet, egg wash generously.
8 Lightly score the surface into portion sizes to lessen the risk of the pastry breaking up when cut for service. If the joint is to be presented whole, further decoration can be added from the pastry trimmings at this stage.
9 Allow to rest in refrigerator for 1–2 hours.
10 Egg wash again and bake at 220°C (425°F, Reg. 7) approx. 30 mins; the meat should be pink in the centre.
11 Serve whole or cut into portions, as required, accompanied by a suitable sauce, e.g. Madeira.

Notes Variations can include additions to the duxelle, e.g. pâte, sliced or quartered button mushrooms, chopped ham or chicken, or purée of raw chicken or veal.
   Beef Wellington can also be prepared in single or double portions.

10   Fillet of beef en croûte Richelieu   *Filet de boeuf en croûte Richelieu*

The prepared fillet is larded, the duxelle omitted and it is wrapped in pastry and cooked in the same way as beef Wellington, garnished with stuffed tomatoes and mushrooms, braised lettuce and château potatoes.
   Other classical garnishes can also be used, for example:

Bouquetière – artichoke bottoms filled with carrot, turnips, dice of French beans and peas, sprigs of cauliflower coated with hollandaise sauce and château potatoes.
Forestière – morels tossed in butter, dice of bacon, and Parmentier potatoes.
Mascotte – quarters of artichoke bottoms tossed in butter, cocotte potatoes, and slices of truffle.

Alternatively, garnishes can be prepared from selected seasoned vegetables according to one's own choice and an appropriate name given to the dish.

11   Peppered steak in cream sauce   *4 portions*

4 × 100–150 g	4–6 oz	steaks (fillet, rump or sirloin)
50 g	2 oz	crushed peppercorns
50 g	2 oz	butter
30 ml	1/16 pt	brandy
125 ml	¼ pt	double cream
		1–2 teaspns French mustard (optional)

1 Lightly salt the steaks and press them firmly into the peppercorns on each side, ensuring that the peppercorns stick. Leave for 30–45 mins.
2 Shallow fry steaks on both sides in hot butter to just below required degree of cooking, remove and keep warm.
3 Pour off surplus fat, deglaze pan with brandy, add cream and boil to required consistency. Mix in mustard, correct seasoning.
4 Pour over steaks and serve.

Notes
Variations include:

a) A thin demi-glace in place of cream, with the sauce finished by mixing in 50–75 g (2–3 oz) butter.
b) 25–50 g (1–2 oz) finely chopped shallots placed in the pan and cooked for 20 seconds before adding the steaks.

12   Chopped beef and onion steaks (using raw meat)
Fricadelles   *4 portions*

250 g	10 oz	freshly chopped or minced lean beef
150 g	6 oz	white breadcrumbs, soaked in milk and squeezed dry
50 g	2 oz	butter
		1 egg
50 g	2 oz	chopped onion, cooked without colour
		salt, pepper and grated nutmeg

1 Combine all ingredients, mould into flat cakes.
2 Shallow fry in hot butter and/or oil on both sides. (Complete cooking in oven if necessary.)
3 Serve with a suitable sauce e.g. piquante, Robert etc.

Note A dish of pasta, e.g. buttered noodles, or a vegetable purée, make a suitable accompaniment.

13 Chopped beef and onion steaks (using cooked meat)
Fricadelles   *4 portions*

250 g	10 oz	chopped or minced lean cooked beef
150 g	6 oz	dry mashed potato
50 g	2 oz	chopped onion, cooked without colour
		1 egg
5 g	¼ oz	chopped parsley
		salt and pepper

1 Combine all ingredients.
2 Proceed as in recipe 12.

Notes Fricadelles can be made with veal or a mixture of pork and veal.
    Various herbs and spices can be added to give variety.

Veal
14 Veal sauté with mushrooms   *4 portions*

500 g	1 ¼ lb	stewing veal
25 g	1 oz	seasoned flour
25 g	1 oz	butter
		1 tablespn oil
100 g	4 oz	chopped onion
		1 crushed clove of garlic ⎫ optional
		1 tablespn tomato purée ⎭
125 ml	¼ pt	white wine
500 ml	1 pt	brown stock
		bouquet garni
		salt and pepper
200 g	8 oz	button mushrooms

1 Trim meat, cut into even pieces, pass through seasoned flour.
2 Quickly brown on all sides in hot butter and oil, drain off excess fat.
3 Add onion and garlic and cook for a few minutes.
4 Mix in tomato purée, add white wine and reduce by half.
5 Add stock and bouquet garni, cover with lid and simmer gently until almost cooked.
6 Pick meat into a clean pan, discard bouquet garni, correct the seasoning

and strain on to the meat. If there is too much sauce, allow to reduce before straining.

7 Bring to boil, add whole or quartered button mushrooms, cover with lid and simmer until tender, then serve.

Notes

The mushrooms can be cultivated or wild.

If button mushrooms are used, they may be sliced and added for the last 1–2 minutes of cooking.

This recipe will produce a very thin sauce. If a thicker sauce is required use half brown stock and half demi-glace.

15 Veal sauté with white wine, button onions, mushrooms and tomatoes   *Sauté de veau Marengo*   *4 portions*

500 g	1¼ lb	prepared stewing veal
25 g	1 oz	seasoned flour
25 g	1 oz	butter
		1 tablespn oil
100 g	4 oz	chopped onion
		1 crushed clove garlic
125 ml	¼ pt	white wine
500 ml	1 pt	brown stock
1 kg	2 lb	tomatoes, skinned, deseeded, diced
		bouquet garni
		16 button onions
		16 button mushrooms
		salt and pepper
		8 heart-shaped bread croûtons fried in butter
		chopped parsley

1 Proceed as for recipe 14 stages 1–6, adding the tomatoes with the stock.
2 Add button onions, simmer 15 mins, add button mushrooms and cook until tender.
3 Serve with tips of croûtons dipped in sauce and chopped parsley.

16 Veal escalope with tomatoes, cheese and white wine

4 portions

		4, 8 or 12 escalopes, according to size, slightly batted
25 g	1 oz	seasoned flour
100 g	4 oz	tomatoes, skinned, deseeded, diced
50 g	2 oz	butter
125 ml	¼ pt	white wine
		4 thin slices mozzarella cheese
		chopped parsley

1 Pass the escalopes through the flour.
2 Cook the tomatoes in a little butter for 5 mins, season.
3 Cook the veal to a golden brown on both sides in butter, remove from pan.
4 Pour off any fat, deglaze with white wine, reduce by half, strain and season.
5 Lay a slice of cheese on each escalope, place under salamander until cheese has melted, add the tomatoes and heat through.
6 Dress the escalopes on a serving dish, pour the reduced wine around the edge of the dish, sprinkle with chopped parsley and serve.

Note Variations can include the addition of sliced mushrooms, double cream, rosemary, tarragon, basil or chives.

17 Shallow-fried veal chops with mushrooms   *4 portions*

		4 veal chops
50 g	2 oz	butter
200 g	8 oz	mushrooms (cultivated or wild), sliced
125 ml	¼ pt	dry white wine
125 ml	¼ pt	veal stock
100 g	4 oz	butter
		salt and pepper
		chopped parsley

1 Shallow fry the chops in butter, remove from pan and keep warm.
2 Lightly brown mushrooms in the same pan, remove and keep warm.
3 Pour off any fat, then add wine, stock and strained juice from the chops.
4 Reduce by half, incorporate butter, season, and add parsley.
5 Correct seasoning, pour over chops and serve.

18 Veal chops with mushrooms, onions and potatoes
4 portions

		4 veal chops
50 g	2 oz	butter
		16 small button mushrooms
		16 small button onions
		16 small potatoes
		salt and pepper
60 ml	⅛ pt	dry white wine

1 Brown chops on both sides in butter and place in an earthenware dish.
2 Quickly brown mushrooms, onions and potatoes, and add to chops.
3 Season lightly, cover and cook in oven at 180°–190°C (350°–375°F, Reg. 4–5) for approx. ½–1 hour.
4 Remove the chops and garnish; dress on a serving dish.
5 Deglaze the pan with the wine, strain over chops and serve.

19   Veal chops with cream and mustard sauce   *4 portions*

		4 veal chops
50 g	2 oz	butter or oil
125 ml	¼ pt	dry white wine
125 ml	¼ pt	veal stock
		bouquet garni
		salt and pepper
60 ml	⅛ pt	double cream
		French mustard, to taste
		chopped parsley

1 Shallow fry the chops on both sides in hot butter, pour off the fat.
2 Add white wine, stock, bouquet garni and season lightly; cover and
   simmer gently until cooked.
3 Remove chops and bouquet garni, reduce liquid by two-thirds, then add
   cream, the juice from the chops and bring to boil.
4 Strain the sauce, mix in the mustard and parsley, correct seasoning,
   pour over chops and serve.

20   Veal escalopes with lemon   *4 portions*

		4, 8 or 12 veal escalopes, according to size, slightly batted
25 g	1 oz	seasoned flour
100 g	4 oz	butter
125 ml	¼ pt	veal or chicke:. stock
		juice of 1 lemon
		chopped parsley
		salt and pepper

1 Pass the escalopes through the flour, fry quickly in butter on both sides
   and remove from pan.
2 Add stock, lemon juice, bring to boil and strain.
3 Reboil and reduce by two-thirds. Incorporate remaining butter, add
   parsley, correct seasoning, pour over escalopes and serve.

21   Veal kidneys with mustard and cream sauce   *4 portions*

400 g	1 lb	skinned and trimmed kidneys, cut in walnut-sized pieces
100 g	4 oz	butter
250 ml	½ pt	double cream
		grated zest of 1 lemon
		1–2 tablespns French mustard, according to taste
		salt and pepper

1 Sauté the kidneys in a little hot butter for 3–4 mins, drain in a colander.
2 Boil the cream, lemon zest, mustard, salt and pepper for 2–3 mins.

3 Strain into a clean pan and incorporate remaining butter. Add kidneys, do *not* re-boil, correct seasoning and serve.

Notes Variations can include: brandy, chopped shallots, a chopped herb, e.g. tarragon, chervil or chives, and cultivated or wild mushrooms, either singly or in combination.

22   Veal kidneys with ceps   *4 portions*

		2 tablespns oil
200 g	8 oz	fresh ceps
		or
50 g	2 oz	dried ceps
50 g	2 oz	finely chopped shallots
		salt and pepper
		few drops of lemon juice
		1 tablespn chopped parsley
200 g	8 oz	tomatoes, skinned, deseeded, diced
25 g	1 oz	butter
100 g	4 oz	lardons of streaky bacon
400 g	1 lb	skinned and trimmed kidneys, cut in walnut-sized pieces

1 Heat the oil and cook the ceps for 4–5 mins until brown.
2 Reduce heat, continue cooking until tender, and add shallots and season.
3 Add lemon juice and chopped parsley.
4 Cook the tomatoes in a little oil until soft, then add to ceps.
5 Heat the butter and a little oil and brown the lardons.
6 Drain and mix lardons with ceps and tomato.
7 Quickly sauté the kidneys in butter for 4–5 mins until brown but slightly pink in the centre, season lightly and drain.
8 Place the cep mixture on a serving dish with the kidneys on top and serve.

23   Fricassée of kidneys and sweetbreads with flageolets and broad beans   *4 portions*

200 g	8 oz	heart-shaped sweetbread
25 g	1 oz	butter
		1 tablespn oil
200 g	8 oz	veal kidneys, skinned, trimmed, cut in 1 cm (½ in) dice
60 ml	⅛ pt	white wine
25 g	1 oz	finely chopped shallot
125 ml	¼ pt	double cream
		salt and pepper
		chopped parsley, tarragon or chervil
50 g	2 oz	cooked flageolet beans
50 g	2 oz	cooked broad beans

1 Blanch sweetbread for 5 mins, drain, refresh, skin, remove any fat or gristle, and cut into walnut-sized pieces.
2 Heat butter and oil in a frying pan, add sweetbreads and cook for 2–3 mins, then add kidneys and cook for 4–5 mins to a golden brown, drain and keep warm.
3 Add white wine and shallot to the pan, strain and reduce by half, add cream and simmer 3–4 mins.
4 Correct seasoning, add sweetbreads, kidneys, flageolets and broad beans. Mix carefully, correct seasoning and serve sprinkled with chopped herbs.

24   Grenadines of veal

Grenadines are smaller, thicker escalopes, approximately 4 cm (1½ in.) thick, larded with thin strips of fresh pork fat. They are usually pot-roasted or braised and can be cooked and garnished in a variety of ways, for example:

Beauharnais – stuffed mushrooms and quarters of artichoke bottoms.
Jardinière – carrots, turnips, French beans, peas and cauliflower coated with hollandaise sauce.
Nemours – green peas, carrots and duchess potatoes.

The above are examples of the many classical garnishes but there are other ways of garnishing, such as:

1. A type of pasta, e.g. noodles or spaghetti, either with butter or butter and cheese, or with a sauce.
2. One or two carefully selected vegetables.
3. A variety of vegetables.

The sauce made from the cooking liquor of the grenadines can also be varied in many ways, with imagination and careful thought.

25   Veal sweetbreads with white wine, tomato and mushrooms

4 portions

500 g	1¼ lb	heart-shaped sweetbreads
25 g	1 oz	seasoned flour
25 g	1 oz	chopped shallot
100 g	4 oz	sliced mushrooms
30 ml	1/16 pt	brandy
60 ml	⅛ pt	white wine
100 g	4 oz	tomato, skinned, deseeded, diced
		juice of 1 lemon
		salt and pepper
60 ml	⅛ pt	double cream
		chopped parsley, chervil, tarragon

1 Soak, blanch and refresh the sweetbreads, remove skin, fat and gristle.
2 Dry the sweetbreads well, pass through seasoned flour, and cook gently in butter on both sides until golden brown.
3 Add shallots, cover with a lid and cook for 2–3 mins, then add mushrooms, cover with a lid and cook 4–5 mins.
4 Add brandy and flame, add white wine, tomatoes, lemon juice and season lightly.
5 Simmer gently until cooked.
6 Add cream, re-boil, correct seasoning, and serve sprinkled with herbs.

Note This is a dish that lends itself to many variations. For example:
– lemon juice may be omitted or reduced in quantity,
– red wine can be used in place of white,
– tomatoes can be omitted and the quantity of mushrooms increased,
– wild mushrooms can be used in place of cultivated,
– jus-lié can be used in place of cream.

Pork
26 Roast stuffed suckling pig

Suckling pig is young milk-fed pig, 8–10 weeks old, weighing 3–5 kg (6–10 lb), which takes approximately 2–2½ hours to roast. If the stuffing is cooked separately allow about half an hour less.
  A golden-brown, crisp skin is essential, therefore the cooking must always be timed so that the pig does not have to stand for too long before serving. Brush the skin with oil frequently during cooking to ensure its crispness.

Basic stuffing

1 kg	2 lb	finely chopped onion, cooked without colour in pork fat or butter
400 g	1 lb	fresh bread cubes, soaked in milk and squeezed dry, or fresh breadcrumbs
100 g	4 oz	butter
50 g	2 oz	freshly chopped sage
		or
25 g	1 oz	dried sage
50 g	2 oz	parsley
		grated nutmeg, salt and pepper
		2 eggs

Thoroughly mix all the ingredients.
Variations can include the addition any of the following: 200 g (8 oz) chopped chestnuts; 200 g (8 oz) chopped dessert apple or stoned cherries or cranberries; 100 g (4 oz) chopped mushrooms; 100 g (4 oz) chopped bacon, ham or pork sausage meat; juice of 2 crushed cloves of garlic; rosemary or basil in place of sage, or a combination of all three; 60 ml (⅛ pt) brandy.

1 Stuff the pig loosely with the stuffing mixture and sew up the opening securely with string.
2 Truss the forelegs and hindlegs so that the pig lies flat on its belly during cooking.
3 Place a block of wood in its mouth to keep it open, and cover the ears and tail with foil to prevent burning.
4 Score the pig's back to allow fat to escape.
5 Brush with oil or melted butter and roast at 200°C (400°F, Reg. 6), basting frequently. Allow 25 mins for every ½ kg (1 lb).
6 A few minutes before the pig is cooked, remove foil from ears and tail.
7 When cooked, transfer the pig to a wooden board, deglaze the pan and make roast gravy. Apple sauce should also be served.
8 Place a red apple in the mouth, cherries or cranberries in the eye sockets and serve.

27   Fillet of pork in pastry   *Filet de porc en croûte*

This can be prepared, cooked and served in the same way as Beef fillet en croûte or Wellington, recipe 9, page 109.

As pork fillets are smaller, two or three can be pressed together, with stuffing in between, before covering with pastry.

Alternatively, the lean meat from a loin completely trimmed of all fat and sinew can be used.

A variety of sauces may be offered but a slightly piquant sauce is particularly suitable, e.g. Robert, charcutière.

28   Pork escalopes with prunes   *4 portions*

Escalopes can be taken from prime cuts of pork, e.g. fillet, loin, best-end and leg, cut into 75–100 g (3–4 oz) slices, free from fat and sinew and batted. They may then be cooked plain, with prunes as here, or egg and crumbed and served in a wide variety of ways with different sauces, garnishes or accompaniments.

		12–16 prunes
250 ml	½ pt	white wine
		piece of cinnamon stick or pinch of ground cinnamon
25 g	1 oz	seasoned flour
		4 pork escalopes (if small allow 2–3 per portion)
50 g	2 oz	butter
75 ml	1/6 pt	double cream
		1 tablespn redcurrant jelly
		salt and pepper

1 Soak prunes overnight in wine.
2 Remove and discard stones from prunes and simmer with the liquid and cinnamon until soft.

3 Flour the escalopes, shallow fry in butter on both sides until cooked through.
4 Remove from pan and keep warm.
5 Drain off prunes (reserving liquid) and add to the escalopes.
6 Add prune liquid to the pan in which escalopes were cooked and reduce by half.
7 Incorporate cream and redcurrant jelly, bring to boil and correct seasoning. If sauce is too sweet, add a few drops of lemon juice.
8 Strain sauce over pork and serve.

Note Well-trimmed pork chops can also be cooked in this way.

29 Pork escalopes with apples, cream and calvados
Escalopes de porc à la normande *4 portions*

25 g	1 oz	seasoned flour
		4 escalopes (if small allow 2–3 per portion)
50 g	2 oz	butter
100 g	4 oz	sliced onions
200 g	8 oz	cooking apples, peeled and sliced
60 ml	⅛ pt	calvados
125 ml	¼ pt	stock
75 ml	1/6 pt	double cream
		salt and pepper

1 Flour escalopes and shallow fry in butter on both sides until cooked through. Remove from pan, keep warm.
2 Gently cook the onions in the same pan, add the apples, cover with a lid and cook gently until apples are soft.
3 Drain off the fat, add the calvados and flame.
4 Add the stock, simmer 5 mins, liquidise, or pass firmly through a strainer, and return to a clean pan.
5 Add the cream, bring to boil, correct seasoning and consistency, pour over the escalopes and serve.

Note Well-trimmed pork chops can also be cooked this way. Caramelized apple slices can be served with this dish and are prepared as follows:

50 g	2 oz	butter
		2 medium-sized cooking apples, cored, unpeeled, cut in thick slices
25 g	1 oz	sugar

1 Heat the butter in a thick-bottomed pan.
2 Dip one side of the apple slices in the sugar. Place sugar side down in the hot butter.
3 Cook over high heat until caramelized.
4 Sprinkle with the rest of the sugar, turn the slices over and brown on the other side.

30   Pork chops with rum and fruit   *4 portions*

```
              4 pork chops, well trimmed of almost all fat
100 g  4 oz   butter
25 g   1 oz   brown sugar
              2 bananas, peeled and halved
              2 cooking apples, peeled and quartered
              2 slices of pineapple (tinned or fresh), halved
60 ml  ⅛ pt   rum
```

1 Cook the seasoned chops in a little of the butter on both sides, then remove from pan.
2 Add the remainder of the butter to the pan, heat and add sugar.
3 Fry the fruits on both sides and add the rum.
4 Dress the fruit around the chops, strain the liquid over and serve.

31   Sauté of pork with leeks   *4 portions*

```
500 g  1 ¼ lb  boned shoulder of pork
25 g   1 oz    seasoned flour
               1–2 tablespns oil
400 g  1 lb    sliced leeks
250 ml ½ pt    stock
               bouquet garni, including a little sage
               1–2 cloves garlic (optional)
               salt and pepper
```

1 Trim meat, cut into even pieces and pass through seasoned flour.
2 Thoroughly brown on all sides in hot oil.
3 Transfer to an ovenproof dish, mix in the leeks, cover with a lid and cook for 3–4 mins.
4 Mix in the stock, add bouquet garni and garlic, bring to boil and simmer until tender.
5 Remove bouquet garni and garlic, check consistency and seasoning and serve.

9

Poultry and game

Chicken

1   Chicken mousse, mousselines and quenelles

These chicken dishes are smooth and light in texture and easy to digest. They are made from a mixture known as chicken forcemeat.

Mousses are cooked in buttered moulds in a bain-marie in a moderate oven, then turned out of the mould for service. Therefore the basic mixture must be fairly firm so that the mousse does not break up. They can be cooked in individual or 2- or 4-portion moulds.

Mousselines are moulded using two tablespoons which are dipped into hot water to prevent the mixture sticking to the spoons. The mousselines are then placed into a buttered shallow dish and carefully covered with chicken stock. They are then covered with a buttered paper and cooked gently in the oven. Usually two mousselines are served to a portion.

Quenelles are shaped with two spoons as for mousselines but the sizes can be varied by using different sized spoons, according to requirement, e.g. using teaspoons if the quenelles are required for vol-au-vent. The mixture can also be piped into pea-sized shapes and used to garnish soups.

2   Chicken forcemeat

400 g	1 lb	prepared chicken
		salt and pepper
		nutmeg
		3 whites of egg
375–500 ml	¾–1 pt	double cream, very cold

1 Remove all the sinew from the flesh of chicken.
2 Lightly season and liquidise in a food processor.
3 Gradually add the egg whites, mixing thoroughly, and then pass through a sieve.
4 Place mixture in a bowl on ice until very cold.
5 Whilst on ice gradually combine the cream, mixing thoroughly. Test a little of the mixture by gently cooking in simmering water. If the mixture is too light add a little more white of egg, if too stiff, add a little more cream. Check seasoning.

3   Mousseline of chicken using a panada

A panada is used primarily as a cost-saving factor and to extend the flavouring ingredient. There are three basic panadas:
1 Equal quantities of white breadcrumbs and milk soaked and squeezed dry.
2 A basic choux pastry mixture without the addition of eggs.
3 A frangipan panada.

Frangipan panada

50 g	2 oz	butter or margarine
100 g	4 oz	flour
		4 egg yolks
250 ml	½ pt	milk

1 Cream the butter, flour and yolks together well; boil the milk and add to the mixture, then return to the saucepan and bring back to the boil.
2 Allow to cool.

Allow all panadas to cool before adding to the basic mixture.

Chicken forcemeat using a panada

400 g	1 lb	raw chicken flesh
		3 egg whites
150–200 g	6–8 oz	panada (the most suitable is frangipan because of its lightness)
500 ml	1 pt	double cream
		seasoning, mace, nutmeg

1 Remove all sinew, bones and skin from the chicken.
2 Purée in a food processor.
3 Beat in egg whites and panada.
4 Pass through a fine sieve then place into a basin over a bowl of ice.
5 Add the cream slowly, beating well between each addition.
6 Season with salt, pepper, mace and nutmeg. Use as required.

4   Chicken soufflé

300 g	10 oz	raw chicken, without skin or sinew
50 g	2 oz	butter
250 ml	½ pt	thick velouté
		salt and pepper
		3 eggs, separated

1 Finely dice the chicken and cook in the butter.
2 Add to the velouté and purée in a food processor.
3 Pass through a fine sieve and season.
4 Beat the yolks into the warm mixture.
5 Fold in the stiffly beaten whites carefully.
6 Place into 4 buttered moulds or one 4-portion mould.
7 Bake at 220°–230°C (425°–450°F, Reg. 7–8) for approx. 15 mins and serve. For a 4-portion soufflé cook at 180°C (350°F, Reg. 4) for approx. 20–25 mins.
8 Serve a suitable sauce separately, for example mushroom or suprême sauce.

Note For a lighter soufflé use 3 egg yolks and 4 egg whites.

5   Introduction to chicken sauté

Chickens 1¼–1½ kg (2½–3 lb) in weight are suitable to cut into 8 pieces for 4 portions. The pieces can be prepared on the bone or skinned and bone out. Boning out slightly increases shrinkage, the portions look smaller and preparation time is increased, but it facilitates ease of eating.

Chicken is prepared in this manner for fricassée, blanquette and chicken pies; the winglets, giblets and carcass are used for chicken stock. There are many classical garnishes for chicken sauté and a few examples follow. Further variety can be introduced by using herbs, e.g. tarragon, basil, rosemary etc., wines, e.g. dry white, dry sherry, vermouth, and different garnishes, such as wild mushrooms and ceps.

6 Chicken sauté with mushrooms and curry-flavoured sauce
4 portions

		1 chicken cut for sauté
50 g	2 oz	butter
150 g	6 oz	finely chopped onions
		1 dessertspn curry powder
100 g	4 oz	button mushrooms
125 ml	¼ pt	cream

1 Allow seasoned chicken to cook for a few minutes in butter without colour.
2 Add the onion, curry powder and cayenne and cover with a lid to finish cooking in the oven.
3 Cook the mushrooms in butter without colour and place with the chicken on the serving dish and keep warm.
4 Add the cream to the pan, cook for several minutes and pass through a sieve.
5 Finish with 25 g (1 oz) of the butter and pour over the chicken.

Note When garnished with slices of truffle this dish is called Poulet sauté Stanley.

The following recipes are examples of the different ways of using chicken cut for sauté:

1 Shallow fried and coloured brown with jus-lié (e.g. provençale)
2 Cooked without colour and a sauce (e.g. Archiduc)
3 Crumbed and fried (e.g. Maryland, page 130)

7 Chicken sauté with tomatoes, olives and anchovies *Poulet sauté provençale*
4 portions

1 ¼ – 1 ½ kg	2 ½ – 3 lb	chicken cut for sauté
50 g	2 oz	butter
60 ml	⅛ pt	white wine
		1 clove garlic
200 g	8 oz	tomatoes, skinned, deseeded, diced
		4 anchovy fillets chopped
		12 black olives (stoned)
250 ml	½ pt	jus-lié or demi-glace
		basil

1 Season the chicken and cook in the butter in a sauté pan to a golden brown on all sides.
2 Cover with a lid and complete the cooking until tender.
3 Dress the chicken in the serving dish.
4 Drain off the fat from the pan, deglaze with the wine and add the crushed garlic, tomatoes, anchovies, olives and jus-lié and chopped basil.
5 Simmer for a few mins and correct the seasoning.
6 Pour over the hot chicken, and finish with chopped basil.

8   Chicken sauté in whisky-flavoured cream sauce
Poulet sauté archiduc   *4 portions*

50 g	2 oz	butter or margarine
1 ¼ – 1 ½ kg	2 ½ – 3 lb	chicken cut for sauté
50 g	2 oz	finely chopped onion
50 g	2 oz	carrots ⎫
50 g	2 oz	celery ⎬ cut in brunoise
50 g	2 oz	leek ⎭
60 ml	⅛ pt	whisky or port wine
250 ml	½ pt	chicken velouté
125 ml	¼ pt	single cream or non-dairy unsweetened creamer
		2–3 drops of lemon juice
		seasoning, chopped parsley

1 Heat the butter or margarine in a sauté pan.
2 Season the chicken and place in the pan: legs, then breasts and wings.
3 Set quickly on both sides without colour, remove from the sauté pan, then add to the pan in which the chicken has been cooked the finely chopped onion and the brunoise of vegetables, sweat without colour.
4 Deglaze with whisky or port wine, add chicken velouté and bring to the boil.
5 Replace the chicken into the pan with the velouté and vegetables, cover with a lid and gently simmer until cooked.
6 Finish with lemon juice and single cream or non-dairy creamer.
7 Arrange the pieces of chicken neatly in a suitable dish and coat with sauce. Sprinkle with chopped parsley and serve.

9   Chicken sauté with ceps   *Poulet sauté aux cèpes*

Proceed as for chicken sauté. Before swilling the pan add 50 g (2 oz) chopped shallots and 200 g (8 oz) ceps and cook for a few minutes, add the jus-lié and finish with chopped parsley.

10 Chicken sauté with button onions and potatoes *Poulet sauté champeaux*

Deglaze the pan with white wine and just-lié, strain and finish with butter. Garnish with 100 g (4 oz) button onions cooked in butter and 100 g (4 oz) cocotte potatoes.

11 Chicken sauté with tarragon *Poulet sauté à l'estragon*

Infuse the jus-lié with tarragon and garnish the finished dish with blanched tarragon leaves.

12 Chicken sauté with vegetables and ham *Poulet sauté fermière*

Garnish with 50 g (2 oz) each of carrots, turnips, celery and onion cut in paysanne and sweated in butter and 50 g (2 oz) ham cut in dice. Add to the chicken when cooked and finish with jus-lié.

13 Breast and wing of chicken (suprême)

The word suprême is traditionally used to describe half of the white meat of a whole chicken. In contemporary menu practice the word wing or breast is often used in place of suprême.

Therefore there are two suprêmes to a chicken. Each has a fillet which is lifted off, the sinew is removed, an incision is made along the thick side of the suprême and the fillet inserted, then the suprême is lightly batted.

Suprêmes can be poached or shallow fried in butter, oil or margarine. When shallow fried they can be garnished as for sauté of chicken. For certain dishes the breasts can be floured or crumbed before shallow frying.

14 Poached chicken breast with mushrooms *Suprême de volaille aux champignons* *4 portions*

		4 suprêmes of chicken
100 g	4 oz	button mushrooms
		juice of 1 lemon
500 ml	1 pt	allemande sauce (see overleaf)

1 Gently poach the chicken in mushroom cooking liquor, produced by cooking the mushrooms in water containing lemon juice.
2 Place the suprêmes on the dish with the mushrooms and keep warm.

3 Reduce cooking liquor and add to the allemande sauce.
4 Correct the seasoning and consistency and strain over the chicken and mushrooms.

Sauce allemande

500 ml	1 pt	chicken or veal stock	
50 g	2 oz	flour	velouté
50 g	2 oz	butter, margarine or oil	
50 g	2 oz	mushrooms	
		juice of 1 lemon	
		2 egg yolks	
25 g	1 oz	butter	

1 Make the velouté.
2 Cook the mushrooms just covered with water and lemon juice.
3 Add the mushroom liquor and the yolks to the velouté, whisking in thoroughly.
4 Reduce to the required consistency, season and pass through a strainer, then finish by adding the butter.

15   Poached chicken breast with cheese sauce and asparagus

Poach the breast of chicken in chicken stock and add the reduced cooking liquor to the cheese sauce. Mask the suprême with the finished sauce, glaze and garnish with asparagus.

Note When slices of truffle are added this dish is known as Suprême de volaille Alexandra.

16   Poached chicken wing in chicken cream sauce and mushrooms

Poach the breast of chicken and add the reduced cooking liquor to the chicken cream sauce (suprême sauce). Mask the chicken with the sauce, which contains 50 g (2 oz) julienne of mushrooms cooked in a little butter.

Note When a julienne of truffle is also added this dish is called Suprême de volaille Polignac.

17   Fried chicken breast with mushrooms and chicken sauce   *Suprême de volaille aux champignons à brun*

Shallow fry the chicken in butter to a golden colour on both sides, garnish with mushrooms cooked in butter and coat with allemande sauce (above).

18 Fried chicken wing with asparagus and nut brown butter *Suprême de volaille aux asperges*

Shallow fry the chicken, garnish with asparagus tips and finish with nut brown butter.

19 Fried chicken breast with artichokes *Suprême de volaille aux fonds artichauts*

Shallow fry the chicken, garnish with sliced cooked artichoke bottoms and finish with nut brown butter and chopped parsley. Jus-lié is served separately.

20 Fried suprême of chicken with vegetables *Suprême de volaille jardinière*

Shallow fry the chicken, garnish with batons of vegetables and finish with nut brown butter.

21 Crumbed breasts or wings of chicken

Prepare the chicken by passing through seasoned flour, egg and crumbs. Shallow fry to a golden colour on both sides.

22 Fried crumbed chicken wing with cucumber and nut brown butter *Suprême de volaille Doria*

Shallow fry the chicken, garnish with turned pieces of cucumber cooked in butter and finish with nut brown butter.

23 Fried crumbed chicken breast with asparagus and artichokes

Shallow fry the breast of chicken, garnish with asparagus and artichoke bottoms and coat with nut brown butter.

Some examples of garnishes and sauces suitable for use with these dishes include the following:

Vegetables	*Sauces*
stir-fry vegetables	wine sauces
chicory	asparagus
courgettes	broccoli
sugar peas (mange-tout)	leek
peppers	watercress
spinach	

24   **Suprême of chicken Maryland**   *4 portions*

1¼–1½ kg	2½–3 lb	chicken suprêmes
100 g	4 oz	breadcrumbs
		2 eggs
		4 tomatoes
		4 rashers streaky bacon
		2 bananas
100 g	4 oz	sweetcorn

1 The suprêmes, after being egg and crumbed, may be deep or shallow fried to a golden colour ensuring that they are cooked through.
2 Garnish with grilled tomatoes, grilled bacon, fried halved bananas and fried sweetcorn fritters. (Not all establishments serve tomato, however it does add colour to the presentation.)

Sweetcorn fritters
The sweetcorn is bound in a thick white sauce, or a little flour and egg, and shallow fried on both sides. Alternatively, the mixture can be made into croquettes, flour, egg and crumbed and deep fried.

Note Hot horseradish sauce is served separately. The horseradish sauce is made from cream sauce with freshly grated horseradish.
   The banana may also be crumbed and deep fried.

25   **Chicken Kiev**   *Suprême de volaille à la kiev*

4 portions

		4 suprêmes of chicken
100 g	4 oz	butter
25 g	1 oz	seasoned flour
		2 eggs
100 g	4 oz	breadcrumbs

1 Make an incision along the thick sides of the suprêmes.
2 Insert 25 g (1 oz) cold butter into each. Season.
3 Pass through seasoned flour, eggwash and crumbs, ensuring complete coverage. Eggwash and crumb twice if necessary.
4 Deep fry, drain and serve.

Note
To vary the flavour, garlic, parsley, tarragon or chive butter can be used.
   The chicken could be stuffed, for example, with duxelle, chopped yellow, green and red peppers (pimentos), or lemon or thyme stuffing, in which case it would not be named à la kiev and so leaves room for personal interpretation and names to suit.

26   Breast of chicken in cream sauce under glass   *Suprême de volaille sous clôche*   *4 portions*

		4 suprêmes
50 g	2 oz	butter
125 ml	¼ pt	sauce suprême
125 ml	¼ pt	cream

1 Season the chicken and sweat in butter without colour.
2 Place each suprême on a suitable heatproof dish e.g. a round egg dish.
3 Coat with the sauce suprême which has been finished with cream;
  butter and white wine may be added if required.
4 Cover with the bell-shaped glass cover and allow to cook gently on the
  side of the stove for approx. 8 mins.
5 Serve covered with the glass bell.

Note This dish can be cooked with button mushrooms, or wild
mushrooms, and the sauce can be finished with 60 ml (⅛ pt) of dry white
wine, sherry or vermouth.

27   Stuffed crumbed fried breast of chicken   *Suprême de volaille farci*   *4 portions*

		4 suprêmes of chicken	
		salt and pepper	
100 g	4 oz	stuffing	
		seasoned flour	⎫
		1 egg	⎬ if crumbed
25 g	1 oz	breadcrumbs	⎭
50 g	2 oz	oil	
50 g	2 oz	butter	

1 Make an incision along the thick side of the suprêmes and season.
2 Add the stuffing and enclose.
3 Flour or, if to be breadcrumbed, pass through flour, eggwash and
  breadcrumbs.
4 Shallow fry gently to a golden colour on both sides.
5 Ensure that the chicken is thoroughly cooked, if necessary by finishing
  in the oven.
6 Finish with nut brown butter or serve with parsley or garlic butter.

Note Suggested stuffings include: duxelle; pimentos or leeks, chopped and
cooked in butter; ham; and liver paté. Always add the stuffing cold unless
the suprêmes are to be cooked immediately.

28   Chicken fricassée in cream and wine sauce   *Fricassée de volaille au vin blanc*   *4 portions*

1¼–1½ kg	2½–3 lb	chicken cut for sauté
75 g	3 oz	butter
100 g	4 oz	leeks ⎫
100 g	4 oz	celery ⎬ cut into ¼ cm (⅛ in.) dice
100 g	4 oz	onions ⎭
250 ml	½ pt	white wine
250 ml	½ pt	double cream

1 Gently cook the seasoned chicken in 50 g (2 oz) butter without colour in a sauté pan.
2 Add the diced vegetables, cover with a lid and cook until tender on top of the stove or in the oven.
3 Remove the chicken and keep warm.
4 Deglaze the pan with wine.
5 Add the cream, simmer for 2 mins, whisk in the remaining butter and correct the seasoning. (Alternatively, use 125 ml (¼ pt) chicken velouté and 125 ml (¼ pt) double cream.)
6 Pour over the chicken to serve.

Note Various garnishes can be used which would be added to the sauce before being poured over the chicken. For example:

100 g (4 oz) julienne of leek, cooked in butter
100 g (4 oz) diced pimento
150 g (6 oz) turned blanched cucumber
100 g (4 oz) peeled white grapes without pips

Yoghurt may be used in place of cream and English wine can also be considered.

29   Stuffed legs of chicken with vegetable garnish
Ballottines de volaille fermière   *4 portions*

		4 legs of chicken
		stuffing (see page 133)
		salt and pepper
50 g	2 oz	butter
100 g	4 oz	carrots ⎫
100 g	4 oz	onion � half cut in paysanne,
100 g	4 oz	celery ⎬ remainder in mirepoix
100 g	4 oz	leeks ⎭
375 ml	¾ pt	jus-lié

1 Bone out the chicken legs: first, remove the thigh bone.
2 Scrape the flesh off the bone of the drumstick towards the claw joint.
3 Sever the drumstick bone, leaving 2–3 cm (¾–1 in.) at the end.

4 Fill legs with a savoury stuffing, neaten the shape and secure with string using a trussing needle. Season with salt and pepper.
5 Pot-roast in butter with mirepoix in a covered pan or sauté until cooked.
6 Ensure that the stuffing is cooked through, approx. 20–30 mins.
7 Remove the ballottines and keep warm in a clean pan.
8 Deglaze the pan with wine, if desired, add the jus-lié and simmer for several mins.
9 Strain, correct the seasoning and consistency.
10 Add to the sauce the paysanne of vegetables which have been sweated together in a little butter.
11 Pour the sauce on to the chicken, simmer gently for a few mins and serve.

Stuffing for ballottines

25 g	1 oz	chopped onion (cooked)
50 g	2 oz	breadcrumbs
50 g	2 oz	butter or margarine
		salt and pepper
		or use
100 g	4 oz	minced chicken and veal, in place of the breadcrumbs, seasoned and bound with an egg

Mix all the ingredients together, adding the required herb or flavouring e.g. thyme, parsley, rosemary etc. If desired, chopped crushed garlic, chopped chicken livers and chopped mushrooms could also be used.

Note Wines such as Madeira, Marsala or white port could also be added to the sauce.

Duck

30 Braised duck with celery *Caneton braisé au céleri*

4 portions

50 g	2 oz	butter or oil	
50 g	2 oz	bacon trimmings	
50 g	2 oz	carrots	mirepoix
50 g	2 oz	onions	
200 g	8 oz	celery	
2 kg	4 lb	duck	
375 ml	¾ pt	brown stock	
375 ml	¾ pt	demi-glace	
		bouquet garni	
		4 pieces of braised celery	

1 Place the butter in a braising pan and lightly fry the mirepoix.
2 Add the seasoned, trussed duck and brown on all sides.

3 Drain off the fat, add the stock and demi-glace so as to three-parts cover the duck, add the bouquet garni and bring to the boil.
4 Cover with a lid and cook in a moderate oven (200°C, 400°F, Reg. 6 approx.) and allow to simmer until cooked, approx. 1½ hours.
5 Put the duck aside to keep warm, remove the string.
6 Degrease the sauce, strain and correct the seasoning and consistency.
7 Cut the duck into portions, mask with the sauce, garnish with braised celery and serve.

Note
a) In place of demi-glace, jus-lié may be used or the stock thickened slightly with cornflour.
b) 1 or 2 heads of celery, according to size, would be required for braising for the garnish.
c) In place of celery, braised duck could be served with, for example, chicory, salsify, leeks or spring vegetables.

31 Duckling with gooseberries   *Canéton poëlé aux groseilles à maquereau*   *4 portions*

2 kg	4 lb	duckling
50 g	2 oz	butter
50 g	2 oz	carrots ⎫
50 g	2 oz	onions ⎬ mirepoix
25 g	1 oz	celery ⎭
		bayleaf
		thyme
250 ml	½ pt	brown stock
10 g	½ oz	arrowroot
200 g	8 oz	gooseberries, topped and tailed

1 Clean, truss and season the duckling for pot-roasting.
2 Place the duck in a buttered pan with mirepoix and coat with butter. Cover pan with tight-fitting lid.
3 Cook in the oven at 200°C (400°F, Reg. 6) for 1 hour, basting occasionally.
4 Remove the lid, continue cooking for a further half hour until tender and baste frequently.
5 Remove the duck and keep warm.
6 Drain all fat from pan, deglaze with the brown stock and thicken with arrowroot.
7 Add the gooseberries to the sauce and simmer gently for a few minutes, until just cooked.
8 Carve the duck, coat with sauce and serve.

Note
a) If gooseberries are very tart, a little sugar or honey can be added to to the sauce.

b) In place of gooseberries, blackcurrants or peaches, cut into quarters, could be used.

c) For service the duck can be cut into pieces retaining the bone or by removing the legs, boning out and cutting into slices, and by removing the breast from the bone and carving into slices.

32   Stuffed leg of duck

Proceed as for stuffed chicken legs, page 132.

The stuffing recommended for chicken can be used for duck as well but consider also sage and onion, and sauces such as orange, and port wine.

33   Breast of duck

Remove the breast of duck in a similar manner to suprême of chicken (page 127). Grill, sauté or roast in a hot oven and cook as required, either slightly underdone or cooked through.

Serve whole or sliced and garnish as required.

Note The fat and skin may be removed from the breast: discard the fat and tie the skin back on to the breast to protect it during the cooking.

34   Breast of duck with pineapple   *Suprême de canard à l'ananas*   *4 portions*

		4 duck suprêmes
100 g	4 oz	oil or butter
		4 slices pineapple
250 ml	½ pt	jus-lié

1 Shallow fry the duck in butter or oil.
2 Carefully fry the pineapple to colour. If canned pineapple is used, shallow fry quickly; if fresh pineapple is used, cook until tender.
3 Quarter the pineapple and neatly arrange three-quarters on the duck; cut remaining quarter into dice and add to the jus-lié.
4 Deglaze the pan with the jus-lié, strain and pour over the duck to serve.

Note Variations to this garnish may be kiwi fruit, mango, and banana, and a liquor such as curaçao or rum may be added to the jus-lié.

Turkey

35 Stuffed leg of turkey

Ensure that the sinews are withdrawn from the turkey leg, remove the leg from the turkey and bone out, season and stuff, then tie with string. Roast, braise or pot roast, remove the string and allow to stand before carving in thick slices.

Suitable stuffings include chestnut, walnut, peanuts or mixed nuts in pork sausage meat or those stuffings suggested for chicken or duck ballottines.

Sauces such as jus-lié containing cranberries, blackcurrants or red currants may be served.

36 Breast and wing of turkey

Suprêmes of 100–150 g (4–6 oz) can be cut from the boned-out breast and wing of turkey and used in a similar manner to chicken (see pages 127–131).

Guinea fowl

Guinea fowl can be used in a similar manner to chicken. The flesh is of a dry nature and has little fat, therefore when roasted or pot roasted (poêlé), it is usual to bard the guinea fowl and not to over-cook it.

37 Breast of guinea fowl with bacon and mushrooms
Suprême de pintarde forestière   *4 portions*

		4 suprêmes of guinea fowl
100 g	4 oz	oil or butter
100 g	4 oz	lardons of bacon, blanched
200 g	8 oz	button mushrooms
100 g	4 oz	potatoes (diced and shallow fried)

1 Season and sauté the suprêmes in oil or butter on both sides for 3 to 4 mins.
2 Remove and keep warm.
3 Fry the lardons for a few minutes, add the quartered mushrooms and cook quickly for a minute or two. Add the cooked potatoes.
4 Add the garnish to the suprêmes and finish with nut brown butter.

Note In place of button mushrooms, wild mushrooms could be used and a jus-lié containing chopped mushrooms could be served separately.

38 Sauté of guinea fowl with tomatoes and herbs

Pintarde sauté aux tomates   *4 portions*

1 ¼ – 1 ½ kg	2 ½ – 3 lb	guinea fowl, cut for sauté
50 g	2 oz	butter
100 g	4 oz	chopped onion or shallots
60 ml	⅛ pt	Madeira
250 ml	½ pt	jus-lié
200 g	8 oz	tomatoes, skinned, deseeded, diced
		salt and pepper
		chopped tarragon, chervil and parsley

1 Shallow fry the seasoned pieces of guinea fowl in the butter to a golden colour.
2 Cover with a lid and cook on the stove or in the oven until tender.
3 Remove the guinea fowl and keep warm.
4 Add the shallots or onions and cook for 2 mins.
5 Drain off the fat, add the wine, jus-lié and tomatoes.
6 Bring to the boil and simmer for 3–4 mins.
7 Correct the seasoning, add the herbs and pour over the guinea fowl to serve.

Note In place of Madeira, Marsala, port or sherry could be used.

Game

39 Partridge with apple, cream and calvados   *4 portions*

		4 young partridges, trussed and barded
200 g	8 oz	butter
		4 large dessert apples, peeled and cored
		1 dessertspn calvados
125 ml	¼ pt	double cream

1 Season the partridges, rub all over with butter and place in an ovenproof dish. Brown in a hot oven 220°C (425°F, Reg. 7) and remove from the dish.
2 Cut apples in thick slices and half-cook them by shallow frying in butter on both sides.
3 Place apples in the ovenproof dish, add calvados and place the partridges on top (removing the bards and trussing strings).
4 Pour over the cream, leave uncovered and return to the oven at 190°C (375°F, Reg. 5) for approx. 20 mins. Ensure the dish is clean and serve.

Note Variations can include: pears in place of apples; alternatives to calvados, e.g. white wine, vermouth or cider; cultivated or wild mushrooms; peeled and pipped grapes.

40 **Braised partridge with cabbage** *Perdrix au chou*

4 portions

Older or red-legged partridges are suitable for this dish.

		2 old partridges
100 g	4 oz	lard, butter, margarine or oil
400 g	1 lb	cabbage
100 g	4 oz	belly of pork or bacon (in the piece)
		1 carrot, peeled
		1 studded onion
		bouquet garni
1 litre	2 pts	white stock
		8 frankfurter sausages or pork chipolatas

1 Season the partridges, rub with fat, brown quickly in a hot oven and remove.
2 Trim the cabbage, remove the core, separate the leaves and wash thoroughly.
3 Blanch the cabbage leaves and the belly of pork for 5 mins. Refresh and drain well to remove all water. Remove the rind from the pork.
4 Place half the cabbage in a deep ovenproof dish; add the pork rind, the partridges, carrot, onion, bouquet garni, the remaining fat, and stock, and season lightly.
5 Add the remaining cabbage and bring to the boil, cover with greased greaseproof paper, a lid and braise slowly until tender, approx. 1½–2 hrs.
6 Add the sausages half-way through the cooking time by placing them under the cabbage.
7 Remove bouquet garni and the onion and serve everything else, the pork and carrot being sliced.

41 **Pheasant in casserole** *Faisan en casserole*

4 portions

100 g	4 oz	carrot ⎫
100 g	4 oz	onion ⎬ sliced
50 g	2 oz	celery ⎭
		small sprig of thyme
1 × 1½–2 kg	3–4 lb	pheasant, cleaned, trussed and barded
		salt and pepper
50 g	2 oz	butter
		1 tablespn brandy
125 ml	¼ pt	game stock

1 Place vegetables and thyme in casserole.
2 Add the seasoned and buttered pheasant.
3 Cover with a lid and place in oven at 200°C (400°F, Reg. 6), basting occasionally until cooked.
4 Remove pheasant, pour off fat and deglaze casserole with brandy and gravy.

5 Bring to the boil (in a saucepan if necessary), correct the seasoning, skim off any fat, strain and serve.

Note This is a basic recipe which can be garnished in a variety of ways, for example:
a) button onions, olive-shaped potatoes and lardons of bacon
b) button or wild mushrooms
c) braised celery

42 **Pheasant with cream** *Faisan à la crème*

1 Three-quarters cook the pheasant as in previous recipe.
2 Add 125 ml (¼ pt) double cream and a few drops of lemon juice and continue cooking without a lid, basting frequently until tender.
3 Remove pheasant, strain off the liquid, degrease, correct seasoning and consistency and serve.

Note This is also a basic recipe to which other garnishes may be added, such as:
   wild or button mushrooms
   a little meat glaze to alter the colour and flavour of the sauce
   peeled and pipped grapes
   quennelles of game etc.
   Pheasant can also be cooked with apples, as on page 137.
   Old pheasants should only be braised, e.g. as in Partridge with cabbage, page 138.
   Pheasant may be cut up raw and cooked as a sauté with a variety of sauces and garnishes.
   Pheasant can also be prepared as suprêmes, left plain or stuffed, e.g. with a mousseline-type mixture, and shallow fried, e.g. Stuffed breasts of pheasant with a cream, brandy and mushroom sauce. Pheasant may be stuffed in a variety of ways, e.g. Pheasant stuffed with mushrooms and chestnuts.

43 **Pheasant stuffed with mushrooms and chestnuts**

		1 young pheasant	
150 g	6 oz	finely minced pork (half lean, half fat)	⎫
		2 finely chopped shallots or 1 small onion	
		oil	⎬ duxelle
150 g	6 oz	finely chopped mushroom	
		1 teaspn chopped parsley	
		salt, pepper	⎭
200 g	8 oz	peeled chestnuts cooked in stock	
		1–2 tablespns brandy	
		chopped pheasant liver	

1 Truss and bard the pheasant.
2 Use the remaining ingredients to make a stuffing.
3 Stuff the pheasant and either roast or pot-roast it.
4 Prepare a gravy from the pan juices after the pheasant is cooked and serve.

44   Pigeon

As pigeons do not have gall-bladders it is not necessary to remove the livers when they are drawn and cleaned.

Tender young pigeons (pigonneaux) less than 12 months old can be roasted, pot-roasted or split open and grilled and served, for example, with a Robert, charcutierè or devilled sauce.

Young pigeons can be cut in halves, flattened slightly, seasoned, shallow fried in butter and cooked and finished as for sautés of chicken e.g. chasseur, bordelaise etc.

Pigeons may be cooked in casserole, as recipe 41 page 138 or as a salmis. Older pigeons should only be braised.

See also the recipe for breast of pigeon, herb ravioli, page 165.

45   Saddle of hare   *Râble de lièvre*

This joint is cut from the back of the hare, usually in a similar way to a short saddle of lamb, that is, a pair of uncut loins. All sinew must be removed, the joint trimmed and, if desired, the joint may be larded with pork fat.

It is not essential to marinade the saddle if obtained from a young hare, but if in doubt as to its tenderness, or if it is required to be kept for a few days, then the joint should be marinaded in the following:

Raw marinade for furred game e.g. venison, hare, etc.

200 g	8 oz	carrot ⎫
200 g	8 oz	onion ⎬ finely sliced
100 g	4 oz	celery ⎭
		2 cloves garlic
25 g	1 oz	parsley stalks
		sprig of thyme, half bay leaf
		2 cloves
		12 peppercorns
500 ml	1 pt	red wine
125 ml	¼ pt	wine vinegar
125 ml	¼ pt	oil

1 Season the joints with salt and pepper.
2 Place the joints in a suitable container, e.g. stainless steel or china.
3 Cover with the marinade, keep in the refrigerator and turn the joint over frequently.

46 Saddle of hare, German style *Râble de lièvre à l'allemande*

1 saddle yields 1–2 portions according to size

1 Remove the saddle from the marinade and dry thoroughly.
2 Place the saddle on a bed of vegetables from the marinade and roast in the oven at 220°C (425°F, Reg. 7).
3 When the saddle is three-quarters cooked, remove the vegetables.
4 Add 125 ml (¼ pt) cream and, basting frequently with the cream, complete the cooking, keeping the meat pink.
5 Remove the saddle, add a few drops of lemon juice to the sauce, correct seasoning and consistency, pass through a fine strainer and serve with the saddle.

Examples of classical variations include:
Grand veneur – poivrade sauce mixed with redcurrant jelly and cream.
Smitaine – as for German style, the sauce well flavoured with onion and soured by the addition of more lemon or wine vinegar.
Montmorency – garnished with glazed cherries.
There are many other variations that can be made, for example, after the saddle is removed from the roasting tray, the tray can be deglazed with brandy, whisky or gin. Sliced mushrooms (cultivated or wild) can be added to the sauce.
Suitable accompaniments include: braised chestnuts, or chestnut purée, or Brussels sprouts with chestnuts; purée of celeriac, or celeriac or parsnips, or celeriac and onion; buttered noodles etc.

47 Quails

Only plump birds with firm white fat should be selected. They may be roasted, spit-roasted, cooked 'en casserole' or poached in a rich well-flavoured chicken or veal stock (or a combination of both).

Quails may also be boned-out from the back, stuffed with a forcemeat made as follows, then cooked by any of the above mentioned methods.

Forcemeat

200 g	8 oz	finely minced pork (half lean, half fat)
400 g	1 lb	quail and chicken livers
50 g	2 oz	chopped shallot or onion
25 g	1 oz	chopped mushroom
		pinch of thyme, half bay leaf
		salt, pepper, mixed spice

1 Gently fry the pork to extract the fat.
2 Increase the heat, add the livers and the remainder of the ingredients.
3 Fry quickly to brown the livers but keep them pink.
4 Allow to cool and pass through a sieve or mince finely.

48   Quails with cherries

100 g	4 oz	carrot	
100 g	4 oz	onion	sliced
50 g	2 oz	celery	
		small sprig of thyme	
		4 quails, cleaned and trussed (stuffing optional)	
50 g	2 oz	butter	
		1 tablespn brandy	
		2 tablespns port wine	
125 ml	¼ pt	veal or chicken stock	
		juice of ¼ orange and 3–4 drops lemon juice	
		36–40 morello or black cherries, stoned and poached in stock syrup	

1 Place vegetables and thyme in casserole.
2 Add seasoned and buttered quails and cover with a lid.
3 Place in a hot oven (230°C, 450°F, Reg. 8), basting frequently until cooked.
4 Remove quails, pour off fat, deglaze with brandy, port and stock.
5 Add orange and lemon juice, correct seasoning, strain and allow to simmer.
6 When reduced to the required quantity, add the cherries, pour over the quails and serve.

49   Quails with grapes

Prepare as in previous recipe, stuffing quails if required, substituting white wine for port and peeled and pipped grapes for cherries.

50   Quails in aspic

The quails are boned, stuffed and gently poached. When cold they are lightly coated with a well-flavoured aspic in which the cooking liquid from the quails has been incorporated.

51   Venison

Venison is the meat of the red deer, fallow deer and roebuck. Of these three, the meat of the roebuck is considered to have the best and most delicate eating quality. The prime cuts are the legs, loins and best ends. The shoulder of young animals can be boned, rolled and roasted but if in any doubt as to its tenderness, it should be cut up and used for stewed or braised dishes.

After slaughter, carcasses should be well hung in a cool place for several

days and when cut into joints are usually marinaded before being cooked
(see page 140 for marinade).

52   Roast leg or haunch of venison

1 Prepare and trim leg, removing pelvic or aitch bone.
2 After marinading for 24 hours, remove, dry well and roast, basting
  frequently. The cooking time will vary according to the weight of the
  joint which is generally kept slightly pink in the centre. As a guide
  allow approx. 15–20 mins per 400 g (1 lb).
3 Deglaze the roasting pan and incorporate the juices in the
  accompanying sauce, which is traditionally peppery and spicy, e.g.
  poivrade, Grand veneur.
Roast haunch of venison is popular served hot or cold.

53   Venison cutlets, chops and steaks

1 Venison cutlets, cut from the best-end, and chops, cut from the loin, are
  usually well trimmed and cooked by shallow frying, provided that the
  meat is tender. If in doubt they should be braised.
2 After they are cooked they should be removed from the pan, the fat
  poured off and the pan deglazed with stock, red wine, brandy, Madeira,
  or sherry, which is then added to the accompanying sauce.
3 A spicy peppery sauce is usually offered, which can be varied by the
  addition of any one or more extra ingredients, e.g. cream, yoghurt,
  redcurrant jelly, choice of cooked beetroot, sliced button or wild
  mushrooms, cooked pieces of chestnut, etc.
4 Accompaniments can include, for example, a purée of green, brown or
  yellow lentils, a purée of any other dried bean, purée or braised
  chestnuts, braised red cabbage, or purée of a root vegetable, e.g.
  celeriac, turnip, swede, carrot, parsnip or any combination of the five.
5 Venison steaks or escalopes are cut from the boned-out nuts of meat
  from the loins, well trimmed and slightly thinned with a meat bat.
6 The escalopes can be quickly shallow fried and finished as for cutlets
  and chops, with a variety of accompanying sauces and garnishes. (Some
  example of these will be found in Chapter 10 British dishes.)

10

British dishes

Introduction

The aim of this chapter is to give practical examples illustrating the style and type of dishes of a number of leading British chefs. The recipes follow in course sequence. Many of the first courses may be increased in size for a main course and the fish dishes (suitably adjusted to size) can be served as a first, fish or main course.

All those who have contributed recipes are in charge of their kitchens and all have established reputations for producing and serving good food.

Every dish in this chapter has proved to be popular with customers. The type of establishment using the recipes varies from restaurants that are wholly or partly owned by the chef and with less than fifty seats to large restaurants and hotel dining rooms.

It is hoped that the examples in this chapter will stimulate readers to be innovative and creative in their own cooking. Before doing so, however, it is important that the theory and practice of basic skills and classical-based practices are mastered, as these form the foundation knowledge of almost all successful chefs.

The authors and publishers are grateful to all the chefs who so willingly contributed their recipes.

1   Brioche bun filled with seafood perfumed with sauternes and orange   *4 portions*   (David Pitchford)

500 ml	1 pt	fish stock
250 ml	½ pt	double cream
125 ml	¼ pt	fresh orange juice
125 ml	¼ pt	Sauternes
100 g	4 oz	tomatoes, skinned, deseeded and quartered
50 g	2 oz	julienne of the green part of leek
		brioche buns (see overleaf)
		4 fresh scallops (with roes)

100 g	4 oz	Dover sole fillets, cut into 8 goujons
100 g	4 oz	salmon, cut into 8 slices
100 g	4 oz	red mullet, cut into 8 slices
50 g	2 oz	clarified butter
		chopped chives

1 Reduce the fish stock, double cream, orange juice and Sauternes to the consistency of oil.
2 Cut the tomatoes into neat diamonds.
3 Lightly blanch the leek in boiling water and refresh.
4 Remove the top of each brioche and hollow out a little of the centre, retaining the lids. Keep warm.
5 Carefully toss the prepared fish in clarified butter and remove from the pan, discarding any excess butter.
6 Pass the Sauternes and orange reduction through a very fine chinois into the pan used for cooking the fish.
7 At service time add the fish to the reduction and gently reheat.
8 Place the warm brioche buns on hot plates.
9 Add the tomato diamonds, julienne of leek and chopped chives a few seconds before spooning the fish in and around the brioche buns.
10 Place the lids at an attractive angle and serve.

Notes This dish may be served as a first or fish course.
   Any suitable combination of fish may be substituted for those given. In a professional kitchen this dish may provide the means to use previously prepared fish, e.g. lobster.

Brioche paste   (Makes 10 small buns)

12 g	½ oz	yeast
25 g	1 oz	milk
225 g	9 oz	sieved strong flour
		pinch of salt
125 g	5 oz	butter
12 g	½ oz	sugar
125 g	5 oz	beaten eggs

1 Dissolve the yeast in warm milk.
2 Make a leaven with 100 g (4 oz) of the flour, salt and dissolved yeast. Ferment for approx. 1½ hours in a warm place.
3 Cream the butter and sugar and add the beaten eggs.
4 Make the paste with the remaining flour and butter and egg mixture. Knead for 5 mins.
5 Add the leaven to the paste and knead for a further 2 mins. Cover and ferment for a further 20 mins, beating on completion.
6 Use to one-third fill lightly greased brioche moulds and prove to the top of the moulds in a warm place.
7 Bake for 20 mins in a hot oven (220°C, 425°F, Reg. 7).

2 Spinach soufflé with anchovy sauce *6 portions*
(Richard Shepherd)

75 g	3 oz	butter
75 g	3 oz	flour
500 ml	1 pt	warm milk, infused with onion, bay leaf and clove
100 g	4 oz	washed spinach
		4 eggs, separated
		cayenne, ground nutmeg and salt

1 Make a roux from the butter and flour. Cook gently without colour, add the infused milk slowly and, stirring constantly, allow to cook out slowly.
2 Cook the spinach in a little boiling salted water and refresh in cold water. Squeeze thoroughly and chop finely.
3 Add a pinch of salt to the egg whites and beat until very stiff.
4 Season the sauce with cayenne, nutmeg and salt. Add egg yolks and mix thoroughly, then add spinach, continuing to mix and fold in little by little the beaten egg whites.
5 Fill 6 well buttered soufflé moulds and cook in a pre-heated oven at 220°C (425°F, Reg. 7) for about 20 mins. Serve with anchovy sauce (below).

Note This is served as a first course.

Anchovy sauce

		3 egg yolks
200 g	8 oz	clarified butter
		cayenne, salt and lemon juice
		1 small tin anchovy fillets

1 Add 1 tablespn water to the egg yolks and cook over a gentle heat, whisking continuously to a sabayon.
2 Allow to cool slightly and slowly add the warm clarified butter. When combined add a little cayenne, salt and squeeze of lemon juice.
3 Squeeze the anchovy fillets free from oil and blend with a drop of water to a smooth paste. Place into a bowl and add sauce, whisking continuously until thoroughly mixed.
4 Pass through a fine chinois and use to accompany spinach soufflé.

3 Salad of salmon and avocado mousse with mango and sherry sauce   *8 portions*

(Jack Philips)

400 g	1 lb	fresh salmon, without skin or bone, cut into 8 slices
100 g	4 oz	fresh salmon
50 ml	2 fl oz	double cream
		¼ egg white
		teaspn of iced water
		salt and pepper
		1 avocado
25 ml	1 fl oz	béchamel
		½ lemon
		2 leaves gelatine
		salt and pepper

salmon mousse — { double cream, ¼ egg white, teaspn of iced water, salt and pepper }

avocado mousse — { 1 avocado, béchamel, ½ lemon, 2 leaves gelatine, salt and pepper }

1 Place the raw slices of salmon on silver foil.
2 Spread on the raw salmon mousse which has been liquidised in the order of fish, cream, egg white, water and seasoning.
3 Place on top of this the avocado mousse, liquidised in the order of avocado, béchamel, lemon juice, dissolved gelatine and seasoning and then piped onto a piece of tin foil and semi frozen.
4 Roll and seal with 'wrap-fast' and poach or steam for 15 mins. Cool.
5 Serve when cold by slicing, each slice showing a round of salmon on the outside, salmon mousse to follow and avocado mousse in the centre.
6 Place three thin slices on each plate, decorate with radicchio and serve with the sauce.

Mango and sherry sauce
Liquidise half a mango, add 50 ml (2 fl oz) sherry vinegar, 150 ml (6 fl oz) soya oil, a touch of French mustard and castor sugar to taste.

Notes The unique feature of this dish is to have the salmon cooked yet retain the greenness of the avocado.
   It may be served as a first or fish course.

4 Salad Belinda   *4 portions*

(Martin Davis)

200 g	8 oz	fresh duck livers (cleaned, gall removed)
		salt and ground black pepper
50 g	2 oz	butter
		oil
		1 small head radicchio
		¼ head of curly chicory
		corn salad
		½ head round lettuce
125 ml	¼ pt	vinaigrette (using half sunflower oil, half walnut oil)
		½ avocado
		½ ogen melon

½ avocado, ½ ogen melon } skinned and thinly sliced lengthways

100 g	4 oz	fresh redcurrants (frozen if not available)
100 g	4 oz	streaky bacon lardons (small batons), blanched and coloured in butter
		1 bunch watercress (well cleaned)

1 Prepare duck livers by generously seasoning then sauté in the butter and oil so that when cooled they remain pink inside. Cool until needed.
2 Wash and separate leaves of radicchio, chicory, corn and lettuce and carefully tear into bite-size pieces. Drain and mix together, sprinkling lightly with vinaigrette.
3 Mound salad leaves artistically onto 4 plates.
4 Thinly slice duck livers and arrange on top of salad mound.
5 Arrange avocado and melon slices around livers.
6 Sprinkle with redcurrants and lardons, and finish with a small bouquet of watercress in the centre of the salad.

Note This salad can be served warm in the winter months and is offered as a first course.

5 Stilton and port mousse with walnuts   *4 portions*
(Murdo Macsween)

		5 leaves gelatine
		aspic and garnish as needed
100 g	4 oz	stilton
50 ml	2 fl oz	port
25 g	1 oz	walnuts, chopped
125 ml	¼ pt	double cream
		4 egg whites
		seasoning

1 Soak gelatine in cold water.
2 Line 4 individual moulds with a little aspic and garnish, e.g. slices of stuffed olives.
3 Liquidise stilton and port together, adding a little single cream if necessary, and add walnuts.
4 Half-whip double cream and fold into stilton mixture.
5 Whip up egg whites.
6 Squeeze all the water from gelatine and melt over a low heat, then add to egg whites while still whipping.
7 Fold egg whites into stilton mixture and season.
8 Place mousse into moulds and allow to set for 2 hours.

This is served as a first course.

6   **Mousseline of duck**   *4 portions*   (Philip Britten)

150 g	6 oz	breast of duck
		chopped garlic, shallots, juniper berries, peppercorns and thyme
		½ tablespn port
		½ tablespn brandy
		½ large beaten egg
		½ teaspn salt and pepper
		2 tablespns reduced duck and juniper-flavoured veal stock
125 ml	¼ pt	double cream
125 ml	¼ pt	whipping cream

1 Slice raw breast and marinate together with chopped garlic, shallots, juniper berries, peppercorns, thyme, port and brandy for 12 hours.
2 Remove duck from marinade and dry thoroughly on kitchen paper.
3 Chop finely in a food processor and add the egg, salt and pepper, the brandy and port from the marinade, and the reduction and mix well.
4 Whilst the machine is in motion slowly add all the cream until well amalgamated. Correct seasoning.
5 Place into 4 equal-sized well greased moulds, cover with tin foil and cook in a bain-marie at 160°C (325°F, Reg. 3) until firm for approx. 25 mins.
6 Serve with a rich juniper berry sauce.

Notes This is served as a first course.

1 The reduction must be of a very intense flavour and consistency in order to balance the lack of flavour in the cream, without impairing the texture of the mousseline. Therefore the quality of the reduction is of paramount importance to achieve the best result.
2 All ingredients, barring the reduction, which must be kept warm to prevent setting, must be kept very cold to compensate, as the cream is vulnerable to curdling when warm.
3 A ragoût of diced mushrooms with a little reduction, cooled until set, can be placed into the centre of each mousseline prior to cooking. Be sure this is well enclosed all round. This little touch can give a very nice effect when being cut open.

7   **Endive and hazelnut soup**   *8 portions*   (David Nicholls)

1 kg	2 lb	Belgian endive
150 g	6 oz	potatoes
50 g	2 oz	onions
50 g	2 oz	leeks
50 g	2 oz	celery
100 g	4 oz	butter
1 litre	2 pt	chicken stock
1 litre	2 pt	milk
		salt and pepper

100 g	4 oz	roasted whole hazelnuts (skins removed)
50 g	2 oz	bacon
		2 slices bread cut into 1 cm (½ in.)
150 g	6 oz	double cream

1 Cut out the root from the endives and chop roughly – wash well.
2 Peel and prepare the potatoes, onions, leeks and celery and chop roughly.
3 Sweat the vegetables in butter until soft, without colour.
4 Moisten with chicken stock, reduce by half, add the milk and reduce by half again. Adjust the seasoning and add the nuts.
5 Liquidise all together and pass through a coarse chinois.
6 Cut the bacon into small strips without the fat or rind. Blanch well and pan-fry until crisp.
7 Prepare the croûtons in the usual way.
8 Re-heat the soup and add the cream, adjust seasoning and if too thick thin with chicken stock.
9 Pour into soup plates or bowls and sprinkle with croûtons and lardons to serve.

Note This is a thick 'country style' soup and should not be too refined.

8 Steamed sea bass with angel-hair pasta, bean sprouts and mango *4 portions* (Stanley Berwick)

For enriched stock

200 g	8 oz	cleaned and chopped carrot	
50 g	2 oz	white of leek	liquidised, raw
50 g	2 oz	onions	
100 g	4 oz	unsalted butter	
125 ml	5 fl oz	dry white wine	
500 ml	1 pt	fish stock	
125 ml	5 fl oz	white chicken stock	

1 Place vegetables in a heavy saucepan with the butter and cook on a low heat until tender.
2 Add the wine and cook until nearly dry.
3 Add the fish and chicken stock and cook out until half the quantity has evaporated.
4 Pass through a sieve into a clean pan and continue cooking until only 250 ml (½ pt) remains.

4 × 150 g	6 oz	sea bass fillets with scales and bones removed and cut into 3 diamonds
		salt and pepper
100 g	4 oz	taglioni or vermicelli pasta
250 ml	½ pt	enriched fish stock

100 g	4 oz	bean sprouts
100 g	4 oz	firm mango, diced
50 g	2 oz	unsalted butter

1 Place the sea bass, skin side up, in a container for steaming (or poach if necessary) and season.
2 Cook the pasta and set to one side, lightly seasoned and buttered.
3 Rapidly boil the stock while the fish is cooking.
4 When reduced by half, add the bean sprouts and mango and beat in the butter.
5 Remove from the heat and correct seasoning.
6 Place the hot pasta in the centre of four pre-heated plates and arrange the sea bass diamonds, skin side up, around this.
7 Spoon the sauce, with its garnish between each piece of sea bass and serve.

9   Fillet of monkfish in fresh lime sauce   *4 portions*
(Somerset Moore)

1 kg	2 lb	trimmed monkfish fillets (1 per person)
		salt and pepper
		juice of 3 limes and zest of 1 lime
		1 tablespn finely chopped shallots
250 ml	½ pt	double cream
100 g	4 oz	unsalted butter
100 g	4 oz	puff pastry fleurons
		sprigs of dill or parsley

1 Score the fillets, season and sauté until cooked through. Remove and keep warm.
2 Add lime juice and zest and shallots to pan, simmer until soft, not coloured. Reduce until 2 tablespoons remain.
3 Add cream, boil until thickened.
4 Remove from heat, whisk in cubes of cold butter.
5 Slice monkfish, coat plates with sauce and arrange monkfish in a circle.
6 Garnish with fleurons and dill or parsley to serve.

10   Envelope of salmon and turbot   *4 portions*
(David Dorricott)

100 g	4 oz	diced avocado
100 g	4 oz	diced tomato
5 g	¼ oz	chopped tarragon
10 g	½ oz	fresh white breadcrumbs
		2 tspns walnut oil
		salt and pepper

4 × 75 g   3 oz   turbot ⎱
4 × 75 g   3 oz   salmon ⎰ batted out
250 ml   ½ pt   fish cream sauce (see below)

1 Mix 85 g (3½ oz) avocado, 85 g (3½ oz) tomato, half the tarragon, all the breadcrumbs and walnut oil and season.
2 Place in a dome shape in the centre of the turbot.
3 Cover with salmon and gently seal around the edges.
4 Sauté quickly in a hot non-stick pan.
5 Finish cooking under the salamander.
6 Heat the fish cream sauce.
7 Add the remaining tarragon, avocado and tomato, and correct the seasoning.
8 Place fish on a plate, coat with sauce and garnish with a sprig of tarragon.

Note This dish is served as a first course.

Fish cream sauce

5 g   ¼ oz   butter
                 1 medium shallot, sliced
375 ml   ¾ pt   fish stock
                 ½ bay leaf
                 7–8 peppercorns
125 ml   ¼ pt   white wine
60 ml   ⅛ pt   Noilly Pratt vermouth
250 ml   ½ pt   double cream
                 salt and pepper

1 Melt butter and add shallot, sauté without colour for 1 min.
2 Add fish stock, bay leaf, peppercorns and reduce by three-quarters.
3 Add white wine and Noilly Prat, reduce by two-thirds.
4 Add double cream, simmer and reduce until of a sauce consistency.
5 Pass through a fine strainer, correct seasoning and use as above.

11   Salmon parcels   (Anthony Marshall)

                2 tbs double cream   ⎫
                1 egg white   ⎬
150 g   6 oz   cod fillet   cod mousse
                1 bunch of chives (chopped) ⎭
600 g   1½ lb   salmon trout (wild Scotch), boned, de-blooded
                1 beef tomato
500 ml 1 pt   fish stock   ⎫
                ½ bottle white wine   ⎬ white wine sauce
250 ml ½ pt   double cream   ⎭

1 Prepare the cod mousse: place in a food processor 2 tablespoons of double cream, 1 egg white, chilled minced cod and seasoning, and

process until smooth. Then remove from the machine, push through a hair sieve, stir in chopped chives and rest in a cool place.

2 Cut salmon trout into thin slices, 12 cm (5 in.) square, and place to one side. (Bat out if necessary.)

3 Spread a little cod mousse onto each square of thinly sliced salmon trout and wrap into small cushions. Turn over (so the weight helps to keep the cushions in shape) and return to fridge.

4 Blanch the beef tomato, peel, de-pip and cut into 5 cm (2 in.) strips.

5 Make the white wine sauce. Reduce fish stock, skimming frequently until almost reduced, then add white wine and repeat the process.

6 Add the cream, reduce until of a sauce consistency and pass through a tammy cloth or fine strainer.

7 Steam the salmon parcels for approx. 4 mins.

8 Ensuring all ingredients are hot, pass hot sauce onto a plate, place salmon parcels on top and neatly arrange tomato petals around.

9 Brush salmon with a little clarified butter.

10 Blanch two chives, tie into a bow and place on top of the salmon parcel. If so desired, place onto a napkin.

12   Ceviche of sea bass or red mullet   *4 portions*

(Stephen Bull)

		juice of 1 lemon and 2 limes
		1 heaped teaspn crushed coriander seeds
40 g	1 ½ oz	castor sugar
300 g	12 oz	sea bass or red mullet fillets (leave skin on some)
		chives, finely chopped
50 g	2 oz	diced tomato flesh, skinned and seeded
		2 small shallots, finely chopped

1 Mix juices, coriander and sugar to dissolve sugar. Salt lightly.

2 Slice fish very thinly (flatten with heavy knife if necessary).

3 Lay in wide shallow dish and pour marinade over. Leave for 3 hours.

4 Serve on individual plates, sprinkled with chives, tomato and shallots.

Note Cerviche is a word of Spanish/Peruvian origin, meaning 'fish marinaded in lime and lemon juice'.
    This dish is served as a first course.

13   Scotch salmon terrine layered with scallops, served on a lime yoghurt dressing   *10–12 portions*   (Stephen Goodlad)

1 kg	2 lb	scallops, cleaned out of shell
200 g	8 oz	sole flesh
		3 egg whites

625 ml	1 ¼ pt	double cream
100 g	4 oz	brunoise vegetables (carrot, leek, celery)
50 g	2 oz	soft butter
		1 tablespn fine herbs
25 ml	1 fl oz	dry sherry
		1 side fresh salmon (from 4 kg (8 lb) wild salmon)*
400 g	1 lb	cooked leaf spinach
100 ml	4 fl oz	single cream ⎞
		juice of 1 lime ⎟ sauce and garnish
125 ml	¼ pt	natural yoghurt ⎟
		3 sprigs of picked chervil ⎠

*A 1 ½ kg (3 lb) side yields 1 kg (2 lb) salmon to line terrine after trimming

1 Purée 200 g (8 oz) scallops and the sole flesh in a food-processor, add the egg whites and seasoning, then slowly blend in 125 ml (¼ pt) double cream.

2 Remove the purée and push it through a fine drum sieve.

3 Beat the remaining double cream into the purée, and leave the bowl to rest on ice for 30 mins.

4 Add the brunoise of vegetables, which have been sweated down in the butter and herbs and deglazed with the dry sherry. Cool and add to the purée.

5 Fillet the salmon, remove the skin, bones and the brown pieces of flesh. Cut into the same size as the terrine and butterfly.

6 Place the salmon between a piece of lightly greased clingfilm (with oil) and gently tap it out using a cutlet bat. This will lubricate the salmon and make flattening it easier.

7 Grease the terrine with clarified butter and silicone paper, then line the salmon into the mould.

8 Cover with spinach, lay the spinach out flat and place fresh scallops down the middle. Spread a thin layer of mousse over the scallops to hold them in place.

9 Roll the spinach into a sausage shape the same length as the terrine.

10 Place a layer of mousse half-way up the lined terrine, lay the spinach sausage into the mousse, cover with the remaining mousse, then fold the overlapping salmon.

11 Cover with greaseproof paper, place the lid on and poach in a bain-marie for 1 hour in a low oven (160°C, 325°F, Reg. 3).

12 Remove from the oven and allow to cool. Leave overnight in the terrine to set.

13 Stir the single cream and lime juice into the yoghurt. Use to sauce 12 medium-sized plates.

14 Remove the terrine from the mould. Slice with a warm thin bladed knife and lay on top of the sauce on a 12 in. (30 cm) plate. Place a sprig of chervil at the top of the plate and serve.

Note It is advisable to use wild salmon when available and in season at its cheapest, but farmed salmon or salmon trout can also be used. It is a good idea to lay the salmon onto greased silicone paper. This will make it easier to line the terrine and to turn it out when set.

14   Escalope of salmon with fine herb sauce   *6 portions*
(Michael F. Sullivan)

25 g	1 oz	butter
200 g	8 oz	mirepoix, excluding carrots
		thyme, 2 bay leaves, 2 garlic cloves, parsley and herb stalks
		4 crushed peppercorns
10 g	½ oz	strong fish glaze
		¼ bottle dry white wine
500 ml	1 pt	double cream
		salt to taste
		3 egg yolks
		6 tablespns whipped cream
		1 teaspn of chopped dillweed, tarragon, chives, chervil and parsley (may be pre-chopped and mixed)
1 kg	2 lb	fresh salmon, prepared – cut into 6 thin escalopes

1 Melt butter and sweat mirepoix and herbs, stirring frequently.
2 Add fish glaze when mirepoix is well cooked.
3 Deglaze with white wine and reduce to syrup stage.
4 Add cream and reduce by one-third, stirring frequently.
5 Season to taste, remembering the sauce will be diluted with the addition of the whipped cream and egg yolk. Pass through a fine strainer and keep at blood temperature.
6 As each portion is ordered, pour 50 ml (2 fl oz) white wine sauce into a warm bowl.
7 Add whipped cream, egg yolk and chopped herbs, making sure that no lumps of whipped cream remain in the sauce.
8 Spoon sufficient sauce on to warmed dinner plates to cover the centre and place a salmon escalope in the middle. Avoid getting sauce on to the top side of the salmon.
9 Give 1 twist of black mill pepper over the escalope then glaze under the salamander.
10 The salmon will be cooked once the sauce is lightly glazed. Serve at once.

15   Sliced fillet of lamb with fresh herbs   *8 portions*

(Nick Gill)

		1 double loin of young English lamb
		olive oil, salt and pepper
		tarragon, chervil, mint, thyme and parsley
		watercress and spinach
1 litre	2 pt	strong lamb stock
		5 shallots, finely chopped
		1 glass dry vermouth
500 ml	1 pt	double cream
1 kg	2 lb	French turnips and 2 carrots
1 kg	2 lb	potatoes (Dutch binje)
200 g	8 oz	young mange-tout
		12 fresh asparagus tips

1 Prepare the lamb a day in advance. Strip it of all bone, fat, and sinew, producing 2 long fillets.
2 Marinade the fillets overnight in olive oil, seasoning and finely chopped herbs. Reserve the bones.
3 To prepare the herb sauce: blanch bunches of fresh tarragon, chervil, mint, thyme, parsley (reserving a few leaves), watercress and spinach, by plunging into rapidly boiling water, then almost immediately into cold water. Drain, purée, put into a clean bowl and refrigerate.
4 Reduce the lamb stock, with the lightly roasted and finely chopped lamb bones, to a syrupy residue. Remove the bones.
5 In a clean saucepan, sweat the shallots with the vermouth and the lamb glaze until almost evaporated.
6 Add the cream and simmer gently for 5–10 minutes until slightly thickened. Sieve and keep warm.
7 To prepare the vegetable garnish: using a small Parisienne cutter, cut balls out of the turnips, carrot, and potatoes. Top and tail the mange-tout and bundle the asparagus. Cook carrot and turnip glacé, fry the potato, blanch the asparagus and mange-tout.
8 Heat a little olive oil in a heavy pan, add the drained and seasoned fillets of lamb, and cook over a fairly fierce heat, turning occasionally, until the lamb is well sealed and nicely pink inside. Remove from the pan and keep warm.
9 Add the herb purée to the stock and cream until a deep green colour and good flavour is obtained.
10 Sieve and adjust seasoning and consistency to taste.
11 To serve: coat 8 large hot plates with the sauce. Slice the lamb into thin medallions and lay these around the plate. Decorate with the vegetables and herb leaves.

16   Lambs' kidneys with juniper and wild mushrooms
4 portions   (Paul Gayler)

		12 English lambs' kidneys
25 g	1 oz	chopped shallots
		12 crushed juniper berries
60 ml	⅛ pt	gin, marinaded with the berries for one day
125 ml	¼ pt	English white wine
½ litre	1 pt	strong lamb stock
50 g	2 oz	selected wild mushrooms (trompettes, girolles, piéd de mouton, depending on seasonal availability)
		2 large potatoes

1 Remove fat and thin film of tissue covering the kidneys.
2 Season well and sauté in a hot pan, keeping them pink. Remove and keep warm.
3 Add the shallots and some crushed juniper berries to the pan, flambé with a little gin, pour in the white wine and reduce well. Add the lamb stock and reduce by half. Pass and finish with butter.
4 Prepare the mushrooms and sauté in hot oil, adding butter to maintain their earthy flavour, then keep warm.
5 Finely shred the potatoes into matchsticks on a mandolin, dry in a clean cloth, season and cook in butter as a fine potato cake.
6 To serve, place the potato cake in the centre of a serving dish, slice the kidneys and arrange attractively in a circle on the potato. Garnish the kidneys with the wild mushrooms, cordon the dish with the sauce and serve immediately.

17   Trio of roast farmed rabbit with braised cabbage and thyme sauce   *4 portions*
(Robert Mabey)

1 × ¾–1 kg	1½–2 lb	Savoy cabbage
150 g	6 oz	butter
		salt, mill pepper
100 ml	4 fl oz	dry white wine
2 × 1–1½ kg	2–3 lb	whole farmed rabbits
		24 whole cloves of garlic
		3 sprigs of fresh thyme
500 ml	1 pt	veal and rabbit stock

1 Discard the outside leaves of the cabbage, cut into four quarters, discard the stalk and finely slice the cabbage.
2 Heat 50 g (2 oz) of butter in a casserole dish, add the cabbage and season. Gently sweat the cabbage until soft, then cover with butter papers and cook in the oven at 190°C (375°F, Reg. 5) for 1 hour (turning every 15 mins).
3 When the cabbage is cooked, add half a glass of white wine and keep warm.

4 Remove the legs from the rabbits at the ball joint. Then cut the saddle from the ribs, remove the sinews and flap from the saddles and set aside for the sauce. Keep the kidneys in the fat to be served later. Cut the first seven ribs from the rabbit and prepare as for a miniature version of rack of lamb. Chop the rest of the carcass for making stock. This should leave 4 legs, 2 saddles, 4 baby racks and 4 kidneys.
5 Heat 50 g (2 oz) butter in a large sauteuse, add the seasoned pieces of rabbit and trimmings and fry to obtain colour; the kidneys and racks will need about 2 mins on each side.
6 Add the unpeeled cloves of garlic and thyme (reserving some picked leaves for the garnish). Cover with butter papers and roast in a hot oven.
7 Remove the saddle after 10 mins and the legs after 20 mins. Allow to relax in a warm place on a wire rack.
8 Drain off the fat, add the rest of the wine, reduce by half, add the stock, simmer and remove any scum.
9 Pass the stock and reduce by half (or to the consistency of single cream). Peel the cloves of garlic and keep warm.
10 Place the cabbage in a circle in the middle of the warmed dish.
11 Remove the bones from the rabbit thighs, cut into 4 slices and place in the centre of the dish.
12 Cut the loins and the fillets from the saddles and slice lengthways, fanning the pieces around the leg.
13 Cut the kidneys in 2 and arrange with the cloves of garlic around the dish.
14 Finish the sauce with 50 g (2 oz) butter, check the seasoning, pour the sauce over the meat and serve immediately.

18 Sautéed breast of pheasant with wild mushrooms and pheasant mousse in a horseradish and shallot sauce
4 portions (Allan Garth)

		2 pheasants
		1 egg, separated
500 ml	1 pt	double cream
		salt and pepper
		1 dessertspn brandy
100 g	4 oz	onions
100 g	4 oz	carrots
100 g	4 oz	leeks
50 g	2 oz	celery
		bouquet garni
		3 finely chopped shallots
		1 root of horseradish grated
200 g	8 oz	wild mushrooms
		1 tomato, skinned, deseeded and diced
		1 teaspn chopped chives

1   Remove the breasts and the legs from the pheasant.
2   Remove the meat from the thighs, you will need this for the mousse.
3   To make the mousse: place the thigh meat in the food processor and blend until the meat becomes a paste. Add the egg white.
4   Remove, place into a bowl over ice and beat in half the double cream, seasoning and the brandy.
5   Butter 4 small timbales, fill with the mousse and cook in a bain-marie for about 10 mins at 190°C (375°F, Reg. 5).
6   To make the sauce: chop the pheasant bones and place in a pan with the roughly chopped onions, carrots, leeks and celery, and a bouquet garni.
7   Cover with cold water and simmer for about 2 hours.
8   Strain and reduce the stock to 500 ml (1 pt).
9   Sauté the chopped shallots, add the remaining cream and the stock, and reduce to 500 ml (1 pt).
10   Add the horseradish and season.
11   Clean and wash the mushrooms, sauté in hot butter. When cooked, add the diced tomato and chives. Keep warm.
12   Sauté the seasoned breasts of pheasant in a pan until coloured.
13   Place in a very hot oven for about 5 mins, depending on the size of the breasts. When cooked the pheasant should be pink inside.
14   Slice the pheasant breasts onto the wild mushrooms on a serving dish, turn out the mousses and accompany with the sauce.

19   Stuffed breast of pheasant Aviona   *4 portions*

(Keith Podmore)

		2 hen pheasants
750 ml	1½ pt	cold water
50 g	2 oz	onion
50 g	2 oz	carrot
		1 stick celery
50 g	2 oz	leek
		bouquet garni
		salt and pepper
10 g	½ oz	each of parsley, chervil, chives and tarragon, chopped
40 g	1½ oz	carrot
40 g	1½ oz	white of leek } in julienne
40 g	1½ oz	celery
60 ml	2½ fl oz	dry white wine
75 g	3 oz	butter
40 g	1½ oz	mange-tout } in julienne
40 g	1½ oz	beetroot

1   Remove the legs and suprêmes from the pheasants and bone the thighs. Make pockets in the suprêmes.
2   Prepare stock from the carcass, bones and drumsticks, using the water and vegetables and bouquet garni.

3 Finely mince the thigh meat, incorporating the herbs and season. Use to fill the suprêmes.
4 Prepare a fine julienne of the carrot, celery and leek, keeping each separate.
5 Butter and season a suitable pan and sprinkle with the julienne of vegetables.
6 Lay on the suprêmes, sprinkle with the white wine and season.
7 Heat the pan on top of the stove, cover and cook in the oven till ready.
8 Strain the pheasant stock and reduce till lightly syrupy. Strain in the cooking liquor from the pheasant and further reduce if needed.
9 Finish with butter and season.
10 Dress the suprêmes on plates, sprinkling the cooked julienne garnish over.
11 Blanch the mange-tout and beetroot separately.
12 Pour the sauce over the pheasant, sprinkle with the mange-tout and beetroot and serve.

20 Baked suprême of chicken with sage mousse
4 portions   (Michael Coaker)

4 × 150 g	6 oz	chicken breasts
100 g	4 oz	chicken mousseline
25 g	1 oz	sweated brunoise of vegetables (carrot, celery, leek, courgette) } combined
10 g	½ oz	freshly chopped sage
		4 pieces crepinette (thin pig's caul)
50 g	2 oz	wild mushrooms
50 g	2 oz	butter (unsalted)
125 ml	5 fl oz	Madeira sauce
25 ml	1 fl oz	double cream

1 Season and seal the chicken breasts very quickly on their presentation sides.
2 Remove, allow to cool, and spread the prepared mousse evenly on top of the breasts, keeping to their shape.
3 Cover each with crepinette and bake in oven until cooked.
4 Pan-fry the wild mushrooms in butter and season.
5 Cut each suprême in half across the breast at a slight angle.
6 Serve on a bed of Madeira sauce finished with cream and butter, garnished with a small bouquet of wild mushrooms.

Note A dash of Grand Marnier can be added to the sauce as a slight variation.

21   Breast of maize-fed chicken with two sauces
4 portions   (Tim McEntire)

2 × 1½ kg	3 lb	maize-fed chickens
		1 egg white
		salt, cayenne pepper
500 ml	1 pt	double cream
300 g	12 oz	broccoli
50 g	2 oz	unsalted butter

1 Remove suprêmes from the chickens and bone out the thighs.
2 Make a good stock from the bones, adding a veal bone if available.
3 Process the flesh from the thighs in a food processor with the egg white, season and cool thoroughly.
4 Beat in half of the cream.
5 Cook and refresh the broccoli, reserve 4 good florets for garnish and purée the rest.
6 Add half the broccoli purée to the chicken mousse, test for consistency and seasoning.
7 Place into 4 buttered dariole moulds, poach and keep warm.
8 Strain and reduce the chicken stock, add the remaining half of cream, reboil, correct seasoning and divide into two portions.
9 Add the remaining broccoli purée to one of the portions of chicken sauce.
10 Finish both sauces with butter, and correct seasoning and consistency.
11 Slice the suprêmes, reform and dress neatly onto plates. Turn out a dariole mould of mousse onto each plate.
12 Coat the green mousses with chicken sauce, the suprêmes with broccoli sauce and garnish with one floret of broccoli on each plate.

22   Fanned breasts of duckling with strawberry essence
4 portions   (John King)

2 × 2 kg	5 lb	fresh ducks or 4 duckling breasts
125 ml	¼ pt	cooking oil
		salt
125 ml	¼ pt	strawberry syrup
60 ml	⅛ pt	strawberry vinegar
		1 punnet fresh strawberries
500 ml	1 pt	jus-lié (thickened veal stock)
		1 bunch mint leaves
50 g	2 oz	butter

1 Remove the breasts from the ducks. Clean off any sinews and excess fat but leave the small cleaned wing bone attached, season lightly with salt.
2 Heat sufficient oil to cover the bottom of a thick-bottomed, shallow pan.

3 Add the duck breasts, flesh side down and just seal, then turn over on the fat side and place in the oven, at 220°C (425°F, Reg. 7), and cook until the meat is pink (medium-cooked). Remove the breasts from the pan when cooked and keep warm.
4 Pour off the excess oil and fat and place the pan back on the heat. Pour in half the strawberry syrup and half the strawberry vinegar, bring to the boil and reduce heat slightly.
5 Slice each breast of duck thinly on the angle, keeping the wing bone.
6 Slice one strawberry per breast, place the breast or breasts on plates, with a sliced strawberry on top of each breast, and keep warm.
7 Bring the sauce back to the boil. Ensure that it is not too thick and thin with stock as necessary. Work in the butter. The sauce should have a sweet but slightly sharp (vinegar) taste.
8 Run the sauce around the hot fanned duck breast.
9 Decorate with whole strawberries with little wedges cut out and fresh mint leaves.

Note Extra strawberry syrup or vinegar can be used in the sauce if necessary, but the sauce should not be too thick.

23 Guinea fowl with yellow pepper sauce *4 portions*
(Terry Farr)

2 × 1¼ kg	2½ lb	cleaned guinea fowl
		salt and pepper
100 g	4 oz	veal or chicken forcemeat
		1 level teaspn pink peppercorns
25 g	1 oz	unsalted butter
75 g	3 oz	chopped shallots
200 g	8 oz	cleaned and diced yellow pepper
125 ml	¼ pt	dry white wine
125 ml	¼ pt	thin chicken velouté or béchamel
125 ml	¼ pt	double cream
100 g	4 oz	julienne of red, green and yellow pepper

1 Remove suprêmes and legs from carcasses.
2 Remove bones from legs and tap out lightly with cutlet bat.
3 Season insides of legs, and spread with forcemeat, combined with peppercorns. Roll up legs and tie lightly.
4 Melt the butter in a thick-bottomed pan, add the seasoned suprêmes and legs, and cover with a lid.
5 Cook gently for 8–10 mins, remove suprêmes and cook legs for a further 5–6 mins. Keep the joints in a covered dish in a warm place.
6 Add the shallots to the juices in the pan and cook without colour.
7 Add the diced yellow pepper and cook gently for about 5 mins.
8 Add white wine and reduce by half.

9 Add velouté and cream and cook gently for 5 mins.
10 Liquidise the sauce (or rub through a sieve), strain through fine chinois, adjust seasoning and consistency.
11 Arrange the suprêmes on one side of 4 warmed plates and the leg, cut into 5 slices, on the other.
12 Surround the joints with the sauce and garnish the centre with the julienne of mixed peppers.

24 Roast pigeon or chicken with glazed garlic and broad beans *4 portions* (Alan Hill)

4 × 150g	6 oz	milk-fed pigeons
		salt and freshly-ground pepper
25 g	1 oz	butter
10 g	½ oz	ginger stem
10 g	½ oz	rosemary
10 g	½ oz	apple
100 ml	4 fl oz	red wine
125 ml	5 fl oz	wild game stock
25 g	1 oz	butter
10 g	½ oz	shallots
50 g	2 oz	broad beans
50 ml	2 fl oz	double cream
		pinch nutmeg
50 g	2 oz	back bacon
		12 garlic cloves
25 g	1 oz	butter, to finish

1 Remove the legs from the pigeon breasts, season and sauté in a little hot butter.
2 Add the ginger, rosemary and apple and sauté until golden brown.
3 Deglaze the pan with red wine and add the wild game stock and braise the legs.
4 Once the legs are cooked, remove them from the stock and keep warm.
5 Pass the sauce through a fine sieve.
6 Sauté the pigeon breasts in a little butter to taste and remove from the pan. Keep warm.
7 Deglaze the pan with the sauce, pass and finish with butter.
8 Sauté the shallots in a little butter without colour and add the broad beans. Add the cream and season.
9 Fry the bacon until golden and crispy and add the poached garlic cloves; remove from the pan and dry.
10 Place the garnish upon the plate and place the legs upon the beans and bacon.
11 Place the sauce upon the plate and slice the pigeon into thin strips and fan around the garnish.

12 Top with the garlic cloves and place two cutlet frills upon the legs. Serve immediately.

Note Individual spring chickens, weighing 300–400 g (12 oz), or pieces of chicken cut as for sauté, may be used in place of pigeons, in which case chicken stock should be used in place of game stock.

25 **Breast of pigeon with herb ravioli** *4 portions* (Shaun Hill)

75 g	3 oz	strong flour	
25 g	1 oz	semolina	
		1 egg	ravioli paste
		1 teaspn oil	
25 g	1 oz	chopped fresh herbs	
		salt	
		2 plump pigeons	
250 ml	½ pt	chicken stock	
250 ml	½ pt	veal jus-lié	
50 g	2 oz	chicken livers	
25 g	1 oz	chopped fresh herbs	ravioli filling
		salt, pepper, nutmeg	

1 First, combine the ingredients for the herb ravioli paste and allow to rest in the fridge or freezer for 30 mins.
2 Pluck and draw the pigeons, remove the suprêmes and livers. Discard the other giblets.
3 Chop the pigeon bones and legs, then colour them in a copper pan.
4 Add the chicken stock and jus-lié, then reduce by half and strain through a muslin.
5 Make the ravioli filling by chopping all the livers and mixing with the chopped herbs and seasoning.
6 Roll out the ravioli paste as thinly as possible and egg wash lightly.
7 Using one half of the pasta, spoon the filling into 16 mounds at about 5 cm (2 in.) intervals. Fold across the other half of the pasta to cover and cut out the ravioli with a round 4 cm (1.5 in.) diameter cutter. Press the edges together.
8 Colour the seasoned pigeon breasts in a pan and then finish in a hot oven for 3–4 mins until rare.
9 Poach the ravioli for 1 minute in salted boiling water, then carefully lift into sauce.
10 Slice the pigeon breasts horizontally into thin escalopes and lay onto herb ravioli in sauce to serve.

26   Crust of venison Count Peter   *4 portions*   (Keith Stanley)

4 × 125 g	5 oz	fillet of venison
250 ml	½ pt	red wine
75 g	3 oz	chopped carrot
75 g	3 oz	chopped onion } marinade
		2 bay leaves
10 g	½ oz	peppercorns
50 g	2 oz	pâte de foie gras
150 g	6 oz	game farce (see below)
50 g	2 oz	redcurrant jelly
200 g	8 oz	4 × 9 cm (3½ in.) shortcrust tartelettes
50 g	2 oz	diced pear
50 ml	2 fl oz	oil
50 g	2 oz	butter
125 ml	¼ pt	red wine
250 ml	½ pt	sauce grand veneur (see page 167)
		pear tips/redcurrant bouquet

1 Trim venison of all nerves and sinews. Cut into 15 cm (12 in.) lengths and soak in marinade overnight.
2 Heat pâté and game farce in a small sauteuse.
3 Spread jelly in tartelettes. Pipe in a ring of pâté. Place diced pear in the middle and keep warm.
4 Drain, dry and season venison, reserving marinade. Seal in hot oil and half the butter. Reduce·heat and cook slowly – very pink. When cooked, take out and keep warm.
5 Drain off fat, deglaze with red wine, add marinade and reduce by half.
6 Add sauce grand veneur, bring to boil, simmer 5–10 mins and season.
7 Strain through chinois. Finish with remaining butter, strain and keep hot.
8 To serve: ensure that both tartelettes and venison are hot and slice fillets on an angle 5 cm (3/16 in.) thick. Dress on tartelettes, slightly overlapping each other. Set on plate, pour sauce around and inside, top with the tips of poached pears and a bouquet of redcurrants.

Game farce

50 g	2 oz	butter or margarine
100 g	4 oz	game livers
25 g	1 oz	chopped onion
		sprig of thyme
		1 bay leaf
		salt, pepper

1 Heat 25 g (1 oz) butter in a frying-pan.
2 Quickly toss the seasoned livers, onion and herbs, browning well but keeping underdone. Pass through a sieve or mincer.
3 Mix in the remaining 25 g (1 oz) butter. Correct the seasoning.

Sauce grand veneur

25 g	1 oz	margarine, butter or oil
50 g	2 oz	onion
50 g	2 oz	carrot
50 g	2 oz	celery
		1 bay leaf
		sprig of thyme
		2 tablespns white wine
		2 tablespns vinegar
5 g	¼ oz	mignonette pepper
250 ml	½ pt	demi-glace
		1 tablespn redcurrant jelly
		2 tablespns cream

mirepoix (bracketing onion, carrot, celery, 1 bay leaf, sprig of thyme)

1 Melt the fat or oil in a small sauteuse.
2 Add the mirepoix and allow to brown.
3 Pour off the fat.
4 Add the wine, vinegar and pepper.
5 Reduce by half. Add the demi-glace and the redcurrant jelly.
6 Simmer 20–30 min. Correct the seasoning.
7 Pass through a fine chinois and finish with the cream.

Notes
a) Recipe is given with fillet of venison but a short saddle or half a loin can be used.
b) Any trimmings of venison should be incorporated in the game farce.
c) Special care is needed with the simmering and skimming of the sauce to achieve a clear and shiny finish.
d) Be careful to seal the venison, then cook to very pink – not rare – otherwise the two different stages of cooking will be visible when slicing.

27 Fillets of venison with beetroot *4 portions*

(David Fellowes)

8 × 75 g	3 oz	thin slices of venison fillet*
150 g	6 oz	very thinly sliced beetroot
		1–2 tablespns red wine vinegar
250 ml	10 fl oz	sauce grand veneur (above)
100 ml	4 fl oz	double cream

*Venison should be marinaded for 48 hours in a cooked game marinade (see overleaf)

1 Flash fry the thin slices of venison, remove and keep hot.
2 Add the thinly sliced beetroot to the same pan, moisten with the vinegar and toss over the beetroot carefully.
3 Evaporate the vinegar, remove the beetroot and keep hot.
4 Add the sauce grand veneur to the pan and then the double cream.

5 Dress the beetroot, with the venison on top, pour the sauce around the venison and serve.

Note Beetroot may be enhanced with caraway seeds or fresh green herbs if desired.

Cooked marinade for venison

25 g	1 oz	carrot ⎞
25 g	1 oz	onion ⎬ chopped
10 g	½ oz	celery ⎠
50 ml	2 fl oz	oil
		1 small clove garlic
		½ bay leaf
		sprig of thyme
		3 peppercorns
		1 clove
125 ml	5 fl oz	vinegar

1 Lightly colour carrot, onion and celery in the oil.
2 Mix in garlic, bay leaf, thyme, peppercorns and clove.
3 Add vinegar, simmer for 25 mins, allow to cool. Do not use until completely cold.

28   Baby vegetables in a pastry case with butter sauce
4 portions   (Aidan McCormack)

200 g	4 oz	carrots
200 g	4 oz	turnips
200 g	4 oz	potatoes
		2 courgettes
		2 sticks celery
		24 French beans
250 g	6 oz	puff pastry
		egg wash
25 g	1 oz	shallots
		4 tablespns vinegar
		4 tablespns water
125 ml	¼ pt	cream
150 g	6 oz	unsalted butter
		salt and white pepper
		juice of 1 lemon
		assorted green herbs
		2 tomatoes, chopped

1 Prepare the vegetables: turn carrots, turnips and potatoes into regular sizes. Turn courgettes to the same size, leaving a little green skin on one side. Peel the celery, then baton to the size of a matchstick. Top and tail the French beans and cut to the same size as the celery.
2 Boil 1 litre (2 pints) salted water and cook the vegetables separately

until crisp, then refresh in iced water and keep until needed. Retain the water to re-heat the vegetables when required.

3 Roll out the puff pastry and cut into 4 10 × 5 cm (4 × 2 in.) squares, egg wash the top of the squares and mark with a fork from corner to corner each way.

4 Rest for 10 minutes then bake at 220°C (425°F, Reg. 7) until golden brown, remove and leave to cool. When cool remove the tops and hollow out the pastry cases. Be careful not to damage the sides. Keep in a warm place until needed.

5 To make the sauce: reduce the shallots, vinegar and water in a pan until the shallots are just moist. Add the cream and bring to the boil.

6 Whisk in the butter and season with salt and white pepper. Add the lemon juice and keep warm, but do not boil.

7 Reheat the vegetables in the salted water, drain and add to the hot butter sauce.

8 Place the warm pastry cases onto 4 plates and divide the vegetables between the pastry cases, letting them flow over the sides. Use sufficient sauce to cover the plate. Place the pastry lid to one side of the case, sprinkle with fresh herbs and add a little chopped, fresh tomato flesh to serve.

Note Any vegetables may be used, providing they are cut to the same size.

29 Fennel casserole *4 portions* (Robert Jones)

450 g	1 lb	or 3 bulbs of fennel
		2 tablespns olive oil
200 g	8 oz	finely diced onion
		2 cloves garlic, crushed
400 g	1 lb	tomato concassée (or 1 tin)
		salt and freshly ground black pepper
50 g	2 oz	wholemeal breadcrumbs
50 g	2 oz	grated cheddar cheese

1 Prepare the fennel by removing the outer leaves and trim the root base. Slice the bulbs thinly, reserving the green ends for decoration.

2 Heat the oil and gently fry the chopped onions and garlic in a frying pan without colour for a few mins.

3 Add the slices of fennel and cook for a few mins.

4 Add the tomatoes, season well, cover the pan and slowly cook for about 15 mins.

5 Transfer the mixture to an ovenproof dish, mix the breadcrumbs and cheese together and sprinkle over the fennel mixture.

6 Bake in a pre-heated oven at 200°C (400°F, Reg. 6) for about 15–20 mins until the top is golden brown and crisp. Serve immediately.

Note This dish is suitable for quick freezing.

Desserts

30   Drambuie chocolate charlotte with coffee bean sauce

4 portions   (David Miller)

60 g	2 ½ oz	plain eating chocolate
		4 egg yolks
100 g	4 oz	castor sugar
125 g	5 oz	unsalted butter, softened
60 g	2 ½ oz	cocoa powder
		1 miniature bottle of Drambuie
250 ml	½ pt	double cream ⎱ whipped until stiff
25 g	1 oz	icing sugar ⎰
		12–18 sponge fingers
25 ml	1 fl oz	cold black coffee (not instant)
125 ml	5 fl oz	double cream ⎫
10 g	½ oz	icing sugar ⎬ decoration
35 g	1 ½ oz	plain eating chocolate, grated ⎭
1 × 10 cm	4 in.	mould, refrigerated

1 Place plain chocolate in a bain-marie to melt slowly.
2 Whisk egg yolks and castor sugar together until light and thick.
3 Add melted chocolate to eggs slowly, keeping warm and not allowing chocolate to set.
4 In a separate bowl, cream unsalted butter and cocoa powder until light and creamy. Add half the Drambuie.
5 Fold together the eggs and butter, mixing until smooth. Fold in whipped cream.
6 Use mixture to half-fill the mould.
7 Soak 5 sponge fingers with the remaining Drambuie and a little black coffee.
8 Cover the mixture evenly with the sponge fingers. Add the rest of the mixture and refrigerate for 2 hours.
9 To remove, run mould under hot water and turn out onto a plate. Cut the remaining sponge fingers to size and place round the sides. Decorate the top of the charlotte with whipped cream and grated chocolate, and serve with coffee bean sauce (see below).

Coffee bean sauce

125 ml	¼ pt	milk
125 ml	¼ pt	double cream
35 g	1 ½ oz	castor sugar
		1 teaspn freshly ground fine coffee
		3 egg yolks
25 g	1 oz	castor sugar

1 Bring milk, cream and 35 g (1½ oz) sugar to boil.
2 Remove, add ground coffee and cover to infuse for 15 mins.
3 Meanwhile, whisk egg yolks and remaining sugar until light.

4 Bring coffee infusion to the boil, add to eggs and whisk. Then return to pan and cook slowly on a low heat for 5 mins without boiling.
5 Transfer coffee cream to cool bowl and allow to cool, stirring occasionally.

Note If necessary, in order to speed up cooling, place bowl into cold water with ice cubes.

31 **Burnt lemon tart** *8–10 portions*   (Brian Turner)

100 g	4 oz	sugar	
200 g	8 oz	butter	
		zest of 1 orange	flan pastry
300 g	12 oz	flour	
		16 eggs	
350 g	14 oz	sugar	
		juice of 4 lemons	filling
300 g	12 fl oz	double cream	
		icing sugar	

1 To make pastry: cream sugar, butter and orange zest. Fold in flour and leave to rest.
2 Use pastry to line a 30 cm (12 in.) flan case, bake blind and cool.
3 Mix together the eggs and sugar. Add lemon juice, then double cream and pass.
4 Pour mixture into cooked flan case. Bake at 160°C (325°F, Reg. 3) for 40 mins until set.
5 Sprinkle the flan with icing sugar and burn in a pattern to caramelise the sugar. Remove and cool.

Note Do not refrigerate. This flan must be eaten fresh.

32 **Mango mousse with fresh coconut sauce** *4 portions*
(Anthony Blake)

		2 egg yolks	
75 g	3 oz	castor sugar	
250 ml	½ pt	milk	
10 g	½ oz	gelatine (dissolved in a little water)	
		1 mango (peeled and puréed)	
250 ml	½ pt	double cream, whipped	
		1 coconut	
50 g	2 oz	castor sugar	
125 ml	¼ pt	milk	sauce
50 g	2 oz	coconut cream	
250 ml	½ pt	whipped cream	
		12 marshmallows dipped in coconut	

1 Whisk the egg yolks and sugar together until very light and fluffy.
2 Heat the milk to just below boiling point in a heavy-based pan then slowly pour onto the egg yolks, whisking constantly.
3 Return the mixture to a clean pan and cook gently until thick enough to coat the back of a spoon, but do not allow mixture to boil.
4 Whisk in the gelatine and mango purée then pass through a fine sieve. Leave to cool, then chill until it just begins to set.
5 Gently fold in the whipped cream then pour into moulds (timbales or ramekins) and chill for about 4 hours.
6 Make the sauce by first cracking open the coconut, scraping out the flesh and reserving the milk. Cut the flesh into small pieces and cook with the sugar, coconut milk, milk and coconut cream until slightly soft.
7 Pass through a fine sieve and fold in the whipped cream.
8 To serve: unmould the mousse onto cold plates, spoon some of the sauce around and add marshmallows which have been dipped in toasted coconut.

33 Cinnamon soufflé with Drambuie cream *4 portions*
(Chris Oakes)

550 g	1 lb 6 oz	pears, roughly chopped	
500 ml	1 pt	water	
		1 level teaspn cornflour	panada
		1 level tablespn water	
		3 level tablespns cinnamon	
250 ml	½ pt	whipping cream	
10 g	½ oz	sugar	
		½ measure Drambuie	
		5 egg whites	
75 g	3 oz	sugar	

1 To make the panada: place the pears in a saucepan, barely cover with water and cook until soft.
2 Liquidise and pass. Reheat in a clean pan and simmer until thick, stirring occasionally (approx. 10 mins).
3 Mix the cornflour and water together. Whisk into pear mixture and leave on a low heat for approx. 10 mins.
4 Add ground cinnamon and whisk. This mixture can now be used immediately or kept in the fridge for later use.
5 Whisk the cream until it peaks. Add sugar and Drambuie to taste.
6 To make the soufflé: warm the panada gently in a bain-marie.
7 Whisk the egg whites in a copper bowl until they peak, adding the sugar a little at a time.
8 Mix a spoonful of the egg whites into the panada, then fold in the rest.
9 Spoon soufflé mixture into 4 buttered and sugared ramekin moulds.

Smooth off around the edge at an angle with a palette knife, finishing with a flat top.
10 Place on a baking sheet in a pre-heated oven at 220°C (425°F, Reg. 7) for approx. 10–12 mins.
11 Serve *immediately*, dusted with icing sugar and a sauceboat of cream.

Note Any fruit can be used in the soufflé but omit the cinnamon if not using pears.

Introduction

As the multi-ethnic society and the popularity of overseas dishes continue to grow, it becomes increasingly important to have a basic working knowledge of ethnic cookery.

Many countries, such as China, Japan and India, and areas like the

Middle East, have long-established culinary traditions with a wide range of dishes dating back for two to three thousand years. Now, because of customer demands and changes in society, all students of cookery need to have at least a basic but sound understanding of ethnic dishes. The following recipes are examples of such dishes, however these will vary according to different regions etc.

From the many ethnic cookery books available, we consider the following may be helpful:

Cuisines of Asia Jennifer Brennan (Macdonald)
Complete Asian Cookbook Charmaine Solomon (1982, Windward)
A New Book of Middle Eastern Food Claudia Roden (1986, Penguin)
Mediterranean Cookbook Arabella Boxer (1983, Penguin)
Mediterranean Cookery Claudia Roden (Guild Publishing, London)
Foods and Wines of Spain Penelope Casas (1985, Penguin)
Spanish Regional Cookery Macmadhachan (Penguin)
Caribbean Cooking Elizabeth Lambert Ortiz (1977, Penguin)
Greek Food Rena Salamon (1983, Fontana)
Best Book of Greek Cookery Paradissis (1976, Efstathiadis Group)
Mexican Cookery Lourdes Nichols (1986, Collins)
Indonesian Cookery David Scott and Surya Winata (1984, Rider)
Indian Cookery Madhur Jaffrey (1982, BBC Publications)
Indian Cookery Dharamjit Singh (1970, Penguin)
Classic Indian Cookery Sahni (1986, Dorling Kindersley)
Kenneth Lo's New Chinese Cookery School Kenneth Lo (1985, Macdonald)
Yan Kit's Classic Chinese Cookbook So Yan Kit (1984, Dorling Kindersley)
Cook Japanese Masaru Doi (1978, Harper and Row)
Japanese Cuisine for Everyone Yukiko Moriyama (1986, Premier Book Marketing, London)
Taste of American Cooking Clare Walker and Keryn Christiansen (1986, Penguin)
Complete International Jewish Cookbook E. Rose (1978, Pan)

Middle East

1   Hummus   Chick pea and sesame seed paste   *4 portions*

Served with pitta bread as an accompaniment to main dishes.

300 g	12 oz	soaked chick peas
		seasoning
75 g	3 oz	sesame seed paste (tahini)
		1 clove of crushed and chopped garlic
50 g	2 oz	finely chopped onion
		juice of 1 lemon
5 g	¼ oz	paprika

1 Cook the chick peas in simmering water for approx. 2 hours. Drain well.
2 Purée the peas in a food processor, add seasoning, sesame seed paste, garlic and onion. Finish with lemon juice.
3 Place into a suitable serving dish decorated with a line of paprika.

2 Date halva   *4 portions*

Served as a sweetmeat

400 g	1 lb	stoned dates, finely chopped
100 g	4 oz	chopped walnuts
100 g	4 oz	chopped almonds
		icing sugar

1 Place the dates into a food processor and blend to a paste.
2 Place into a basin and mix in the chopped nuts.
3 Knead to a smooth mixture on a table dusted with icing sugar. Roll into a sausage shape, cut into rounds approx. 2 cm, 1 m diameter.
4 Serve dusted with icing sugar.

3 Tabbouleh   Cracked wheat salad   *4 portions*

Serve with hummus or kebabs.

75 g	3 oz	cracked wheat (burghul)
25 g	1 oz	finely chopped onion
50 g	2 oz	diced cucumber
50 g	2 oz	tomato, peeled, deseeded, diced
		salt, pepper
30 mls	1/16 pt	vegetable oil
		juice of ½ lemon
		chopped parsley and mint

1 Cover the cracked wheat with cold water and leave to soak for 10 mins. Drain well, place into a suitable basin.
2 Add the onion, cucumber and tomato, season with salt and pepper.
3 Mix in the oil and lemon juice, stir in the chopped parsley and chopped mint.
4 Serve on individual side plates, dressed in lettuce leaves.

4 Kibbeh bil sanieh   Spiced lamb with cracked wheat   *4 portions*

Eaten with salad, pitta bread, hummus and yoghurt. Served hot or cold.

200 g	8 oz	burghul (cracked wheat)
400 g	1 lb	leg or shoulder of lamb, boned and diced
50 g	2 oz	finely chopped onion
		1 teaspn cinnamon
		seasoning
		2 tablespns of cold water

50 g	2 oz	finely chopped onion	
		1 chopped, crushed clove of garlic	
60 ml	⅛ pt	oil	
200 g	8 oz	minced lamb	filling
		½ teaspn allspice	
50 g	2 oz	pine kernels	
50 g	2 oz	chopped raisins	
50 g	2 oz	melted butter or margarine	

1 Cover the cracked wheat with cold water and allow to stand for 5 mins. Drain well.
2 Place the lamb in a food processor with the finely chopped onion, cinnamon and seasoning, and blend to a smooth paste. Add the cold water, mix well.
3 Add the well drained cracked wheat. Blend in a processor until a smooth paste is formed.
4 For the filling: first, sweat the onion and garlic together in the oil. Add the minced lamb, allow to brown quickly.
5 Mix in the allspice, pine kernels and raisins.
6 In a suitable dish, spread half of the lamb and wheat mixture on the bottom (the kibbeh). Cover with the filling. Finish by topping with the rest of the kibbeh.
7 Cut diagonal lines over the top to make diamond shapes and brush the melted fat over the top.
8 Bake in a moderately hot oven, 190°C (375°F, Reg. 5) for approximately 45 mins. The surface should be brown and crisp. Baste occasionally with a few tablespoons of stock, so that the interior is moist.

5 Couscous
4 portions

This is the national dish of the Maghreb, the North African countries of Morocco, Tunisia and Algeria of Berber origin. A couscous has been adopted by other Arab countries who call it Maghebia which is different from the North African dish. Couscous itself is a type of fine semolina.

The basic process for the preparation of couscous is the steaming of the grain over a stew or broth. This is generally made with lamb or chicken and a variety of vegetables. Chick peas are usually added and sometimes raisins. The broth is often coloured red with tomato purée or yellow with saffron.

The actual process of cooking the couscous is very simple, but calls for careful handling of the grain. The aim is to make it swell and become extremely light, each grain soft, delicate and separate. The grain must never cook in the broth or sauce, but only in the steam. The couscousier, the pot traditionally used, is in two parts: the bottom part is the round pan in which the stew is cooked; the top consists of a sieve which holds the couscous.

The treatment of the grain is always the same, whatever the sauce. This recipe is for a basic Moroccan couscous.

200 g	8 oz	couscous
400 g	1 lb	lean stewing lamb
		or
200 g	8 oz	stewing lamb and
200 g	8 oz	stewing beef
		or
1 × 1½ kg	3 lb	chicken, cut for sauté
		2 tablespns olive oil
50 g	2 oz	finely chopped onion
		1 garlic clove, crushed and chopped
100 g	4 oz	celery
100 g	4 oz	leek
100 g	4 oz	carrot
25 g	1 oz	chick peas
		¼ teaspn ground ginger (optional)
		¼ teaspn saffron (optional)
50 g	2 oz	raisins
100 g	4 oz	courgettes, cut in 1 cm (½ in.) dice
50 g	2 oz	tomato, skinned, deseeded, diced
		chopped parsley
50 g	2 oz	tomato purée
		cayenne pepper
		½ teaspn paprika
50 g	2 oz	butter or margarine

1 Soak the couscous in warm water for 10 mins.
2 Fry the meat in the oil until browned and sealed. Remove quickly, fry the onions and garlic.
3 Drain, place meat, onions and garlic into a saucepan.
4 Add the celery, leeks, carrots cut into 1 cm (½ in.) dice. Add the chick peas, cover with water, season.
5 Add ginger and saffron. Bring to boil and simmer for approx. 1 hour.
6 Drain the couscous, place in the top part of the couscousier and steam for approx. 30 mins. Alternatively, place the couscous in a metal colander lined with muslin. Fit into the top of the saucepan, making sure that the liquid from the stew does not touch the steamer as the couscous will become lumpy. Stir occasionally.
7 Add to the stew the raisins and courgettes, the tomato, chopped parsley and tomato puŕee. Cook for a further 30 mins.
8 Remove approx. 250 ml (½ pt) sauce from the stew and stir in the cayenne pepper, enough to make it strong and fiery. Finish with paprika.
9 To serve pile the couscous into a suitable serving dish, preferably

earthenware, add knobs of butter or margarine and work into the grains with a fork.

10 Carefully arrange the meat and vegetables over the couscous and pour the broth over. Serve the hot peppery sauce separately.

11 Alternatively, the couscous, meat and vegetables, the broth and the peppery sauce can be served in separate bowls.

6   Khoshaf   Dried fruit with nuts, perfumed with rose and orange water

4 portions

During Ramadan, Muslims fast all day and only eat after sunset. This is one of the dishes enjoyed during Ramadan. It is served hot or cold.

100 g	4 oz	dried apricots
100 g	4 oz	prunes
100 g	4 oz	dried figs
100 g	4 oz	raisins
		1 tablespn rose water
		1 tablespn orange blossom water
50 g	2 oz	blanched almonds (halved)
50 g	2 oz	pine kernels

1 Wash the fruit if necessary, soak overnight.
2 Drain, place fruit in a large saucepan, cover with water and bring to boil. Simmer for approx. 10 mins.
3 Add the rose water and the orange blossom water.
4 Place into a serving dish sprinkled with nuts.

7   Muhallabia   Rose-perfumed rice pudding

50 g	1 oz	cornflour
75 g	3 oz	ground rice
500 ml	1 pt	milk
		2 tablespns rose water
50 g	2 oz	castor sugar
100 g	4 oz	ground almonds
		chopped almonds and pistachio nuts to decorate

1 Place the cornflour and ground rice into a basin and add sufficient of the milk to make a smooth paste.
2 Boil the rest of the milk in a saucepan, add the boiling milk to the rice and cornflour.
3 Pour back into the saucepan. Reheat and stir until the mixture reboils and thickens. Add the rose water and sugar, cook for a further 2 mins.
4 Stir in the ground almonds, mix well.
5 Pour into individual serving dishes decorated with chopped almonds and pistachio nuts.

India

8 Chicken palak   Chicken fried with spinach and spices   *4 portions*

1 × 1½ kg	3 lb	chicken, cut for sauté
50 g	2 oz	ghee or butter, margarine or oil
50 g	2 oz	finely chopped onion
		1 clove of garlic, crushed and chopped
25 g	1 oz	fresh ginger
		1 green chilli
		1 teaspn ground cumin
		1 teaspn ground coriander
250 g	10 oz	spinach, washed and finely chopped
200 g	8 oz	tomatoes, skinned, deseeded, diced
250 ml	½ pt	chicken stock

1 Gently fry the chicken in the fat until golden brown.
2 Remove the chicken and fry the onion and garlic until lightly browned. Add the spices, sweat for 3 mins.
3 Stir in the spinach, add the tomatoes and season. Add the chicken pieces.
4 Add the chicken stock, bring to boil.
5 Cover with a lid and cook in a moderate oven (180°C, 350°F, Reg. 4) until the chicken is tender, approx. 30 mins. Stir occasionally, adding more stock if necessary.
6 Serve in a suitable dish with rice, chapatis (see page 186) and dhal (see page 182).

9 Chicken tikka   Chicken marinated in yoghurt and spices and grilled   *4 portions*

1 × 1½ kg	3 lb	chicken, cut for sauté
125 ml	¼ pt	natural yoghurt
		1 teaspn grated ginger
		1 teaspn ground coriander
		1 teaspn ground cumin
		1 teaspn chilli powder
		1 clove of garlic, crushed and chopped
		juice of ½ lemon
50 g	2 oz	tomato purée
50 g	2 oz	finely chopped onion
60 ml	⅛ pt	oil
		4 wedges of lemon
		seasoning

1 Place the chicken pieces into a suitable dish.
2 Mix together the yoghurt, seasoning, spices, garlic, lemon juice and tomato purée.

3 Pour this over the chicken, mix well and leave to marinade for at least 3 hours.
4 In a suitable shallow tray, add the chopped onion and half the oil.
5 Lay the chicken pieces on top and grill under the salamander, turning the pieces over once or gently cook in a moderate oven (180°C, 350°F, Reg. 4) for approx. 20–30 mins.
6 Baste with the remaining oil.
7 Serve on a bed of lettuce garnished with wedges of lemon.

10   **Dahl**   Lentil or split pea purée   *4 portions*

Dahl is made from lentils and is an important part of the basic diet for many Indians. It can also be made using yellow split peas.

200 g	8 oz	lentils
		1 teaspn turmeric
50 g	2 oz	ghee, butter or oil
50 g	2 oz	finely chopped onion
		1 clove of garlic, crushed and chopped
		1 green chilli (optional), finely chopped
		1 teaspn of cumin seeds

1 Place the lentils in a saucepan and cover with water. Add turmeric, bring to boil and gently simmer until cooked. Stir occasionally.
2 In a suitable pan, heat the fat and sweat the onion, garlic, chilli (if using) and cumin seeds. Stir into the lentils and season.
3 Serve hot to accompany other dishes. The consistency should be fairly thick but spoonable.

11   **Pasandeh**   Lamb with yoghurt and spices   *4 portions*

400 g	1 lb	boned loin of lamb, cut into slices approx. 2 cm (1 in.) thick
125 ml	¼ pt	natural yoghurt
		1 teaspn freshly grated ginger
		1 clove of garlic, crushed and chopped
		1 teaspn chilli powder
		¼ teaspn turmeric
		2 teaspns garam masala
		salt
		2 cardamom pods
		1 teaspn black cumin seeds
50 g	2 oz	ground almonds
25 g	1 oz	desiccated coconut
25 g	1 oz	poppy seeds
25 g	1 oz	sesame seeds
125 ml	¼ pt	oil
100 g	4 oz	finely chopped onion
250 ml	½ pt	white stock or water
		2 green chillies, chopped
		fresh coriander leaves, chopped

1 Mix the slices of lamb with the yoghurt, ginger, garlic, chilli powder, turmeric, garam masala, salt, cardamoms and black cumin seeds.
2 Dry-roast the ground almonds, coconut, poppy seeds and sesame seeds until golden brown.
3 Grind the seeds and nuts in a food processor until fine and well mixed and add 1 tablespoon of water. Stir this mixture into the meat and yoghurt.
4 In a sauté pan heat a little oil and fry the onion until golden brown.
5 Remove the onion from the pan. Add a little more oil, heat and quickly stir-fry the lamb, return the onion and continue to stir-fry for approx. 5 mins.
6 Add the stock or water, bring to boil and gently simmer for approx. 20 mins, stirring occasionally. Add the green chillies and coriander leaves.
7 Serve in a suitable dish, accompanied by chapatis (p. 186) and lentils.

Note Beef may be substituted for lamb.

12   Tandoori prawns   Grilled spiced prawns   *4 portions*

		12 king size prawns	
100 g	4 oz	unsalted butter	
		1 teaspn fresh grated ginger	
		1 clove of garlic, crushed and chopped	
		1 teaspn chilli powder	
		1 teaspn ground cumin	
		1 teaspn ground coriander	
		fresh coriander leaves	
		seasoning	
		lettuce leaves	
		onion rings	garnish
		2 chopped chillies	
		1 lemon cut into wedges	

1 Shell and wash the prawns, leaving the head attached. Place in a shallow tray.
2 Melt the butter and add all the spices, including the coriander leaves.
3 Pour this melted butter mixture over the prawns.
4 Gently grill on both sides under the salamander, approx. 5–6 mins.
5 Serve on a bed of lettuce, garnished with onion, chillies and lemon.

Note This dish should be prepared using live prawns, but if unobtainable cooked prawns may be used, in which case the prawns should be reheated for 2–3 minutes.
    Tandoori prawns may be served as a first or fish course.

13   **Pakora**   Batter-fried vegetables and shrimps

A reception or bar snack or as a main course.

125 g	5 oz	bessan (chick-pea flour)
375 ml	¾ pt	water
		¼ teaspn turmeric
		1 teaspn ground coriander
		¼ teaspn cayenne
		salt

batter

vegetables such as: batons of carrot, florets of cauliflower, florets of broccoli, sliced aubergines, batons of celery, slices of par-boiled potato, peeled or unpeeled, batons of parsnip, large cooked shrimps or prawns, peeled and seasoned with salt and curry powder

1 Sieve the flour and slowly add the water, whisking continuously.
2 Pass through a strainer.
3 Add turmeric, coriander and cayenne pepper, season with salt. Allow to stand for 15 mins.
4 Dip vegetables and shrimps or prawns into the batter, coating well.
5 Deep fry in hot oil (approximately 190°C/375°F) until a light saffron colour.
6 Drain well and serve with chutney.

Note Unlike plain wheat flour, batter made with bessan produces a non-porous surface and no fat will penetrate to the food inside.

14   **Vegetable samosas**   Vegetable patties   *4 portions*

May be served as starters or snacks.

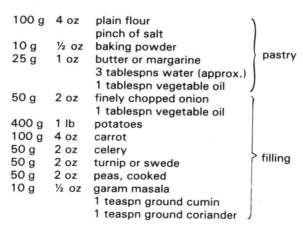

100 g	4 oz	plain flour
		pinch of salt
10 g	½ oz	baking powder
25 g	1 oz	butter or margarine
		3 tablespns water (approx.)
		1 tablespn vegetable oil

pastry

50 g	2 oz	finely chopped onion
		1 tablespn vegetable oil
400 g	1 lb	potatoes
100 g	4 oz	carrot
50 g	2 oz	celery
50 g	2 oz	turnip or swede
50 g	2 oz	peas, cooked
10 g	½ oz	garam masala
		1 teaspn ground cumin
		1 teaspn ground coriander

filling

1 Sieve the flour, salt and baking powder. Add the melted butter and the water to make a smooth dough.

2 Knead well to form an elastic dough and allow to rest before being used.
3 Quickly fry the onion in the oil and cut the remaining vegetables into brunoise.
4 Add the vegetables and spices to the onion, with a little water to prevent burning. Cover with greaseproof paper and a lid and sweat until tender.
5 Add the peas and correct the seasoning.
6 Divide the dough into approx. 10 pieces. Roll out into 8 cm (3 in.) squares.
7 Place a spoonful of filling in the centre of each square, egg wash the edges and fold over to form triangles.
8 Brush with vegetable oil, place on lightly greased baking sheets and bake in a moderate oven (180°C, 350°F, Reg. 4) for approx. 15–20 mins until cooked and golden brown.
9 Alternatively the samosas may be deep fried in hot vegetable oil (375°F, 190°C) until crisp and golden brown.

15 Indian banana fudge   *4 portions*

A sweetmeat.

		3 cardamom pods
100 g	4 oz	banana, puréed
25 g	1 oz	butter or margarine
50 g	2 oz	semolina
50 g	2 oz	ground almonds
50 g	2 oz	brown sugar
		4 tablespns water

1 Grind the seeds from the cardamom pods and add to the banana.
2 Melt the butter in a heavy-based saucepan and add the semolina, gently fry until golden brown.
3 Add the banana, almonds, sugar and water, and bring to the boil. Stir continuously until the mixture leaves the sides of the pan.
4 Pour into a greased shallow tray and place in the refrigerator to set. When set, cut into squares to serve.

16 Kheer   Rice and vermicelli pudding with nuts   *4 portions*

25 g	1 oz	butter or margarine
50 g	2 oz	long grain rice
50 g	2 oz	fine vermicelli
250 ml	½ pt	milk
25 g	1 oz	raisins
50 g	2 oz	condensed milk
		1 teaspn crushed cardamom seeds
		1 teaspn rose water

25 g	1 oz	flaked almonds
25 g	1 oz	pistachio nuts
50 g	2 oz	castor sugar

1 Melt the butter or margarine in a sauteuse, fry the rice and vermicelli until golden.
2 Add the milk, bring to the boil and simmer for approx. 6 mins.
3 Add the raisins, condensed milk and cardamom seeds. Bring back to the boil, stirring frequently until cooked – the mixture should be fairly thick. Finish with rose water.
4 Serve in a suitable dish, sprinkled with nuts and sugar.

17 Chapatis Crisp wholemeal pancakes *4 portions*

Chapatis are cooked on a tawa or frying pan. They are made fresh for each meal, and are dipped into sauces and used to scoop up food.

200 g	8 oz	wholewheat flour
		pinch of salt
125 ml	¼ pt	water
		vegetable oil

1 Sieve the flour and salt, add the water and knead to a firm dough.
2 Knead on a floured table until smooth and elastic.
3 Cover with a damp cloth or polythene and allow to relax for 30–40 mins.
4 Divide into 10 pieces, flatten each and roll into a circle 12–15 cm (5–6 in.) in diameter.
5 Lightly grease a frying pan with oil, add the chapati and cook as for a pancake. Traditionally chapatis are allowed to puff by placing them over an open flame.
6 Just before serving reheat the chapatis under the salamander.

Indonesia

18 Gado gado Vegetable salad with peanut dressing *4 portions*

This dish is popular throughout Indonesia. It may be served as a starter or with a main meal and rice.

200 g	8 oz	white cabbage, finely shredded and washed
100 g	4 oz	bean sprouts, washed
200 g	8 oz	cooked potato, cut in 1 cm (½ in.) dice
50 g	2 oz	tomato, skinned, deseeded, diced
		2 eggs, hard boiled

60 ml	⅛ pt	vegetable oil	
50 g	2 oz	finely chopped onion	
		1 clove garlic, crushed and chopped	
		1 green chilli, finely chopped	sauce or dressing
50 g	2 oz	crunchy peanut butter	
		2 teaspns malt vinegar	
125 ml	¼ pt	coconut milk	

1 Drain the cabbage and bean sprouts and mix together.
2 Add the potato and the tomato, lightly season.
3 Arrange neatly into individual dishes just prior to service and decorate with quarters of hard-boiled egg.
4 Prepare the dressing: heat the oil in a sauteuse and stir fry the onion, garlic and chilli for approx. 2 mins.
5 Stir in the peanut butter, vinegar and coconut milk, simmer for a further 2–3 mins.
6 Pour the hot sauce over the salad or serve separately.

19 Nasi goreng Rice with bacon, chicken and soy sauce

60 ml	⅛ pt	vegetable oil	
100 g	4 oz	finely chopped onion	
		1 clove of garlic, crushed and chopped	
		1 red chilli, finely chopped	
200 g	8 oz	small lardons of bacon	
100 g	4 oz	cooked chicken, cut into 2 cm (1 in.) slices	
		2 tablespns soy sauce	
250 g	10 oz	rice cooked as pilaff, dry and fluffy	
		2 eggs, beaten and seasoned	garnish
50 g	2 oz	finely sliced cucumber	

1 Heat a little oil in a suitable pan, e.g. wok, add the onion, garlic and chilli, and stir-fry. Add the lardons of bacon and cook quickly.
2 Add the cooked chicken and cook for a further 2–3 mins.
3 Add the soy sauce and cooked rice. Reheat the rice thoroughly. Stir occasionally.
4 For the garnish, heat a little oil in a small frying pan. Beat the egg well with seasoning. Pour this into the frying pan, cook one side, turn over and cook the other. Turn out onto a board. Cut into thin strips.
5 Serve in a suitable dish, garnished with strips of the cooked egg and slices of cucumber.

Note Prawns are sometimes added to this dish.

China

20   Walnut chicken   *Yields approx. 20 bite-sized pieces*

Served as an appetizer.

		2 suprêmes of chicken
100 g	4 oz	walnuts, coarsely chopped
		2 egg whites
		1 tablespn dry sherry
		1 teaspn sesame seed oil
50 g	2 oz	plain flour
60 ml	⅛ pt	water
		seasoning

1 Remove the wing bones from the suprêmes. Remove the fillets and take out the nerve from each fillet.
2 Open each suprême out by cutting almost in half horizontally. Open and lay flat. Bat out the suprêmes and each fillet.
3 Mix in a basin the egg whites, sherry, water, sesame seed oil and seasoning. Gradually stir in the sieved flour.
4 Heat sufficient oil in a frying pan to cover the bottom.
5 Dip the 4 pieces of chicken in the flour, coating both sides. Then coat with the chopped walnuts.
6 Gently fry in the hot oil, taking care that the walnuts do not burn. Turn over and cook the other side.
7 When cooked and dried, cut into bite-sized pieces and serve on dish paper.

21   Fried noodles with shredded pork   *4 portions*

100 g	4 oz	pork fillet, cut into batons
		1½ teaspns dark soy sauce
		1 teaspn granulated sugar
10 g	½ oz	cornflour
60 ml	⅛ pt	water
60 ml	⅛ pt	vegetable oil
150 g	6 oz	Chinese egg noodles
150 g	6 oz	bean sprouts
		2 Chinese dried mushrooms
		1 teaspn dry sherry
125 ml	¼ pt	chicken stock
		1 teaspn light soy sauce
		½ teaspn sesame oil
		2 spring onions for garnish

1 Marinade the pork in 1 teaspoon of dark soy sauce, ½ teaspoon of the sugar and cornflour, seasoning, half the water and half the oil. Allow to stand for 15 mins.

2 Blanch the noodles in boiling salted water for 1 min, refresh and drain.
3 In a suitable pan, heat sufficient oil to deep fry the noodles. Drain on kitchen paper or in a cloth.
4 Heat the remainder of the oil in a wok. Add the bean sprouts. Cook quickly and remove.
5 Add the pork and cook until lightly browned.
6 Add the beansprouts to the pork and add the mushrooms.
7 Blend the remaining cornflour with the rest of the water and add all the remaining ingredients. Stir this into the pork and simmer until thickened.
8 Place the noodles in a suitable serving dish, place the pork in the centre and garnish with chopped spring onions.

22 Sole with mushrooms and bamboo shoots   *4 portions*

200 g	8 oz	fillet of lemon or Dover sole, cut into goujons
		2 tablespns sherry
		2 tablespns soy sauce
10 g	½ oz	cornflour
		1 egg white, lightly beaten
10 g	½ oz	fresh ginger (grated)
25 g	1 oz	finely chopped onion
50 g	2 oz	mushrooms, sliced
50 g	2 oz	bamboo shoots, sliced
		pinch of monosodium glutamate (MSG), optional
30 ml	1/16 pt	white stock

1 Place the goujons of fish into a small basin, add half the sherry and half the soy sauce.
2 Season, mix in half the cornflour and stir in the egg white.
3 Carefully take out the goujons and deep fry until golden brown. Drain.
4 Heat a little oil in a frying pan or wok, add the grated ginger and chopped onion, fry for 1 min.
5 Add the mushrooms and bamboo shoots, fry for 1 min.
6 Blend remaining sherry and cornflour together, add monosodium glutamate and stock. Pour into wok and cook, stirring, for 1–2 mins.
7 Place the sole into a suitable serving dish, mask with the mushroom and bamboo shoot sauce and serve.

23 Chinese vegetables and noodles   *4 portions*

400 g	1 lb	Chinese noodles
60 ml	⅛ pt	oil
100 g	4 oz	celery
100 g	4 oz	carrot ⎫ cut in paysanne
50 g	2 oz	bamboo shoots ⎭
75 g	3 oz	mushrooms, finely sliced

75 g	3 oz	Chinese cabbage, shredded
100 g	4 oz	bean sprouts
30 ml	1/16 pt	soy sauce
		garnish: 4 spring onions, sliced lengthways and quickly stir-fried

1 Cook the noodles in boiling salted water for approx. 5–6 mins until *al dente*. Refresh and drain.
2 Heat the oil in a wok and stir fry all the vegetables except the beansprouts, for approx. 1 min. Then add the beansprouts and cook for a further 1 min.
3 Add the drained noodles, stirring well; allow to reheat through.
4 Correct the seasoning.
5 Serve in a suitable dish, garnished with the spring onions.

24 Pork, ham and bamboo shoot soup   *4 portions*

100 g	4 oz	pork fillet, cut into julienne
30 ml	1/16 pt	soy sauce
500 ml	1 pt	brown stock or consommé
100 g	4 oz	cooked ham ⎫
100 g	4 oz	bamboo shoots ⎬ cut into julienne
30 ml	1/16 pt	dry sherry
		seasoning

1 Place the pork fillet into a basin and mix with the soy sauce.
2 Bring the brown stock or consommé to the boil.
3 Add the pork, ham and bamboo shoots to the brown stock or consommé.
4 Bring back to the boil, correct seasoning, add the sherry and serve.

Note This soup may also be lightly thickened with arrowroot or cornflour.

25 Chop suey   *4 portions*

400 g	1 lb	pork fillet
		or
		4 suprêmes of chicken
		or
400 g	1 lb	entrecote steak
60 ml	⅛ pt	soy sauce
30 ml	1/16 pt	sherry
10 g	½ oz	cornflour
5 g	¼ oz	ginger root
200 g	8 oz	green pepper
100 g	4 oz	broccoli florets or cauliflower
50 g	2 oz	carrot
50 g	2 oz	French beans
60 ml	⅛ pt	vegetable oil
		4 spring onions

200 g	8 oz	bean sprouts
100 g	4 oz	tomato, skinned, deseeded, diced
		seasoning
10 g	½ oz	sugar
60 ml	⅛ pt	white stock

1 Cut the meat into scallops or large julienne. Place into a basin with the soy sauce, sherry and cornflour and mix well.
2 Cut the ginger into 1 cm (½ in.) lengths and finely slice.
3 Cut the green pepper into 1 cm (½ in.) dice, the broccoli or cauliflower into small florets, the carrots into large julienne and the French beans into lozenges.
4 Stir fry the meat in half the oil for approx. 1 min. Remove and drain.
5 Add the rest of the oil, the ginger, the spring onions and the remainder of the vegetables. Season and add a pinch of sugar. Stir well.
6 Add the meat and mix well, moisten with a little stock if necessary. Serve in a suitable dish immediately.

26 Chow mein   *4 portions*

400 g	1 lb	egg noodles
250 g	10 oz	pork fillet
10 g	½ oz	cornflour
100 g	4 oz	bamboo shoots
100 g	4 oz	cucumber
100 g	4 oz	spinach leaves
60 ml	⅛ pt	oil
30 ml	1/16 pt	soy sauce
30 ml	1/16 pt	dry sherry
10 g	½ oz	cornflour
30 ml	1/16 pt	sesame seed oil
		pinch salt
		pinch sugar

(soy sauce, dry sherry, cornflour, sesame seed oil, pinch salt, pinch sugar = sauce)

1 Cook the noodles in boiling salted water until *al dente*, refresh and drain.
2 Cut the pork into large julienne, place in a basin, add the cornflour and mix well.
3 Cut the bamboo shoots and peeled cucumber into julienne. Cut the spinach into chiffonade.
4 Heat half the oil in a wok. Reheat the noodles in the oil for 2–3 mins. Season, then drain and place in a serving dish.
5 Heat the remaining oil in a wok, stir fry the pork for approx. 1–2 mins, add the bamboo shoots, cucumber and spinach.
6 Mix all the sauce ingredients in a basin, add to the wok. Cook for a further 2 mins.
7 Carefully arrange the sauce in a serving dish with the noodles. Serve immediately.

Japan

27   Crab and tofu balls

Yield approx. 24

Serve as an appetiser.

```
400 g   1 lb   tofu
100 g   4 oz   cooked white crab meat
               1 egg, beaten
               seasoning
               cornflour
               oil for deep frying
```

1 Squeeze out all the excess moisture from the tofu, place into a mixing bowl and cream well with a wooden spoon.
2 Add the shredded crab meat, beaten egg and seasoning.
3 Mould into small balls. Dip into beaten egg then into cornflour.
4 Deep fry in hot oil, (190°C, 375°F) until golden brown.
5 Serve in a suitable dish on dish paper with hot mustard, or mayonnaise flavoured with horseradish or soy sauce.
6 Alternatively, tofu balls may be dipped into a frying batter then deep fried.

28   Hotate gai shoyu yaki   Scallops grilled with soy sauce   *4 portions*

```
                8 scallops
30 ml   1/16 pt   sake
30 ml   1/16 pt   soy sauce
                4 lemon wedges
                parsley
```

1 Wash the scallops well.
2 Place the scallops shells over a fierce heat to brown.
3 Carefully remove the meat from the shells.
4 Mix the soy sauce and sake together in a basin.
5 Divide the cleaned scallops into 4 china scallop shells and pour the soy sauce and sake over each of the scallops.
6 Place in a suitable tray and grill under the salamander until just cooked.
7 Serve the scallops hot, in the shells, garnished with lemon wedge and parsley.

29   Tonkatsu   Deep-fried pork cutlet   *4 portions*

Tonkatsu is a half-Japanese and half-fragmented English word. *Ton* is a pig or pork and *katsu* is the Japanization of 'cutlet'. The dish itself is of

European origin. It is a popular fast food in Tokyo and other Japanese cities.

		4 slices of loin of pork approx. 1 cm (½ in.) thick
		salt and black pepper
		2 eggs, beaten
		flour
100 g	4 oz	dried breadcrumbs
		vegetable oil
150 g	6 oz	white cabbage
60 ml	⅛ pt	tomato ketchup
		½ lemon
		3–4 drops Worcester sauce
		3–4 drops dark soy sauce
		1 teaspoon English mustard
30 ml	1/16 pt	sake

1 Score the edges of the pork. Season, pass through egg, flour and breadcrumbs.
2 Deep fry the cutlets in oil at 180°C (350°F) for approx. 5 to 7 mins.
3 Remove, drain the cutlets and slice diagonally into 1 cm (½ in.) strips.
4 Shred the cabbage finely. Divide onto 4 plates.
5 Arrange the cutlet pieces on the cabbage and garnish with a lemon wedge. (Cucumber and tomato may also be used.)
6 Mix the tomato ketchup, Worcester sauce, soy sauce, mustard and sake to a paste and place into individual bowls so that the cutlets may be dipped into the sauce.

30 Tempura   Vegetable and shrimp fritters   *4 portions*

Tempura is the Japanese term for frying fish and other foods dipped in batter, normally accompanied by a dipping sauce.

		12 mange-tout, topped and tailed	
100 g	4 oz	white button mushrooms, halved	
100 g	4 oz	carrot, cut in matchstick pieces	
100 g	4 oz	sweet potato, peeled and thinly sliced	
150 g	6 oz	shrimps, shelled, cleaned, tails left attached	
150 g	6 oz	flour	
200 g	8 oz	flour	
10 g	½ oz	baking powder	frying batter
		1 egg yolk	
175 ml	⅓ pt	iced water (approx.)	

1 Heat friture to 175°C (350°F).
2 Ensure all vegetables are dry.
3 Flour the vegetables and shrimps one at a time, shake off surplus, pass through batter, shake off surplus and deep fry for 2–3 mins.

4 Drain vegetables well and keep warm.

5 Increase temperature of friture to 180°C (360°F) and fry the shrimps, drain well.

6 Serve the vegetables and shrimps on dish paper, to ensure they are dry, and accompany with dipping sauce (see below).

Dipping sauce for vegetables, meat, poultry

125 ml   ¼ pt   fish stock
                1 tablespn soy sauce
                ½ tablespn rice wine or sweet sherry
                ½ tablespn rice vinegar or white vinegar

Combine all ingredients and serve in individual bowls.

31 Yakitori

32 Teppanyaki

Yakitori and teppanyaki are Japanese styles of grilling poultry or meat. Grilled fish is known as *shioyaki*.

Restaurants that specialise in serving grilled foods are known as teppanyaki restaurants and in most cases the food is cooked on a table-top grill in front of the diner.

For *yakitori*, small pieces of chicken, duck or other small birds are marinated for 30–45 minutes in a mixture of soy sauce and sake (rice wine) or sherry, pierced on skewers and grilled over charcoal.

For *teppanyaki*, the best quality steaks or pork fillets or chops are marinated for 45 minutes to 1 hour. They are then dried well and grilled on flat metal plates or domed grills of perforated metal.

Marinade

3 tablespns soy sauce ⎫
3 tablespns sweet sherry ⎪
1 tablespn sesame oil   ⎬ mix all ingredients together
1 tablespn white vinegar ⎪
1 tablespn sugar   ⎭

Yakitori and teppanyaki dishes would usually be accompanied by a dish of lightly stir-fried vegetables, e.g. shredded Chinese or ordinary cabbage, mushrooms, sweet peppers, broccoli florets, bean sprouts, asparagus tips, etc. Bowls of dipping sauce would also be served.

33 Sashimi

This is a style of serving raw fish, which must therefore be absolutely fresh. Bream, salmon, trout etc. may be used, either individually or as a mixture of different fish. The thoroughly washed fillets are very thinly sliced with a sharp knife and the slices arranged neatly on the plate. A delicate garnish, such as a decorative leaf, curl of carrot or chopped spring onion may be used.

Sashimi is served with dipping sauce and wasabi paste. This is pungent, like horseradish sauce. It is obtained in powdered form and made up with a little water, as if using dried mustard.

34 Sushi

Sushi (*zushi*) is a style of serving a variety of foods. The main ingredient is vinegared rice, which is served cold with raw fish, shrimps, prawns, vegetables etc. The proportion of rice to water will vary according to the rice used, and the cooking time may also need to be adjusted. Firm short or long grain rice may be used, but not soft pudding rice or brown rice. When cooked the rice will be white and the grains will cohere.

An example of using sushi is *bara sushi* (recipe 36, overleaf).

35 Sushi rice Vinegared rice   *4 portions*

150 g	6 oz	rice
375 ml	¾ pt	water
		salt
		few drops of oil
		3 tablespns rice vinegar
		1 ½ tablespns sugar
		1 teaspn salt
		1 tablespn mirin (sweet sake) or dry sherry

} dressing

1 Thoroughly wash the rice.
2 Place the rice, water, salt and oil in a heavy-based pan.
3 Bring to the boil, cover with a tight fitting lid and reduce the heat.
4 Allow to simmer for 20 mins.
5 Remove from the heat and stand with the lid on for 15 mins.
6 Meanwhile place the dressing ingredients in a pan and bring to the boil.
7 Sprinkle the rice with the dressing whilst both are still warm, and mix thoroughly but lightly.

36 **Bara sushi** Vinegared rice with fish and beans *4 portions*

150 g	6 oz	sushi rice (as recipe 35)
400 g	1 lb	mackerel or shrimps
		6 tablespns vinegar ⎞
		3 tablespns sugar ⎬ seasoned vinegar
		2 teaspns salt ⎠
		2 slices of ginger (optional)
100 g	4 oz	French or runner beans, cooked
		1 tablespn sesame seeds, toasted and chopped

1 Prepare and cook the rice and dressing as in recipe 35.
2 Fillet the fish, sprinkle lightly with salt and leave for 15 minutes.
3 Wash and soak the fish in seasoned vinegar for 10 mins.
4 Remove the skin and slice thinly.
5 If using shrimps, soak the cooked shelled shrimps in the vinegar.
6 Slice the ginger, sprinkle with salt and soak in vinegar.
7 Mix the rice, fish, ginger and sliced beans together, and sprinkle with the sesame seeds to serve.

Note The fish must be very fresh. If rice vinegar is not available a light wine vinegar can be used.

Mexico

37 Tortillas *4 portions*

Tortillas are served with all Mexican meals. Although in Mexico a special flour is used, tortillas may be produced using cornmeal and wholemeal flour.

100 g	4 oz	wholemeal flour
100 g	4 oz	cornmeal flour
250 ml	½ pt	water (approx.)

1 Sieve the flours together into a bowl, add a pinch of salt and sufficient water to make a smooth dough.
2 Knead well until elastic. Divide into 12 or 16 pieces, depending on the size of the tortilla required.
3 Place a ball of dough between two pieces of well oiled greaseproof paper (or use silicone paper). Roll the dough into a circle, diameter 10–15 cm (4–6 in.).
4 Lightly oil a frying pan. Peel off the top layer of paper and place the tortilla in the pan. Cook for approx. 2 mins. Remove the top paper, turn over and cook the other side approx. 2 mins. Both sides should be quite pale and dry.

5 Keep the tortillas warm for service, stacking between pieces of dry greaseproof paper.

Notes The tortilla can be served in different ways. When crisp and golden it is called a *tostada*. These are served with red kidney beans, cheese and a chilli sauce.

Tacos are tortillas curled into a shell shape and fried, usually filled with picadillo (see following recipe) and served with salad and chilli sauce.

Tortillas that are rolled and filled, then served with a sauce, are called *enchiladas*.

Chilli sauce is usually purchased as a commercial product. But it can be made by mixing together tomato ketchup and tabasco sauce or by making a fresh tomato coulis (page 64), strengthened with tomato purée and finished with tabasco.

Tortillas may be made lighter by adding 1 teaspn baking powder.

38 Picadillo   *4 portions*

Used as a filling for tacos

60 ml	⅛ pt	oil
400 g	1 lb	minced lean beef
100 g	4 oz	finely chopped onion
		1 clove of garlic, crushed and chopped
		1 chilli, finely chopped
100 g	4 oz	tomatoes, skinned, deseeded, diced
50 g	2 oz	tomato purée
		¼ teaspn cumin seed
50 g	2 oz	raisins
250 ml	½ pt	brown stock or water
18 g	¾ oz	cornflour
25 g	1 oz	green olives, chopped
25 g	1 oz	capers, chopped
50 g	2 oz	flaked almonds, roasted

1 Heat the oil in a frying pan, add the minced beef and brown quickly.
2 Add the onion, garlic, and the chopped chilli pepper. Season and cook for a further 3 mins.
3 Pour off excess oil and place the meat into a suitable saucepan.
4 Add to the saucepan the tomatoes, tomato purée, cumin seed and raisins.
5 Barely cover with brown stock or water and gently simmer for approx. 30 mins.
6 Lightly thicken with a little diluted cornflour and stir in the olives and capers.
7 Correct the seasoning and consistency. Finish by adding the roasted flaked almonds.

39   **Burritos**   Mexican pancakes   *4 portions*

The pancakes are filled with meat and served with a cheese sauce.

250 ml	½ pt	pancake batter (see below)
		4 portions chilli con carne, page 206
500 ml	1 pt	Mornay sauce flavoured with Dijon-type mustard
		grated cheese, parmesan or cheddar

1 Make the pancakes in the normal way (see below).
2 Fill the pancakes with chilli con carne. Place in a suitable earthenware dish.
3 Mask with Mornay sauce and sprinkle with grated cheese.
4 Glaze under the salamander or in a hot oven and serve.

Pancake batter

100 g	4 oz	flour, white or wholemeal
		pinch of salt
		1 egg
250 ml	½ pt	milk, whole or skimmed
10 g	½ oz	melted butter, margarine or oil
		oil for frying

1 Sieve the flour and salt into a bowl, make a well into the centre.
2 Add the egg and milk, gradually incorporating the flour from the sides, whisk to a smooth batter.
3 Mix in the melted butter.
4 Heat the pancake pan, clean thoroughly.
5 Add a little oil, heat until smoking.
6 Add enough mixture to just cover the bottom of the pan thinly.
7 Cook for a few seconds until brown.
8 Turn and cook on the other side. Turn on to a plate.
9 Repeat until all the batter is used up.

Greece

---

40   **Taramasalata**   Paste of smoked cod's roe   *4 portions*

Served as an hors-d'oeuvre or appetiser. Tarama is the salted roe of the grey mullet, tuna fish or smoked cod's roe.

150 g	6 oz	white bread, without crusts
125 ml	¼ pt	milk
150 g	6 oz	smoked cod's roe, skinned
50 g	2 oz	finely chopped onion } optional
		1 clove of garlic }

250 ml	½ pt	olive or vegetable oil
		seasoning
		stoned olives, lemon, to serve

1 Soak the bread in the milk for 2–3 mins. Squeeze dry.
2 Place all the ingredients except the oil in a food processor, liquidise and gradually add the oil to make a smooth paste.
3 Place into individual ramekin dishes, decorate with stoned olives, garnish with lemon. Serve with hot breakfast toast, or hot pitta bread.

41 Avgolemono soup   Egg and lemon soup   *4 portions*

750 ml	1½ pt	chicken stock
35 g	1½ oz	patna rice
		seasoning
		2 yolks plus 1 egg (the egg is optional)
		juice of ½ a lemon

1 Bring the stock to the boil, add the rice and stir well.
2 Season and cook for 12–15 mins, remove from heat.
3 In a basin thoroughly mix the yolks, egg and lemon juice.
4 Add a tablespoon of the stock a little at a time to the egg and lemon mixture, beating continuously.
5 Add a further 6 tablespoons, mixing continuously. If added too quickly the mixture will curdle.
6 Return the mixture to the stock and heat gently, mixing all the time to cook the egg and to thicken before serving.

42 Spanakopitta   Spinach and cheese wrapped in filo pastry

4 portions

50 g	2 oz	finely chopped onion
		1 clove of garlic, crushed and chopped
250 g	10 oz	butter or margarine
1 kg	2 lb	cooked spinach, chopped
200 g	8 oz	grated feta cheese
		4 eggs
		chopped parsley
		chopped dill weed
		seasoning
		12 sheets of filo pastry (see overleaf)

1 Sweat the onion and garlic in 50 g (2 oz) butter.
2 Add the spinach, stir well and remove from heat.
3 Add the cheese, eggs, herbs and seasoning.
4 Melt the remaining butter. Take a suitable tray or dish, so that the filo pastry will come over the sides.

5 Brush the tray with melted butter or margarine and lay in the filo pastry. Repeat with 5 more sheets of filo pastry.
6 Carefully add the spinach and cheese filling.
7 Brush with melted butter, fold over the edges and cover with the remaining filo pastry. Brush all over with melted butter or margarine.
8 Bake in a moderate oven (180°C, 350°F, Reg. 4) for approx. 40 mins until golden brown.
9 When baked cut into portions to serve.

Filo pastry

1 kg	2 lb	strong flour
250–375 ml	½ – ¾ pt	water
		1 tablespn vinegar
		2 teaspns salt
		4 tablespns olive oil

1 Sift the flour in a bowl.
2 Add water, vinegar and salt to the bowl and mix ingredients to a thick paste.
3 Add the oil, very slowly, while working the mixture.
4 Mix until the dough becomes smooth and elastic. Cover for 30 mins.
5 Split the paste into suitable pieces.
6 First roll out with an ordinary rolling pin, then use a very thin rolling pin or pasta machine, to make the paste wafer thin.
7 The pastry is now ready for use. It must be covered with a damp or oiled cloth when not being rolled out or before use.

Note Always cover filo pastry with a damp cloth or polythene when not using, otherwise it dries quickly and is difficult to handle.
   Filo pastry is usually purchased ready made.

43   **Kalamarakia yemista**   Stuffed squid   *4 portions*

		4 medium-sized squid
50 g	2 oz	finely chopped onion
		1 clove of garlic, crushed and chopped
60 ml	⅛ pt	oil
100 g	4 oz	wholegrain rice
250 ml	½ pt	fish stock
50 g	2 oz	pine kernels
100 g	4 oz	raisins
		chopped parsley
		seasoning
125 ml	¼ pt	dry white wine
200 g	8 oz	tomatoes, skinned, deseeded, diced

1 Prepare the squid: pull the body and head apart, remove the transparent pen from the bag and any soft remaining part. Rinse

under cold water. Pull off the thin purple membrane on the outside.
2 Remove the tentacles and cut into pieces. Remove the ink sac. Reserve the ink to finish the sauce.
3 Sweat the onion and garlic in the oil.
4 Add the rice and moisten with half the fish stock. Stir and add the chopped tentacles, nuts, raisins and chopped parsley. Season. Stir well and allow to simmer for approx. 5–8 mins. so that the rice is partly cooked.
5 Stuff the squid loosely with this mixture. Seal the end by covering with aluminium foil.
6 Lay the squid into a sauté pan with the remaining fish stock, white wine and tomatoes.
7 Cover with a lid and cook in a moderate oven (180°C, 350°F, Reg. 4) for approx. 30–40 mins, turning the squid gently during the cooking. Cook very gently or the squid will burst.
8 When cooked, remove squid and place into a suitable serving dish.
9 Reboil the cooking liquor and reduce by one-third. Strain the ink into the sauce, boil and reduce for 5 mins. Check the seasoning.
10 Mask the squid with the sauce and finish with chopped parsley to serve.

44 Dolmades Stuffed vine leaves   *4 portions*

The word *dolmades* comes from a Turkish verb meaning 'to stuff'.

		10 vine leaves	
50 g	2 oz	finely chopped onion	
		1 clove garlic, crushed and chopped	
60 ml	⅛ pt	olive oil	
100 g	4 oz	brown rice	
25 g	1 oz	tomato purée	
60 ml	⅛ pt	white stock (approx.)	filling
		seasoning	
25 g	1 oz	pine kernels	
		fresh chopped mint	
		fresh chopped dillweed	
25 g	1 oz	currants	
		1 clove garlic, crushed and chopped	
		juice of ½ lemon	
		pinch of sugar	
		olive oil	

1 Blanch the fresh vine leaves in boiling salted water for 1 min, refresh and drain.
2 To make the filling: sweat the onion and garlic in the oil without colour.
3 Add the brown rice and tomato purée and moisten with the stock. Stir in the nuts, herbs and currants. Simmer on top of the stove, or cover with a lid and place in the oven, until half cooked.

4 Correct the seasoning. Stuff each vine leaf with the rice mixture and roll up, making sure that the ends are closed.
5 In a sauté pan add the other clove of garlic and the lemon juice and sprinkle with sugar and oil.
6 Lay the stuffed vine leaves in the sauté pan and sprinkle with more lemon juice.
7 Add 125 ml (¼ pt) water or white stock and season. Cover with aluminium foil.
8 Bring to the boil, draw to the side of the stove, gently cook until tender. Alternatively, place in a moderate oven (180°C, 350°, Reg. 4) covered with a lid for approx. 30 mins until tender.
9 When cooked, serve in a suitable earthenware dish in their cooking liquor, which has been thickened with egg yolks and finished with lemon juice. This is avgolemono sauce (see below).

Avgolemono sauce

		2 egg yolks
		juice of ½ lemon
250 ml	½ pt	stock (cooking liquor)

1 Beat egg yolks and lemon juice over a bain-marie until light.
2 Add the stock gradually and return to the saucepan.
3 Cook over a low heat until the sauce thickens but does not boil.

Note Dolmades may also be eaten cold, served with a lemon vinaigrette dressing, and as part of an assorted hors-d'oeuvre.

45   **Baklavas**   Filo pastry with nuts and sugar   *4 portions*

		12 sheets filo pastry	
200 g	8 oz	clarified butter or ghee	
100 g	4 oz	hazelnuts (flaked)	
100 g	4 oz	almonds (nibbed)	
100 g	4 oz	castor sugar	
10 g	½ oz	cinnamon	
		grated nutmeg	
200 g	8 oz	unrefined sugar or castor sugar	⎫
		grated zest and juice of 2 lemons	⎬ syrup
60 ml	⅛ pt	water	⎪
		grated zest and juice of 1 orange	
		1 cinnamon stick	⎭
		rose water	

1 Prepare a shallow tray slightly smaller than the sheets of filo pastry by brushing with melted clarified butter or ghee.
2 Place on 4 sheets of filo pastry, brushing each with the fat.
3 Now prepare the filling by mixing the nuts, sugar and spices together,

and place into the prepared tray, layered alternatively with filo pastry. Brush each layer with the clarified fat so that there is at least 2–3 layers of filling separated by filo pastry.

4 Cover completely with filo pastry and brush with the clarified fat.

5 Mark the pastry into diamonds, sprinkle with water and bake in a moderately hot oven (190°C, 375°F, Reg. 5) for approx. 40 mins.

6 Meanwhile make the syrup: place all the ingredients in a saucepan and bring to the boil. Simmer for 5 mins, strain through a fine chinois and finish with 2–3 drops of rose water.

7 When the baklavas are baked, cut into diamonds, place on a suitable serving dish and mask with the syrup.

Spain

46 Paella Savoury rice with chicken, fish, vegetables and spices

4 portions

1 × 400 g	1 lb	cooked lobster
200 g	8 oz	squid
400 g	1 lb	gambas (Mediterranean prawns), cooked
400 g	1 lb	mussels
1 litre	2 pts	white stock
		pinch of saffron
50 g	2 oz	finely chopped onion
		1 clove of garlic, finely chopped
50 g	2 oz	red pepper ⎫ cut in ½ cm (¼ in.) dice
50 g	2 oz	green pepper ⎭
1½ kg	3 lb	roasting chicken, cut for sauté
60 ml	⅛ pt	olive oil
200 g	8 oz	short grain rice
		thyme, bayleaf and seasoning
200 g	8 oz	tomatoes, skinned, deseeded, diced

1 Prepare the lobster: cut in half, remove claws and legs, discard sac and trail. Remove meat from the claws and cut the tail into 3–4 pieces, leaving the meat in the shell.

2 Clean the squid, pull the body and head apart. Extract the transparent 'pen' from the body. Rinse well, pulling off the thin purple membrance on the outside. Remove the ink sac. Cut the body into rings and tentacles into 1 cm (½ in.) lengths.

3 Prepare the gambas by shelling the body.

4 Shell the mussels and retain the cooking liquid.

5 Boil the white stock and mussel liquor together, infused with saffron. Simmer for 5–10 mins.

6 Sweat the finely chopped onion in a suitable pan, without colour. Add the garlic and the peppers.

7 Sauté the chicken in olive oil until cooked and golden brown, then drain.

8 Add the rice to the onions and garlic and sweat for 2 mins.
9 Add approx. 200 ml (⅜ pt) white stock and mussel liquor.
10 Add the thyme, bayleaf and seasoning. Bring to the boil, then cover with a lightly oiled greaseproof paper and lid. Cook for 5–8 mins, in a moderately hot oven (180°C, 350°F, Reg. 4).
11 Add the squid and cook for another 5 mins.
12 Add the tomatoes, chicken and lobster pieces, mussels and gambas. Stir gently, cover with a lid and reheat the rice in the oven.
13 Correct the consistency of the rice if necessary by adding more stock, so that it looks sufficiently moist without being too wet. Correct seasoning.
14 When all is reheated and cooked, place in a suitable serving dish, decorate with 4 gambas and 4 mussels halved and shelled. Finish with wedges of lemon.

Note For a traditional paella a raw lobster may be used, which should be prepared as follows.

Remove the legs and claws and crack the claws. Cut the lobster in half crosswise, between the tail and the carapace. Cut the carapace in two lengthwise. Discard the sac. Cut across the tail in thick slices through the shell. Remove the trail, wash the lobster pieces and cook with the rice.

Raw prawns may also be cooked with the rice.

47 Cocido madrileno   Pork with chick peas   *4 portions*

100 g	4 oz	garlic sausage or Spanish chorizo
50 g	2 oz	smoked bacon
400 g	1 lb	loin of pork
100 g	4 oz	chick peas (dried)
100 g	4 oz	potato ⎫ large brunoise
100 g	4 oz	carrot ⎭
100 g	4 oz	finely chopped onion
		seasoning

1 Cut the sausage into 1 cm (½ in.) dice, the bacon into lardons and the boned loin of pork into 2 cm (1 in.) dice.
2 Place the sausage, bacon and pork into a large saucepan, cover with water or white stock, and add the chick peas. Bring to the boil and skim.
3 Simmer gently for approx. 30 mins, then add the vegetables. Add more water or white stock if necessary, season well and simmer for another hour until the meat is very tender.
4 Traditionally the broth is served first, then the vegetables and meat.

Caribbean

48 Metagee   Saltfish with coconut and plantains

200 g	8 oz	saltfish pieces
400 g	1 lb	green plantains
100 g	4 oz	yam
100 g	4 oz	sweet potato
100 g	4 oz	shredded onion
100 g	4 oz	tomato, skinned deseeded, diced
		sprig of thyme
100 g	4 oz	desiccated coconut
250 ml	½ pt	white stock
		4 okra

green plantains, yam, sweet potato } peeled and cut into 1 cm (½ in.) dice

1 Soak the saltfish in cold water for approx. 30 mins.
2 Place the diced plantain, yam and sweet potato into a pan with the onion and tomato.
3 Sprinkle with thyme. Arrange pieces of saltfish on top. Sprinkle with desiccated coconut. Cover with white stock.
4 Top and tail the okra. Do not cut otherwise the starchy substance will be released. Place the okra in with the fish and vegetables.
5 Bring to the boil and simmer gently until the vegetables and fish are cooked.
6 Serve hot in a suitable dish, decorated with the okra on top.

Note When possible it is preferable to use coconut milk in place of white stock and desiccated coconut.

49 Rabbit with prunes   *4 portions*

1 × 1½ kg	3 lb	rabbit, cut into pieces
250 ml	½ pt	red wine
		bayleaf
		½ teaspn thyme
60 ml	⅛ pt	oil
100 g	4 oz	lardons of bacon
50 g	2 oz	plain flour
100 g	4 oz	finely chopped onion
		chopped parsley
100 g	4 oz	celery, cut in 1 cm (½ in.) dice
200 g	8 oz	stoned prunes, soaked in red wine
50 g	2 oz	tomato purée
60 ml	⅛ pt	dark rum

1 Marinade the pieces of rabbit in red wine, bayleaf and thyme for 24 hours.
2 Heat the oil in a sauté pan, fry off the lardons of bacon, drain and reserve.

3 Remove the rabbit from the marinade, dry well in a cloth and dust with seasoned flour.
4 Sauté the rabbit in the sauté pan using the same oil in which the lardons were cooked until lightly browned on all sides. Remove and set aside.
5 Sauté the onions until lightly browned.
6 Place the pieces of rabbit in a suitable braising pan, add the marinade, chopped parsley, celery, the prunes and the wine in which they have been soaked, tomato purée and seasoning.
7 Bring to the boil, cover with a lid and cook in a moderate oven (180°C, 350°F, Reg. 4) for approx. 1½–2 hours until the rabbit is tender.
8 Correct the seasoning and consistency. Stir in the rum.
9 Serve in a suitable earthenware dish, sprinkled with parsley.

50 Almond chicken   *4 portions*

60 ml	⅛ pt	peanut oil
		4 suprêmes of chicken, thinly sliced
100 g	4 oz	finely chopped onion
25 g	1 oz	chopped chives
100 g	4 oz	cucumber ⎫ cut in paysanne
100 g	4 oz	carrot ⎭
200 g	8 oz	water chestnuts, sliced
50 g	2 oz	bamboo shoots, sliced
100 g	4 oz	mushrooms, finely sliced
60 ml	⅛ pt	soy sauce
100 g	4 oz	whole blanched almonds
50 g	2 oz	butter, margarine or oil

1 Heat the peanut oil in a sauté pan or wok, season and stir-fry the chicken over a fierce heat for approx. 2–3 mins.
2 Add the onion, chives, cucumber, carrot, water chestnuts, bamboo shoots and mushrooms, and season.
3 Continue to stir-fry over a fierce heat for approx. 5 mins.
4 Add the soy sauce, cook for further 1 min.
5 Meanwhile sauté the almonds in a little butter, margarine or oil until golden brown.
6 Place the chicken and vegetables into a suitable dish for serving and garnish with the almonds.
7 Serve with a braised or pilaff rice.

United States of America

51 Chilli con carne   Beef with beans in chilli sauce   *4 portions*

Originally from Texas and Mexico, chilli con carne is now eaten throughout the United States.

200 g	8 oz	dried kidney beans or pinto beans
400 g	1 lb	lean topside of beef
60 ml	⅛ pt	sunflower oil
100 g	4 oz	finely chopped onions
		2 cloves crushed and chopped garlic
		2 teaspns of chilli powder
		1 teaspn oregano
		½ teaspn ground cumin
50 g	2 oz	tomato puree
200 g	8 oz	tomatoes, skinned, deseeded, diced
500 ml	1 pt	white or brown stock

1 Soak the beans in cold water for 24 hours. Drain, cover with cold water and bring to the boil. Boil for 10 mins then gently simmer until tender.
2 Prepare the beef by removing all the excess fat and cutting into batons 5 cm (2 in.) long × ½ cm (¼ in.) wide or mincing.
3 Heat a little of the oil in a frying pan and quickly fry the beef until golden brown.
4 Drain the beef, place in a suitable saucepan.
5 Add a little more oil to the frying pan, add the onions and garlic and quickly fry until a light golden colour.
6 Stir in the chilli powder, oregano and cumin and cook for a further 3 mins. Add to the beef.
7 Stir in the tomato purée, tomatoes and seasoning, and cover with white or brown stock.
8 Gently cook by simmering on the stove or cover and cook in a moderate oven (180°C, 350°, Reg. 4) for approx. 1½–2 hours.
9 Check constantly to make sure that meat does not become too dry. Add a little more stock or water if necessary.
10 When the beans are cooked, drain and add to the cooked beef.
11 Serve in an earthenware dish sprinkled with chopped parsley.

Note This dish must be quite moist, the consistency of a stew.
Chilli powders and chilli seasonings vary in strength, therefore the amount used may be varied.

52 Hash brown potatoes   Grated potatoes fried with bacon

4 portions

600 g	1½ lb	potatoes
25 g	1 oz	butter or margarine
100 g	4 oz	lardons of bacon
		seasoning

1 Wash, peel and rewash the potatoes.
2 Coarsely grate the potatoes, rewash quickly and then drain well.

3 Melt the butter in a suitable frying pan. Add the lardons of bacon, fry until crisp and brown, remove from the pan and drain.
4 Pour the fat back into the frying pan, add the grated potato and season.
5 Press down well, allow 2 cm (1 in.) thickness, and cook over a heat for approx. 10–15 mins or in a moderate oven (190°C, 375°F, Reg. 5) until a brown crust forms on the bottom.
6 Turn out onto a suitable serving dish and sprinkle with the lardons of bacon and chopped parsley.

53 Clam chowder   *4 portions*

A chowder is usually an unpassed shellfish soup. It originated in the USA where there are many regional variations. Clams, oysters, scallops and fresh or frozen crabs may be used.

100 g	4 oz	belly of pork, chopped
150 g	6 oz	potatoes
50 g	2 oz	leek
50 g	2 oz	celery
50 g	2 oz	butter or margarine
1 litre	2 pt	fish stock (or chicken stock)
200 g	8 oz	diced clams, fresh or frozen
		salt, pepper
		bouquet garni
100 g	4 oz	tomatoes, skinned, deseeded, diced
125 ml	¼ pt	cream
		chopped parsley
		4 cracker biscuits

1 Sweat the pork, potatoes, leek and celery in the butter without colour.
2 Add the stock and clams, season, add the bouquet garni, bring to the boil and simmer for 45 mins.
3 Add the tomatoes and simmer for a few mins.
4 Correct the seasoning, add the cream and chopped parsley. Crushed cracker biscuits may be added just before serving or served separately.

Note Garlic, bay leaf and thyme may also be added and small pieces of crisply fried bacon served separately.

54 Succotash Lima beans, sweetcorn and bacon in cream sauce

4 portions

50 g	2 oz	lardons of bacon
25 g	1 oz	butter or margarine
350 g	14 oz	lima beans, cooked
150 g	6 oz	sweetcorn, cooked
125 ml	¼ pt	cream sauce
		seasoning
60 ml	⅛ pt	single cream (or yoghurt)

1 Quickly fry the lardons of bacon in the fat.
2 Add the drained lima beans and sweetcorn.
3 Bind with cream sauce, correct the seasoning and finish with cream.
4 Serve in a suitable dish sprinkled with chopped parsley.

Note Lima beans are more commonly known as butter beans.

55 Carrot cake

		4 eggs
200 g	8 oz	castor sugar
375 ml	¾ pt	vegetable oil
200 g	8 oz	soft flour
10 g	½ oz	baking powder
10 g	½ oz	bicarbonate of soda
		pinch of salt
5 g	¼ oz	ground cinnamon
250 g	10 oz	carrots, grated
50 g	2 oz	walnuts, finely chopped
50 g	2 oz	currants
50 g	2 oz	breadcrumbs (white or brown)

1 Place eggs and sugar into a mixing bowl and whisk until ribbon stage is reached.
2 Gradually add the oil (this is best done on a machine using full speed).
3 Slowly add the sieved flour, baking powder, soda, salt and cinnamon.
4 Add the carrots, walnuts, currants and breadcrumbs.
5 Place into a greased 20 cm (8 in.) round or 400 g (1 lb) loaf tin and cook at (190°C, 375°F, Reg. 5) for approx. 20 mins.

56 Chocolate brownies

100 g	4 oz	butter or margarine
50 g	2 oz	cocoa powder
		2 eggs
200 g	8 oz	castor sugar
50 g	2 oz	self-raising flour
		vanilla essence
100 g	4 oz	chopped walnuts
50 g	2 oz	raisins

1 Melt the butter or margarine, stir in the cocoa powder and remove from heat.
2 Beat the eggs and sugar together until light and white and add the butter and cocoa powder mixture.
3 Add the sieved flour and mix well.
4 Add vanilla essence, walnuts and raisins.
5 Place this mixture into a greased and lined 20 cm (8 in.) square shallow cake tin. Bake at 180°C (350°F, Reg. 4) for approx. 30 mins.

(Contd.)

6 Remove from oven and allow to cool. Cut into approx. 2 cm (1 in.) squares to serve.

57   Pecan pie   *4 portions*

150 g	6 oz	sweet pastry
		3 eggs
200 g	8 oz	soft brown sugar
		vanilla essence
		pinch of salt
75 g	3 oz	melted butter or margarine
		6 tablespoons treacle syrup
200 g	8 oz	coarsely chopped pecan nuts

1 Line an 18–20 cm (7–8 in.) flan ring with the sweet pastry and partly bake blind.
2 Prepare the filling from the remaining ingredients. Lightly heat the eggs and sugar together with the vanilla essence and salt.
3 Stir in the melted butter or margarine and syrup, and add the chopped pecan nuts.
4 Pour this mixture into the flan case and decorate with pecan halves.
5 Bake in a moderately hot oven (180°C, 350°F, Reg. 4) for approx. 30–35 mins until the filling is set. Cover with aluminium foil if the pastry starts to get too dark.
6 Serve with cream, ice-cream or yoghurt.

58   Pumpkin pie   *4 portions*

200 g	8 oz	short pastry
500 ml	1 pt	pumpkin purée, to include 2–3 tablespns apricot purée and juice of 1 lemon
50 g	2 oz	flour
100 g	4 oz	castor sugar
		3 eggs
		pinch of cinnamon
		pinch ground ginger
		pinch of grated nutmeg
170 ml	⅓ pt	milk
50 g	2 oz	butter or margarine, melted

1 Line a 20 cm (8 in.) flan ring with the short pastry.
2 Sieve or liquidise the pumpkin purée and place into a mixing basin.
3 Add the flour, sugar, eggs and spices and mix well. Finally add the milk and melted butter.
4 Mix well and pour into the prepared flan case. Bake at approx. 200°C (400°F, Reg. 6) until the pastry is cooked and golden brown, approx. 40–50 mins, reducing the temperature if necessary.
5 Sprinkle the pie with icing sugar to serve.

Kosher foods

Kosher is a Jewish word meaning 'pure' or 'clean', according to the Jewish religious ordinances or rules.

Kosher foods are governed by the dietary laws which are set out in Leviticus XI, the Third Book of Moses in the Old Testament. These laws state the approved and prohibited foods, for example, that meat and poultry must be slaughtered and processed for human consumption according to the law. All permitted meat or other food is labelled *kosher*.

The laws also govern the way certain foods are stored, the kitchen and its equipment and the cook's personal knives. Knives in use for general catering may not be used for kosher catering.

The supervision of these laws is carried out by a representative of the synagogue, appointed by the rabbi.

59 Potato latkes   *4 portions*

400 g	1 lb	potatoes, washed, peeled and grated
50 g	2 oz	finely chopped onion
		salt and pepper
		1 egg
		1 tablespn plain flour or breadcrumbs

1 Wash the grated potatoes, drain well and mix in a basin with the finely chopped onion.
2 Season with salt and pepper and add the beaten egg, flour or breadcrumbs and season.
3 Heat a little oil in a shallow pan and place potato mixture in 50 g (2 oz) pieces in the pan.
4 Cook on both sides for 3–4 mins until golden brown, serve immediately.

Note A little grated carrot or courgette may be added to the potato.

60 Koenigsberger klops   Meat balls

A reception snack *or* main course.

75 g	3 oz	bread, white or wholemeal
		1 egg
200 g	8 oz	minced beef
200 g	8 oz	minced veal
50 g	2 oz	chopped onion
		salt and pepper
		chopped parsley
		¼ teaspn paprika

		½ teaspn grated lemon rind
		juice of ½ lemon
		1 teaspn Worcester sauce
1 litre	2 pt	brown vegetable stock
		cornflour or arrowroot
		tomato purée
25 g	1 oz	capers
25 g	1 oz	gherkins

1 Remove crusts from bread and soak the bread in water.
2 Mix together the beaten egg and meat.
3 Sweat the chopped onion in a little oil until soft, then allow to cool and add to the meat.
4 Season with salt and pepper and add the chopped parsley.
5 Squeeze out excess water from the bread, add to the meat.
6 Add paprika, lemon rind and juice, and Worcester sauce, and mix well.
7 Form into 18 g (¾ oz) balls for a reception snack or 75 g (3 oz) balls for a main course – 2 per portion.
8 Cook in boiling vegetable stock, cover and simmer until cooked. Remove when cooked and keep warm.
9 Boil the remaining stock, lightly thicken with arrowroot or cornflour and colour slightly by adding a little tomato purée.
10 Season with salt and pepper and add the chopped capers and gherkins.
11 Reheat the meat balls in the gravy. Serve the small balls with cocktail sticks.

61 Chollo bread   Plaited Jewish bread   *2 loaves*

56 g	2¼ oz	butter or margarine
500 g	1¼ lb	strong flour
18 g	¾ oz	castor sugar
		1 teaspn salt
63 g	2½ oz	egg
25 g	1 oz	yeast
185 ml	8 fl oz	tepid water (@ 26°C/80°F)

1 Rub the butter or margarine into the sieved flour in a suitable basin.
2 Mix the sugar, salt and egg together.
3 Disperse the yeast in the water.
4 Add all these ingredients to the sieved flour and mix well to develop the dough. Cover with a damp cloth or plastic and allow it to ferment for about 45 mins.
5 Divide into 125–150 g (5–6 oz) strands and begin to plait.

For 4-strand plait	*5-strand plait*
2 over 3	2 over 3
4 over 2	5 over 2
1 over 3	1 over 3

6 After moulding place on a lightly greased baking sheet and egg wash lightly.
7 Prove in a little steam until double in size. Egg wash again lightly and decorate with maw seeds.
8 Bake in a hot oven, at 220°C (425°F, Reg. 7) for approx. 25–30 mins.

62 Matzo fritters

4 portions

		3 matzos (wafers of unleavened bread)
250 ml	½ pt	milk
		2 eggs, separated
150 g	6 oz	matzo meal
100 g	4 oz	brown sugar
		salt
		cinnamon
60 ml	⅛ pt	vegetable oil

1 Sprinkle warm water over the matzos. Place on a baking sheet and dry in a hot oven for 1 min.
2 In a suitable basin beat the milk and egg yolks together, add the matzo meal, sugar, salt and cinnamon.
3 Fold in the stiffly beaten egg whites.
4 Spread this mixture on one side of each matzo. Fry in hot oil on the batter side until brown.
5 Spread batter on other side and fry again until brown.
6 Serve hot, sprinkled with sugar.

63 Blitz kuchen   Baked fluffy batter with nuts and cinnamon

4 portions

200 g	8 oz	cake flour
10 g	½ oz	baking powder
100 g	4 oz	butter or margarine
100 g	4 oz	castor sugar
		4 eggs, separated
		grated rind of 1 lemon
60 ml	⅛ pt	milk
		1 egg white, diluted with 1 tablespn water
100 g	4 oz	chopped mixed nuts
		cinnamon

1 Sieve flour and baking powder into a suitable bowl.
2 Cream butter and sugar together until light and white.
3 Gradually add the egg yolks to the butter and sugar, beating continuously. Add the lemon rind.
4 Gradually add the flour, beating well, then add the milk. Cream well. (Add a little more milk if necessary.)

5 Beat 4 egg whites until full peak.
6 Gently fold egg whites into the batter.
7 Heat a lightly oiled 20 cm (8 inch) frying pan, suitable for placing in the oven. Pour in sufficient batter to cover the surface and spread with diluted egg white.
8 Sprinkle liberally with castor sugar, cinnamon and chopped mixed nuts.
9 Bake in a moderate oven at 190°C (375°F, Reg. 5) approx. 20 mins. Serve hot or cold.

64   Carrot kugel   *4 portions*

		4 eggs, separated
75 g	3 oz	castor sugar
225 g	9 oz	carrots, finely grated
75 g	3 oz	cooking apple, finely grated
		grated rind and juice of 1 orange
		1 teaspn lemon juice
50 g	2 oz	potato flour or cornflour
25 g	1 oz	butter or margarine

1 Place egg yolks into a suitable basin and beat with sugar until ribbon stage.
2 Squeeze out excess liquid from the carrots and apple.
3 Add this to the egg yolks and sugar with the orange rind and juice, then add the lemon juice, potato flour or cornflour and mix well.
4 Beat egg whites until full peak and fold into carrot mixture.
5 Use butter or margarine to well grease a 4-portion soufflé dish and fill it with the kugel mixture.
6 Bake in an oven at 190°C (375°F, Reg. 5) for approximately 30 mins until golden brown. Serve immediately.

12

Vegetarian dishes

See also

1   White vegetable stock   *(1 litre, 2 pts)*

100 g	4 oz	onion ⎫
100 g	4 oz	carrots ⎬ mirepoix
100 g	4 oz	celery ⎪
100 g	4 oz	leeks ⎭
1 ½ litres	3 pt	water

Place all the ingredients into a saucepan, bring to the boil and allow to simmer for approx. 1 hour, skim if necessary. Strain and use.

2   Brown vegetable stock   *(1 litre, 2 pts)*

100 g	4 oz	onions ⎫
100 g	4 oz	carrots ⎬ mirepoix
100 g	4 oz	celery ⎪
100 g	4 oz	leeks ⎭
60 ml	⅛ pt	sunflower oil
		2 oz tomatoes
		2 oz mushroom trimmings
		6 peppercorns
1 ½ litres	3 pts	water
5 g	¼ oz	yeast extract

1 Fry the mirepoix in the oil until golden brown.
2 Drain and place into a suitable saucepan. Add all the other ingredients except the yeast extract.
3 Cover with the water, bring to the boil.
4 Add the yeast extract, simmer gently for approx. 1 hour. Then skim if necessary and use.

3   Indian bean pâté   *4 portions*

		4 tablespns sunflower oil
50 g	2 oz	finely chopped onion
		1 garlic clove, crushed
		1 teaspn ground coriander

		½ teaspn black mustard seeds
		1 finely chopped chilli
10 g	½ oz	grated root ginger
10 g	½ oz	garam masala
100 g	4 oz	cooked brown beans or haricot beans
25 g	1 oz	tomato purée
		juice of 1 lime
		seasoning

1 Place the sunflower oil into a suitable pan and sweat the onion and garlic until soft but without colour.
2 Add the spices and garam masala, sweat together for 2–3 mins.
3 Add the beans, stir well, place in a food processor.
4 Add tomato purée and lime juice. Season. Blend to a smooth purée.
5 Place mixture in a basin, cover with greaseproof paper and allow to stand in refrigerator for 3–4 hours for flavour to develop.
6 Place pâté into individual containers. Decorate with segments of orange and serve separately a dish of chopped banana in lime juice bound with natural yoghurt.

4 Tofu pâté with raw vegetables   *4 portions*

		1 small cauliflower, in bite-sized florets
		1 small head celery ⎫
		2 large carrots ⎭ cut into batons
100 g	4 oz	sunflower seeds
275 g	10 oz	tofu
15 ml		1 tablespn sunflower oil
75 g	3 oz	wheatgerm
100 g	4 oz	finely grated carrot
		seasoning
10 g	½ oz	dill weed
5 g	¼ oz	paprika

(pâté)

1 Prepare and wash the vegetables.
2 Grind half of the sunflower seeds into a fine powder.
3 Add tofu, sunflower oil, wheatgerm and liquidise until smooth.
4 Place into a basin and add grated carrot, remaining whole sunflower seeds, seasoning, chopped dill and paprika.
5 Place into a suitable serving dish, surrounded by the raw vegetables.

Note Tofu is a bean curd available in 3 types:
a) Silken – soft like junket.
b) Firm – like firm cheese.
c) Soft – between silken and tofu.

5   Vegetarian terrine

300 g	12 oz	fresh washed spinach
		salt and pepper
		1 teaspn ground allspice
25 g	1 oz	chopped chives
400 g	1 lb	carrots } washed and peeled
400 g	1 lb	celeriac }
375 ml	¾ pt	choux pastry (see recipe 28, page 275)
190 ml	⅜ pt	double cream or créme fraîche

1 Cook, refresh and drain spinach, purée in food processor and season with salt, pepper, allspice and chopped chives.
2 Cut carrots and celeriac into even pieces, cook and purée separately.
3 To each purée add 125 ml (¼ pt) of choux pastry and 60 ml (1/8 pt) of double cream. Mix well.
4 Take a large well greased loaf tin, preferably aluminium foil (disposable).
5 Layer carrot purée over the base. Next layer with celeriac and finish with the spinach.
6 Cover with foil. Cook in a bain-marie in the oven at 180°C (350°F, Reg. 4) approx. 1¼ hours.
7 Remove from oven, cool and serve cold, sliced with a suitable sauce, e.g. Green peppercorn and paprika (see below).

Green peppercorn and paprika sauce

200 g	8 oz	plum tomatoes
25 g	1 oz	green peppercorns (crushed)
12 g	½ oz	paprika
250 ml	½ pt	double cream or unsweetened vegetable creamer
		juice of ½ lemon

1 Purée the plum tomatoes, place in a suitable pan with the peppercorns and bring to the boil. Simmer for 5 mins.
2 Add paprika, simmer for a further 5 mins.
3 Finish with cream, bring back to boil. (If using unsweetened vegetable creamer check if product is heat-stable.)
4 Add lemon juice, pass through a fine strainer, cool and serve chilled.

6   Stuffed avocado pears garnished with asparagus

4 portions

		2 ripe avocado pears
		juice of 1 lemon
50 g	2 oz	butter or margarine
25 g	1 oz	finely chopped onion
50 g	2 oz	tomato, skinned, deseeded, diced
50 g	2 oz	chopped mushrooms

100 g	4 oz	chopped hazelnuts
100 g	4 oz	grated cheddar cheese
		seasoning
30 ml	⅛ pt	dry sherry or white wine
		12 cooked asparagus tips
250 ml	½ pt	cheese sauce

1 Cut the avocado pears in half, remove stones and skin, taking particular care that they do not break up.
2 Place on a suitable lightly greased tray and brush all over with lemon juice.
3 Heat the butter or margarine in a small sauté pan, add the finely chopped onion and sweat without colour.
4 Add the tomato and mushrooms and sweat also. Remove from heat.
5 Add the chopped hazelnuts and grated cheddar cheese, season with salt and pepper. Mix in the sherry or white wine.
6 Fill the avocado pears with this mixture, garnish with asparagus tips and mask with cheese sauce.
7 Place avocado pears in the oven and glaze slowly until golden brown, serve immediately.

Note To hold the avocado pears in shape they may be placed in china avocado pear dishes, filled and then glazed.
  With imagination, avocado pears may be served hot with a variety of fillings for vegetarians. For example:
  Spinach and mushrooms in a yoghurt, cream or cheese sauce
  Carrot purée flavoured with fresh ginger
  Stir-fry vegetables cut small
  Pilaff rice with chopped dates, nuts and peppers
  Small pasta shells in a light cream sauce using fromage frais
Remember that for healthy eating – cheese sauce may be made with wholemeal flour, sunflower oil and skimmed milk, natural yoghurt, or fromage frais.

7 Carrot and ginger soufflé   *4 portions*

50 g	2 oz	grated parmesan cheese
300 g	12 oz	carrots
		seasoning
125 ml	¼ pt	béchamel sauce
25 g	1 oz	root ginger (grated)
		3 egg yolks
		4 egg whites

1 Well grease a 4-portion soufflé dish and sprinkle with grated parmesan.
2 Peel the carrots, cut into regular-sized pieces and place into a saucepan. Cover with water, bring to the boil and simmer until tender.
3 Drain, purée, place into a suitable basin and season.

4 Add remainder of cheese. Bind with the béchamel sauce. Mix well.
5 Add grated ginger, allow to cool. Add the egg yolks, mix well.
6 Whisk egg whites to soft peak, beat one-third of the whites into the carrot purée, then carefully fold in the remainder.
7 Pour into the soufflé mould, clean the edges.
8 Bake in a pre-heated oven at 200°C (400°F, Reg. 6) for approx. 20–25 mins. Serve with a suitable sauce e.g. broccoli, asparagus.

Note Alternatively this soufflé may be served in individual soufflé dishes.

8 Almond and polenta roast   *4 portions*

100 g	4 oz	finely chopped onions
60 ml	⅛ pt	sunflower oil
75 g	3 oz	polenta (corn meal)
125 ml	¼ pt	water
150 g	6 oz	ground almonds
5 g	¼ oz	yeast extract
		seasoning
		pinch of dried sage
		1 egg

1 Gently fry the onions in the oil until golden brown.
2 Add polenta and water, bring to boil and cook for 5 mins, stirring continuously.
3 Cool slightly, add the remainder of the ingredients and mix well.
4 Place into a well-greased ovenproof dish, bake in a preheated oven at 190°C (375°F, Reg. 5) for 30–40 mins. approx. Serve with a suitable sauce, e.g. tomato, broccoli (see below).

Broccoli sauce   (*½ litre (1 pint) approx.*)

200 g	8 oz	cooked broccoli
40 g	1½ oz	sunflower seeds
125 ml	¼ pt	smetana or silken tofu
		juice of ½ lemon
		seasoning

1 Place the broccoli, sunflower seeds and approx. 250 ml (½ pint) water into a liquidiser with the smetana and lemon juice. Liquidise until smooth.
2 Strain through a coarse strainer into a small saucepan. Correct seasoning and consistency.
3 Heat *very* gently before serving. *Do not boil.*

9 Brazil nut roast in pastry

100 g	4 oz	chick peas, soaked for 24 hours
5 g	¼ oz	yeast extract
100 g	4 oz	brazil nuts
100 g	4 oz	wholemeal breadcrumbs
25 g	1 oz	butter or margarine
50 g	2 oz	finely chopped onion
		1 clove of garlic, crushed and chopped
150 g	6 oz	button mushrooms
5 g	¼ oz	mixed herbs
		seasoning
		1 egg, beaten
200 g	8 oz	brioche pastry, recipe 57 page 289

1 Drain the chick peas, cover with fresh cold water, bring to the boil and gently simmer until tender.
2 Drain the chick peas when cooked, place into a clean basin and mix in the yeast extract.
3 Chop the brazil nuts in a food processor, mix in with the chick peas, add the breadcrumbs and mix well.
4 Heat the fat in a small sauté pan, sweat the onion and the garlic without colour, add the mushrooms and cook for a few mins then mix with the other ingredients.
5 Add mixed herbs and season, then bind with the egg.
6 Line a well greased 400 g (1 lb) bread tin with brioche pastry.
7 Fill with the chick pea and nut mixture. Lightly egg wash the top and cover with brioche. Make a small hole in the centre.
8 Allow to prove.
9 Bake in a moderately hot oven (200°C, 400°F, Reg. 6) for approx. 10 mins. Turn the oven down to approx. 180°C (350°F, Reg. 4) and bake for a further 30 mins. approx. If the top of the brioche colours too much cover with either a sheet of wetted greaseproof or aluminium foil.
10 When cooked, allow to cool slightly and serve sliced or on individual plates with tomato, asparagus or broccoli sauce (see below and page 220).

Note For healthy eating, the brioche paste may be made from 25%, 50% or 95% wholemeal flour, using hardened sunflower margarine.

Asparagus sauce

300 g	12 oz	cooked asparagus
125 ml	¼ pt	vegetable stock
125 ml	¼ pt	white wine
		seasoning
		4 tablespns smetana or double cream

1 Liquidise asparagus, stock and wine until a smooth sauce is obtained.
2 Gently bring to the boil.   (*Contd.*)

3 Strain through a coarse strainer into a clean saucepan. Season.
4 Add smetana or double cream. *Do not boil.*
5 Correct seasoning and consistency, use as required.

10   Gratin of nuts with a tomato and red wine sauce flavoured with basil
4 portions

100 g	4 oz	finely chopped onion
50 g	2 oz	green pepper, in brunoise
50 g	2 oz	celery, in brunoise
25 g	1 oz	butter or margarine
		2 cloves garlic, crushed and chopped
200 g	8 oz	cooked fresh or canned chestnuts
		or use
75 g	3 oz	dried chestnuts (well soaked then cooked in vegetable stock)
200 g	8 oz	cashew nuts
50 g	2 oz	walnuts
100 g	4 oz	cheddar cheese
60 ml	⅛ pt	red wine
60 ml	⅛ pt	brandy
10 g	½ oz	paprika
5 g	¼ oz	thyme (dried)
		1 egg

1 Sweat the onion, green pepper and celery in the butter or margarine without colour.
2 Add the garlic, continue to sweat for 1 min.
3 Add the finely chopped nuts and grated cheddar cheese, mix well.
4 Add the red wine, brandy and herbs, season well and bind with an egg.
5 Place mixture into a well-greased and silicone paper-lined 400 g (1 lb) loaf tin.
6 Cover with aluminium foil and bake at approx. 190°C (375°F, Reg. 5) for approx. 45 mins. (Alternatively, bake in a bain-marie in the oven.)
7 When cooked turn out and carefully portion into individual plates onto a red wine and tomato sauce with basil (see below). Decorate with fresh basil and a little tomato concassée.

Tomato and red wine sauce flavoured with basil

125 ml	¼ pt	fresh tomato coulis (page 33)
125 ml	¼ pt	red wine
		2 sprigs chopped basil
60 ml	⅛ pt	natural yoghurt or single cream
		seasoning

1 Bring the tomato coulis to the boil, add the red wine and chopped basil. Simmer for 2 mins.
2 Finished with natural yoghurt or single cream, and correct seasoning and consistency. Pass through a fine strainer if necessary before use.

11   Crown of brioche filled with leaf spinach, fennel and pine kernels
4 portions

150 g	6 oz	brioche pastry (recipe 57, page 289)
400 g	1 lb	leaf spinach
50 g	2 oz	margarine or butter
25 g	1 oz	finely chopped onion
		1 clove of crushed garlic
100 g	4 oz	julienne of fennel
250 ml	½ pt	velouté, made with vegetable stock
10 g	½ oz	English mustard
		seasoning
60 ml	⅛ pt	single cream or natural yoghurt
25 g	1 oz	pine kernels

1   Divide the brioche dough into 4, place into 4 well-greased individual savarin moulds, prove and bake in a moderately hot oven at 200°C (400°F, Reg. 6) for approx. 10 mins.
2   When cooked, remove from oven and unmould. Keep warm.
3   Blanch the spinach in boiling salted water, refresh and drain well. Squeeze lightly to remove excess water.
4   Add 1 g (½ oz) butter or margarine to a sauté pan, or sauteuse, and sweat the chopped onion and garlic without colour.
5   Separately sweat the julienne of fennel in the remaining butter or margarine, without colour.
6   Add the leaf spinach to the chopped onion and garlic, and allow to reheat through.
7   Bind with the vegetable velouté, add the diluted mustard and season well.
8   Add the fennel and mix gently. Finish with single cream or natural yoghurt.
9   Place the brioches on suitable plates and fill with the spinach and fennel mixture.
10   Sprinkle with lightly roasted pine kernels and serve.

Note Many variations to this basice recipe may be adopted. Different combinations of cooked vegetables may be used to fill the brioche, e.g. mushrooms, chiffonade of lettuce, salsify in tomato sauce or ratatouille.

12   Gratin of spinach, mushrooms, nuts and cheese
4 portions

This dish is prepared in 3 layers: a) spinach, b) mushrooms, c) cheese.

a)
600 g	1 ½ lb	leaf spinach, cooked and puréed
		3 tablespns fresh double or non-dairy cream

(Contd.)

50 g	2 oz	grated parmesan cheese
		3 egg yolks
		salt, pepper, grated nutmeg

b)

50 g	2 oz	sunflower margarine
150 g	6 oz	button mushrooms
		2 tablespns double or non-dairy cream
		seasoning

c)

150 g	6 oz	cottage cheese
50 g	2 oz	ground cashew nuts
50 g	2 oz	ground blanched almonds
25 g	1 oz	chopped chives
		seasoning
		4 egg whites

1 Mix together the spinach, cream, 25 g (1 oz) cheese, and add the egg yolks and seasoning.
2 Heat the sunflower margarine in a sauteuse, add the sliced mushrooms and sweat for 1–2 mins. Stir in the cream, season.
3 Mix cottage cheese with nuts and chives – season.
4 Place one-third of the spinach in the bottom of an 18 cm (7 in.) well-greased soufflé dish.
5 Place the mushrooms on top, followed by a second spinach layer.
6 Next place on the cottage cheese and finally the rest of the spinach.
7 Bake in a pre-heated oven at 180°C (350°F, Reg. 4) for approx. 15 mins. and remove.
8 Beat the 4 egg whites until full peak, season and carefully fold in remainder of the grated parmesan cheese.
9 Using a forcing bag and 1 cm (3/8 in.) star tube pipe on top of the layered mixture and cook for a further 10 mins. at 200°C (400°F, Reg. 6), then serve immediately.

13 Vegetable, bean and saffron risotto   *4 portions*

185 ml	⅜ pt	vegetable stock
5 g	¼ oz	saffron
50 g	2 oz	sunflower margarine
25 g	1 oz	chopped onion
50 g	2 oz	celery
100 g	4 oz	short-grain rice
		1 small cauliflower
		4 tablespns sunflower oil
		1 large aubergine
100 g	4 oz	cooked haricot beans
50 g	2 oz	cooked peas
50 g	2 oz	cooked French beans
250 ml	½ pt	tomato sauce made with sunflower margarine and vegetable stock
25 g	1 oz	grated parmesan cheese

1 Infuse the vegetable stock with saffron for approx. 5 mins. by simmering gently, whilst maintaining the 185 ml (3/8 pint).
2 Melt the margarine, add the onion and celery and cook without colour 2–3 mins. Add the rice.
3 Cook for a further 2–3 mins. Add the infused stock and season lightly. Cover with a lid and simmer on the side of the stove.
4 While rice is cooking prepare the rest of the vegetables. Cut the cauliflower into small florets, wash, blanch and refresh, quickly fry in the sunflower oil in a sauté pan. Add the aubergines cut into ½ cm (¼ in.) dice and fry with the cauliflower. Add the cooked haricot beans, peas and French beans.
5 Stir all the vegetables together and bind with tomato sauce.
6 When the risotto is cooked, serve in a suitable dish, make a well in the centre. Fill the centre with the vegetables and haricot beans in tomato sauce.
7 Sprinkle the edge of the risotto with grated parmesan cheese to serve.

14 Spaghetti with lentil bolognese   *4 portions*

300 g	12 oz	wholemeal spaghetti
150 g	6 oz	brown lentils
		4 tablespns sunflower oil
50 g	2 oz	finely chopped onion
		1 clove garlic, chopped
300 g	12 oz	diced mushrooms
5 g	¼ oz	dried mixed herbs
400 g	1 lb	tomatoes, skinned, deseeded, diced
25 g	1 oz	tomato purée
125 ml	¼ pt	vegetable stock
10 g	½ oz	yeast extract
25 g	1 oz	sunflower margarine
		seasoning
50 g	2 oz	grated parmesan cheese

1 Cook the spaghetti in boiling salted water, stirring occasionally, until *al dente*, refresh and drain.
2 Place the lentils in a saucepan of cold water, bring to the boil, skim and simmer until tender. Drain.
3 Heat the oil and sweat the onion and garlic until soft, for 4–5 mins.
4 Add the diced mushrooms and mixed herbs, cook for 5 mins.
5 Add the lentils, tomatoes and tomato purée.
6 Add vegetable stock, stir well and add yeast extract. The consistency of the sauce should be thick.
7 Reheat the spaghetti in sunflower margarine, season with salt, pepper and nutmeg.
8 Serve the spaghetti in a suitable dish, make a well in the centre and place in the bolognese sauce. Sprinkle with grated parmesan cheese.

15 Spinach and walnut ravioli   *4 portions*

200 g	8 oz	wholewheat flour
100 g	4 oz	strong flour
		2–3 eggs
		pinch of salt
		1 tablespn sunflower oil

} paste

100 g	4 oz	cooked spinach purée
50 g	2 oz	finely chopped onion
		2 sticks celery, finely chopped
150 g	6 oz	very finely chopped walnuts
5 g	¼ oz	freshly chopped basil
5 g	¼ oz	freshly chopped parsley
25 g	1 oz	tomato purée
		2 crushed chopped cloves of garlic
		seasoning
		egg wash

} filling

1 Sieve flour and salt. Make a well, add eggs and oil.
2 Knead to a smooth paste, adding a little more liquid if required.
3 Leave to rest for approx. 30 mins.
4 Mix all the filling ingredients together and season lightly.
5 Roll out paste to a very thin rectangle 30 cm x 45 cm (12 x 18 in.).
6 Cut in half and egg wash. Mark in 3 cm (1 in.) squares.
7 Place a teaspoon of filling on each square.
8 Carefully cover with the other half of the paste and seal, taking special care to avoid air pockets.
9 Mark each with the back of a plain cutter.
10 Cut in between each line of filling, down and across with a serrated pastry wheel.
11 Separate on a well floured tray and leave to dry for 30 mins.
12 Poach in boiling salted water until *al dente*, drain.
13 Place in an earthenware dish, covered with tomato or mushroom sauce (see below) and sprinkle with grated parmesan cheese.
14 Brown under the salamander and serve.

Piquant mushroom sauce

		4 tablespns sunflower oil
50 g	2 oz	finely chopped onions
200 g	8 oz	button mushrooms (sliced)
125 ml	¼ pt	apple juice
		4 tablespns red wine vinegar
10 g	½ oz	yeast extract
5 g	¼ oz	dried mixed herbs
		seasoning
5 g	¼ oz	arrowroot

1 Heat sunflower oil in suitable pan and fry onions lightly for 5 mins. until just brown. Add mushrooms, sweat for 2 mins.

2 Stir in the remaining ingredients, except the arrowroot, mix well.
3 Bring to the boil, simmer for 15 mins. Correct seasoning.
4 Dilute arrowroot with a little water, stir into sauce, mix well.
5 Correct consistency with apple juice. Simmer for 2 mins, use as required.

16   Tofu and vegetable flan with walnut sauce   *4 portions*

150 g	6 oz	shortcrust pastry
		4 tablespns sunflower oil
50 g	2 oz	carrots, diced
50 g	2 oz	sliced mushrooms
50 g	2 oz	celery, diced into ½ cm (¼ in.)
100 g	4 oz	broccoli florets, blanched and refreshed
3 g	⅛ oz	fresh chopped basil
3 g	⅛ oz	chopped dill weed
125 ml	¼ pt	skimmed milk
		1 egg
200 g	8 oz	tofu
		seasoning

1 Line an 18 cm (7 in.) flan ring with shortcrust pastry and bake blind for approx. 8 mins in a pre-heated oven at 180°C (350°F, Reg. 4).
2 Heat the sunflower oil in a sauté-pan, add the carrots, mushrooms and celery, gently cook for 5 mins without colouring.
3 Add the broccoli, cover and cook gently until just crisp, stirring frequently and adding a little water if the mixture begins to dry.
4 Sprinkle over the herbs. Cook for 1 min. Drain vegetables and allow to cool.
5 Warm the milk to blood heat. Whisk the egg and tofu in a basin, add seasoning then gradually incorporate milk. Whisk well.
6 Fill the flan case with the drained vegetables and add the tofu and milk mixture.
7 Bake for 20 mins. approx. at 180°C (350°F, Reg. 4). Serve with walnut sauce.

Walnut sauce *(approx. 500 ml (1 pt))*

100 g	4 oz	finely chopped onion
		1 clove garlic, chopped
50 g	2 oz	walnut oil
10 g	½ oz	brown sugar
25 g	1 oz	curry powder
		grated zest and juice of 1 lemon
25 g	1 oz	peanut butter
		1 teaspn soy sauce
25 g	1 oz	tomato purée
375 ml	¾ pt	vegetable stock
		seasoning
100 g	4 oz	very finely chopped walnuts
10 g	½ oz	arrowroot

1 Fry the onion and garlic in the walnut oil, add the sugar and cook to a golden brown colour.
2 Add the curry powder, cook for 2 mins.
3 Add zest and juice of lemon, peanut butter, soy sauce and tomato purée. Mix well.
4 Add vegetable stock, bring to boil, simmer for 2 mins, season.
5 Add chopped walnuts.
6 Dilute arrowroot with a little water and gradually stir into sauce. Bring back to the boil stirring continuously. Simmer for 5 mins.
7 Correct seasoning and consistency.

17   Puff pastry cases with vegetables in hollandaise sauce flavoured with horseradish
4 portions

150 g	6 oz	puff pastry
		egg wash
100 g	4 oz	mange-tout
		4 artichoke bottoms cooked in a blanc
100 g	4 oz	button mushrooms, washed and trimmed
		juice of ½ lemon
25 g	1 oz	butter or margarine
30 ml	⅛ pt	béchamel sauce
250 ml	½ pt	hollandaise sauce
25 g	1 oz	grated horseradish

1 Roll out pastry to 3 mm (1/8 in.) and cut out 8 x 8 cm (3 in.) ovals or rounds, using a fluted cutter.
2 Place 4 of the rounds or ovals on a lightly greased baking sheet.
3 With the 4 rounds or ovals proceed to another round or oval in the centre approx. 6 cm (2½ in.) in diameter.
4 Egg wash the first 4, press the second 4 tops lightly on top.
5 Egg wash the edges lightly and allow to relax for at least 20 mins.
6 Bake in a moderately hot oven 200°C (400°F, Reg. 6) for approx. 10–15 mins until golden brown.
7 Remove from oven, allow to cool slightly, then remove the soft centre part.
8 Blanch the mange-tout in boiling salted water, refresh and drain.
9 Cut the artichoke bottoms into quarters or eighths, according to size.
10 Cook the mushrooms in lemon juice and butter in a suitable pan.
11 When the mushrooms are cooked remove, add the béchamel to the pan and boil out.
12 To the béchamel add the grated horseradish, mange-tout, artichoke bottoms and mushrooms.
13 Carefully bind with the hollandaise sauce and use to fill the warmed puff pastry cases. Serve on individual plates, decorated with a cooked turned mushroom if desired.

Note With imagination many variations can be adopted using this basic theme. A combination of different vegetables may be used, for example: small pieces of turned cucumber, French beans, carrots, small turned or in batons, celery, cut into paysanne, wild mushrooms, oyster mushrooms, asparagus and small florets of broccoli.

For healthy eating the puff pastry may be made with 50% wholemeal flour. Béchamel sauce made with skimmed milk and sunflower oil, finished with natural yoghurt, or well-seasoned fromage frais, complements the vegetables well.

18 Leeks in pastry with mushroom duxelle *4 portions*

		4 medium leeks
50 g	2 oz	carrot ⎫
50 g	2 oz	onion ⎬ bed of roots
50 g	2 oz	celery ⎭
		seasoning
6 g	¼ oz	dried mixed herbs
750 ml	1½ pt	vegetable stock
25 g	1 oz	chopped shallot
100 g	4 oz	mushrooms, chopped
25 g	1 oz	wholemeal breadcrumbs
60 ml	⅛ pt	natural yoghurt
		puff pastry made with 30% wholemeal flour

1 Split and wash the leeks, blanch for 5 mins. and refresh.
2 Arrange on a bed of roots in an ovenproof pan or dish.
3 Season lightly, sprinkle with dried mixed herbs.
4 Add vegetable stock to come two-thirds way up the leeks and bring to the boil.
5 Cover with greased greaseproof paper and a lid.
6 Cook in a moderate oven 180°C (350°F, Reg. 4) for approx. ½–1 hr. until tender.
7 When cooked drain, fold leeks carefully into portions and allow to cool.
8 Meanwhile make a mushroom duxelle by sweating the shallot in a little oil without colour, add the mushrooms and sweat together.
9 Season, add breadcrumbs and finish with natural yoghurt. Allow to cool.
10 Roll out puff pastry ¼ cm (1/8 in.) thick and cut into rectangles the same length as the leeks.
11 Spread puff pastry with the duxelle mixture, leaving an edge of approx. ½ cm (¼ in.) all round the outside.
12 Place a leek on top and spread a little duxelle on the leek.
13 Egg wash the edges. Roll up pastry leaving the ends open, but making sure that the joints are well sealed.

(Contd.)

14 Brush with egg wash, allow to relax for 15 mins. Bake in a hot oven (200°C, 400°F, Reg. 6) for approx. 15 mins.
15 Serve on individual plates on a bed of red lentil sauce (see below).

Red lentil sauce

		1 large onion, finely chopped
		1 tablespn sunflower oil
500 ml	1 pt	vegetable stock
75 g	3 oz	red lentils
10 g	½ oz	yeast extract
		seasoning

1 Sweat onion in sunflower oil until tender, then add vegetable stock and washed lentils.
2 Bring to boil, simmer until tender and liquidise.
3 Add yeast extract, correct seasoning and consistency.
4 Pass through a coarse strainer and use as required.

19   Vegetarian Scotch eggs   *4 portions*

100 g	4 oz	finely chopped onion
		4 tablespns sunflower oil
3 g	⅛ oz	dried mixed herbs
50 g	2 oz	roasted chopped hazelnuts
50 g	2 oz	chopped brazil nuts
50 g	2 oz	ground almonds
50 g	2 oz	grated cheddar cheese
25 g	1 oz	tomato purée
		seasoning
		1–2 eggs, beaten
		4 hard-boiled eggs
		seasoned flour
		beaten egg(s) ⎫
		wholemeal breadcrumbs ⎬ coating
		oil for deep frying ⎭

1 Prepare the coating by sweating the onion in the oil, add mixed herbs, cook for 2 mins, allow to cool.
2 Place into a basin with the hazelnuts, brazil nuts, ground almonds, cheese and tomato purée and mix well.
3 Season. Bind with sufficient egg until a moulding consistency is obtained.
4 Dip the hard-boiled eggs into beaten egg and then press the nut mixture round to cover them completely.
5 Flour, egg and crumb the eggs.
6 Deep fry in hot oil, 190°C/375°F until crisp and golden brown and drain.
7 Serve hot with a sauceboat of tomato sauce separately. Alternatively serve cold in halves with salad.

Note It may be necessary, to retain shape, to pass the eggs through egg and breadcrumbs twice.

20 Lentil and mushrooms burgers with groundnut and sesame sauce

4 portions

200 g	8 oz	lentils
50 g	2 oz	finely chopped onion
		2 cloves of garlic, chopped
25 g	1 oz	sunflower margarine
400 g	1 lb	finely chopped mushrooms
75 g	3 oz	wholemeal breadcrumbs
		chopped-parsley
		1 egg
		seasoned flour for coating
		oil for shallow frying

1 Place the lentils in a saucepan of cold water. Bring to boil and simmer until cooked.
2 Sweat the onion and garlic in the margarine until soft. Add mushrooms.
3 Cook over a moderate heat approx. 15–20 mins until all the liquid has been evaporated and the mushrooms are in a thick purée.
4 Allow to cool and mix in the drained, cooked lentils.
5 Add breadcrumbs and parsley, bind with beaten egg and mix well.
6 If the mixture is too slack bind with a little more breadcrumbs. If too dry, add a little more beaten egg.
7 Mould into burgers on a floured board.
8 Pass through seasoned flour and quickly fry in a little hot oil, taking care that the burgers do not break up.
9 Alternatively, place on a lightly greased baking sheet, brush with oil and bake in a pre-heated oven at 180°C (350°F, Reg. 4) for approx. 20 mins, turning them over half way during cooking.
10 When cooked serve on individual plates on a bed of groundnut and sesame sauce (see below).

Groundnut and sesame sauce

100 g	4 oz	raisins
		2 tablespns tahini (sesame seed paste)
100 g	4 oz	peanut butter
		2 tablespns sesame oil
		2 tablespns red wine vinegar
		4 tablespns concentrated apple juice
		pinch of ground cinnamon
375 ml	¾ pt	water
		seasoning

1 Place the raisins in a saucepan of cold water. Bring to the boil. Refresh and drain.

2 Liquidise all ingredients together until a smooth sauce is obtained.
3 Correct seasoning and consistency. Pass through a coarse strainer and use as required.

Note Makes approx. 400 ml (1 pt) sauce.

21   Okra and courgettes in spiced lentil sauce   *4 portions*

400 g	1 lb	okra
400 g	1 lb	courgettes
200 g	8 oz	French beans
750 ml	1 ½ pt	spiced lentil sauce (see below)
		seasoning
50 g	2 oz	sunflower margarine

1 Trim the okra but leave whole, blanch and refresh.
2 Lightly peel courgettes, cut into ½ cm (¼ in.) dice, blanch and refresh.
3 Top and tail French beans, cut into 2 cm (1 in.) lozenges, blanch and refresh.
4 Heat the lentil sauce, correct seasoning and consistency.
5 Reheat the vegetables in the margarine.
6 Bind with the lentil sauce and serve in a suitable dish. Serve basmati rice and poppadoms separately.

Spiced lentil sauce

200 g	8 oz	red or green lentils
100 g	4 oz	shredded onion
100 g	4 oz	carrot
		1 bouquet garni
		1 whole fresh chilli
50 g	2 oz	grated root ginger
10 g	½ oz	turmeric
10 g	½ oz	mixed spice
5 g	¼ oz	ground coriander

1 Place the washed lentils in a saucepan, cover with cold water and bring to the boil.
2 Add the onion, carrot, bouquet garni, chilli and spices.
3 Simmer until tender and remove bouquet garni and chilli.
4 Purée in a liquidiser or food processor, correct consistency.

22   Oriental vegetable kebabs with herb sauce   *4 portions*

		1 small cauliflower
		1 red pepper
		1 green pepper
100 g	4 oz	button mushrooms
		4 small courgettes

```
              4 small tomatoes (very firm)
              2 sticks celery
              1 large aubergine
              1 large leek
125 ml   ¼ pt  sunflower oil    ⎫
250 ml   ½ pt  red wine         ⎬
5 g      ¼ oz  dried mixed herbs⎪ marinade
              4–8 bayleaves     ⎪
              seasoning         ⎭
```

1 Prepare the vegetables as follows: cut cauliflower into small florets; wash peppers, remove seeds and cut into 1½ cm–2 cm (¾–1 in) dice; wash button mushrooms, trim stalks; wash courgettes and cut into 1½–2 cm (¾–1 in.) sections; blanch and peel tomatoes; cut into quarters; trim and wash celery, cut into 1½ cm–2 cm (¾–1 in.); wash aubergine, cut in half then into 2 cm x 1 cm (1 x ½ in.) batons; split leeks, wash, cut into 2 cm (1 in.) lengths.
2 Marinade the vegetables in the sunflower oil, red wine and dried herbs, seasoning and bayleaves for approx. 2 hours. Turn occasionally.
3 Neatly arrange vegetables on skewers.
4 Place on a greased tray, brush with oil and grill under salamander for approx. 10–15 mins. turning occasionally.
5 The vegetables will have different textures, they should, however, be slightly firm. The cauliflower, courgettes, and leek may also be blanched and refreshed before marinading to achieve different textures.
6 Serve kebabs on a bed of pilaff rice garnished with cooked peas.
7 Separately serve a sauceboat of herb sauce made from the marinade (see below).

Herb sauce

```
375 ml   ¾ pt   marinade (from kebabs)
125 ml   ¼ pt   vegetable stock
10 g     ½ oz   yeast extract
50 g     2 oz   tomato purée
50 g     2 oz   finely chopped onion
                1 clove garlic, chopped
10 g     ½ oz   sunflower margarine
10 g     ½ oz   arrowroot
                seasoning
```

1 Place marinade, vegetable stock, yeast extract and tomato purée into a suitable saucepan and bring to boil.
2 Sweat the onion and garlic in the margarine for 2–3 mins without colour.
3 Add the marinade and stock liquid from stage 1. Bring to boil.
4 Dilute the arrowroot in a little cold water.
5 Stir the arrowroot into the liquid and bring back to boil, stirring continuously. Simmer for 2 mins, correct consistency. Season, strain and use as above.

13

Vegetables

See also Chapter 10 British dishes
Chapter 11 Ethnic recipes
Chapter 12 Vegetarian dishes

Introduction

As people are becoming more conscious of healthy eating, the serving of a variety of correctly cooked, colourful, attractively presented vegetables becomes increasingly important.

This can be achieved in a variety of ways: a small selection of vegetables served on a separate plate to the main course is popular when appropriate, as is the practice of placing dishes of vegetables on the table for customers to help themselves. There are also people who would welcome a small selection of vegetables served as a separate course.

As fast world-wide transport is now the norm, the more exotic vegetables – which were previously unknown – are now available and caterers should learn how to prepare, cook and serve them.

However, these should not replace but, rather, supplement freshly picked and cooked local produce, which will always be popular if correctly cooked, of good colour and attractively presented.

1 Artichokes with spinach and cheese sauce *Fonds d'artichauts florentine*

Prepared and cooked artichoke bottoms are filled with leaf spinach, coated with Mornay sauce, browned and served.

(Contd.)

Variations: other vegetables that can be substituted for spinach include asparagus points, cooked peas, and a mixture of peas and carrots; also, a duxelle-based stuffing with various additions, which may be finished either with Mornay sauce or au gratin.

2 Sautéed artichoke bottoms *Fonds d'artichauts sautées*

1 Remove the leaves and chokes from the artichokes.
2 Trim the bottoms and cut into slices.
3 Cook in a blanc, drain well then sauté in butter, margarine or oil until lightly browned.
4 Season lightly and serve sprinkled with chopped parsley.

Note Alternatively the artichoke bottoms may be fried from raw, but they must first be rubbed with lemon to prevent discoloration.

3 Aubergine soufflé   *4 portions*

		2 egg plants (aubergines)
250 ml	½ pt	approx. thick béchamel
50 g	2 oz	grated parmesan cheese
		3 eggs, separated
		salt and pepper

1 Cut egg plants in halves.
2 Slash the flesh criss-cross and deep fry for a few mins.
3 Drain well, scoop out the flesh and finely chop.
4 Lay the skins in a buttered gratin dish.
5 Mix the egg plant flesh with an equal quantity of béchamel.
6 Heat this mixture through, then mix in the cheese and yolks, and season.
7 Fold in the stiffly beaten whites.
8 Fill the skins with this mixture, bake at 230°C (450°F, Reg. 8) approx. 15 mins and serve immediately.

Note For extra lightness use 4 egg whites to 3 yolks.

4 Baby sweetcorn

These are cobs of corn which are harvested when very young. They are widely used in oriental cookery and are available from December to March.

Always select cobs that look fresh and are undamaged. Baby corns are removed from their protective husks, cooked for a few minutes in unsalted water and may then be served whole or cut in slices and coated with butter or margarine. Unlike fully grown sweetcorn, baby corn are not removed from the cob before eating – when cooked the vegetable is tender enough to eat whole.

Baby sweetcorns are used in stir-fry dishes, e.g. with chicken, crab or prawns etc., and may also be served cold with vinaigrette. Baby corn looks attractive when served as one of a selection of plated vegetables.

5 Bamboo shoots

These are the shoots of young edible bamboo, stripped of the tough outer brown skin, so that the insides are eaten. They have a texture similar to celery and a flavour rather like that of globe artichokes. They are also obtainable preserved in brine.

Methods of cooking: chopped bamboo shoots are used in a number of stir-fry dishes, meat and poultry casseroles and as a soup garnish. They can also be served hot with a hollandaise-type sauce or beurre blanc.

6 Bean sprouts

These are the tender young sprouts of the germinating soya or mung bean. As they are a highly perishable vegetable, it is best to select white, plump, crisp sprouts with a fresh appearance.

Methods of cooking: first, rinse well and drain, they may then be stir-fried and served as a vegetable, mixed in with other ingredients in stir-fry dishes, used in omelets and also served as a crisp salad item.

Bean sprouts are available all year round.

7 Stir-fried bean sprouts   *4 portions*

400 g   1 lb   bean sprouts
1 tablespn oil
4–6 spring onions, cut in 2 cm (1 in.) pieces
1 teaspn chopped ginger
2 teaspns soy sauce
salt

1 Trim the bean sprouts.
2 Heat the oil in a frying pan or wok and add the spring onions and ginger.
3 Fry for a few seconds, then add sprouts.
4 Stir continuously and add salt.
5 Keeping the sprouts crisp, add soy sauce and serve.

8   Bean sprout sauté   *4 portions*

		1 tablespn sunflower oil or butter or margarine
125 g	4 oz	bean sprouts, trimmed
		salt and pepper
125 g	4 oz	carrots
125 g	4 oz	courgettes } cut in coarse julienne
		2 spring onions

1 Heat the oil or butter in a frying pan, add bean sprouts and sauté for one minute.
2 Season, add carrots and spring onions, and sauté for one minute.
3 Add courgettes, sauté for one minute, correct seasoning and serve.

9   Broad beans with tomato and coriander   *4 portions*

300 g	12 oz	shelled broad beans
		1 tablespn oil or butter
		2 tomatoes, skinned, deseeded, diced
		salt and pepper
		1 tablespn freshly chopped coriander

1 Cook broad beans, keeping them slightly firm, and drain.
2 Heat the oil in a pan and add the tomatoes.
3 Add the broad beans and correct the seasoning.
4 Add the coriander and toss lightly to mix. Correct seasoning and serve.

10   Braised red cabbage with apples, red wine and
juniper   *Chou rouge a l'ardennaise*   *4 portions*

400 g	1 lb	red cabbage, shredded
		2 tablespns oil
200 g	8 oz	cooking apples, peeled, cored and diced
250 ml	½ pt	red wine
		salt and pepper
		12 juniper berries (optional)

1 Blanch and refresh the cabbage.
2 Heat the oil in a casserole, add the cabbage and apples, and stir.
3 Add the wine, seasoning and juniper berries.
4 Bring to the boil, cover and braise approx. 40–45 mins until tender.
5 If any liquid remains when cooked, continue cooking uncovered to evaporate the liquid.

11 Braised red cabbage with chestnuts *Chou rouge limousine*
4 portions

400 g	1 lb	red cabbage, shredded
250 g	10 oz	good beef stock
200 g	8 oz	shelled raw chestnuts, in pieces
		2 tablespns oil or pork dripping
		salt and pepper

1 Mix all ingredients, cover with buttered paper and a tight-fitting lid.
2 Braise in a covered pan (not aluminium or iron) until tender.

12 Cardoons

These are a long plant, similar to celery, with an aroma and flavour like that of the globe artichoke. Select cardoons with bright leaves, crisp stems and a fresh-looking appearance.

Method of cooking: remove leaves, stalks and tough parts and cut into small pieces; cook in acidulated water for approx. 30–40 minutes. Cardoons may be used as a plain vegetable, in other vegetable dishes or served raw as an appetiser.

13 Cardoons with onions and cheese *Cardoons florentine*
4 portions

400 g	1 lb	cardoons
		juice of 1 lemon
100 g	4 oz	finely sliced onion
25 g	1 oz	butter
		salt
50 g	2 oz	grated parmesan

1 Trim and wash the cardoons, rub with lemon juice and cut into 8 cm (3 in.) pieces.
2 Cook in salted lemon water for approx. 30 mins, drain.
3 Gently cook the onion in the butter until light brown.
4 Add the cardoons and a little of the cooking liquid and simmer gently until tender.
5 Correct seasoning and serve sprinkled with cheese.

14 Cardoon fritters
4 portions

400 g	1 lb	cardoons
		juice of 1 lemon
100 g	4 oz	chopped onion
60 ml	⅛ pt	vegetable oil
		juice of 1 lemon
		1 tablespn chopped parsley
		salt
		frying batter

marinade

1 Prepare and cook cardoons as in recipe 13, stages 1–2.
2 Drain well and place while hot in the marinade for 1 hour.
3 Drain and dry the cardoon pieces thoroughly.
4 Dip in the batter and deep fry at 185°C (360°F) until golden brown.
5 Serve with quarters of lemon.

15   Celery moulds   *Timbales de céleri*   *4 portions*

		1 head celery, braised
200 g	8 oz	dry celery purée (cooked)
60 ml	⅛ pt	thick béchamel
		2 egg yolks
		salt and pepper
		jus-lié, to serve

1 Butter 4 dariole moulds and line with strips of braised celery.
2 Thoroughly heat the celery purée, mix in béchamel and egg yolks, and correct seasoning. Use to fill the prepared moulds.
3 Poach in a bain-marie in a moderate oven (200°C, 400°F, Reg. 6) for approx. 1 hour, covered with buttered greaseproof paper or foil.
4 When cooked, allow to stand for a few minutes before turning out.
5 Serve with a cordon of jus-lié.

16   Chinese cabbage

A wide variety of Chinese cabbage – or Chinese leaves – is grown in China, but the one generally seen in Britain is similar in appearance to a large pale cos lettuce. It is crisp and delicate, with a faint cabbage flavour.
   Always select fresh looking, crisp cabbage.
   Method of cooking: the hard centre stems are removed from outer leaves and they can then be stir-fried, braised, boiled or steamed like cabbage. The inner leaves can be used for salads in place of lettuce.

17   Stir-fried Chinese cabbage   *4 portions*

25 g	1 oz	oil
600 g	1 ½ lb	Chinese leaves, roughly chopped
25 g	1 oz	soy sauce, optional
		salt
30 ml	1/16pt	chicken stock or water

1 Heat oil in a frying pan or wok, add leaves and stir fry for 3–4 mins.
2 Add remainder of ingredients and stir fry until leaves are cooked but still slightly crisp.

18   Spicy stir-fry Chinese cabbage

4 portions

25 g	1 oz	oil
25 g	1 oz	finely chopped ginger
		2 cloves garlic, finely chopped
5 g	¼ oz	curry powder
25 g	1 oz	soy sauce
10 g	½ oz	sugar
		2 tablespns stock or water
600 g	1 ½ lb	Chinese cabbage, chopped

1 Heat oil in a frying pan or wok, add ginger, garlic and curry powder, and toss for a few seconds.
2 Add soy sauce, sugar and stock, and bring to the boil.
3 Add the cabbage and boil for 5 mins, stirring occasionally, and serve at once.

19   Christophine

Christophine, also known as chow-chow, chayote, or vegetable pear, looks rather like a ridged green pear and is available in several varieties including white and green, spiny and smooth-skinned, rounded and ridged, or more or less pear-shaped. Christophines usually weigh between 150–250 g (6–8 oz), the inside flesh is firm and white with a flavour and texture resembling a combination of marrow and cucumber.

Christophines are peeled and the stones removed in preparation and they can be cooked in similar ways to courgettes. They are also suitable for being stuffed and braised.

20   Colcannon (1)

4 portions

This is an Irish dish for which there are many variations.

300 g	12 oz	cabbage, trimmed and washed
200 g	8 oz	peeled potatoes
100 g	4 oz	leeks
250 ml	½ pt	milk or single cream
		salt, pepper and nutmeg
25 g	1 oz	butter

1 Shred the cabbage, cook and drain well.
2 Cook and mash the potatoes.
3 Chop the leeks and simmer in the milk until tender.
4 Mix the leeks in with the potatoes, cabbage and seasoning.
5 Place in a serving dish, make a well in the centre, pour in the melted butter and serve.

21   Colcannon (2)   *4 portions*

An alternative recipe.

300 g	12 oz	cooked chopped cabbage, well drained
200 g	8 oz	dry mashed potato
100 g	4 oz	chopped leeks cooked in 25 g (1 oz) butter
		salt and pepper

1 Mix all ingredients.
2 Form into small cakes, allowing 2 per portion.
3 Lightly pass through flour, shake off all surplus.
4 Shallow fry in hot fat on both sides and serve.

22   Fennel gratinated   *Fenouil au gratin*   *4 portions*

		2 fennel bulbs
500 ml	1 pt	Mornay sauce
100 g	4 oz	chopped mushrooms ⎫
25 g	1 oz	chopped shallot ⎬ duxelle
25 g	1 oz	butter or oil ⎭
50 g	2 oz	grated cheese ⎫
25 g	1 oz	fresh breadcrumbs ⎬ mixed
50 g	2 oz	melted butter ⎭

1 Boil or steam fennel until tender, approx. 30–35 mins.
2 Drain, cut into 5 cm (2 in.) pieces.
3 Mix Mornay sauce with duxelle and place half in an ovenproof dish.
4 Add fennel and cover with remainder of the sauce.
5 Sprinkle with cheese, crumbs and melted butter.
6 Heat through and brown in a moderate oven.

23   Fennel in casserole   *4 portions*

2 fennel bulbs
2 tablespns oil
2 crushed cloves garlic
salt and pepper

1 Trim, wash and cook fennel in salted water, or steam, for 10 mins.
2 Drain and cut into 5 cm (2 in.) pieces.
3 Brown the garlic in the oil in a casserole.
4 Add the fennel, season, and add 2 tablespoons water or chicken stock.
5 Cook and braise until tender.

Note See page 169 for an alternative recipe.

24   French beans in cream sauce with garlic   *Haricots verts*
tourangelle   *4 portions*

400 g	1 lb	French beans
50 g	2 oz	butter or margarine
		1 crushed clove garlic
		salt and pepper
250 ml	½ pt	thin cream sauce

1 Prepare, blanch and drain the beans.
2 Melt the butter and sweat the garlic for 20 seconds.
3 Add the beans, season and sweat gently for 1–2 mins.
4 Add the cream sauce and simmer gently until tender.
5 Correct seasoning and consistency and serve.

25   Hop shoots

Only the young shoots of hops can be used as a vegetable, and they must
be fresh and green.
   Method of cooking: wash well, tie in bundles and cook in boiling salted
water for the minimum time until just tender. They can be served hot
with a hollandaise or butter-type sauce and cold with mayonnaise or
vinaigrette. They may also be used in egg dishes, e.g. omelets, scrambled
eggs.

26   Kohlrabi

This is a stem which swells to a turnip shape above the ground. When
grown under glass it is pale green in colour, when grown outdoors it is
purplish. Select kohlrabi with tops that are green, young and fresh. If the
globes are too large they may be woody and tough.
   Methods of cooking: trim off stems and leaves (which may be used for
soups), peel thickly at the root end, thinly at top end, wash and cut into
even-sized pieces. Young kohlrabi can be cooked whole. Simmer in well-
flavoured stock until tender. Kohlrabi may be served with cream sauce,
baked, or stuffed, and added to casseroles (meat and vegetarian) and stews.

27   Stuffed kohlrabi   *4 portions*

4 × 150–200 g	6–8 oz	kohlrabi, peeled
100 g	4 oz	finely chopped onion
50 g	2 oz	butter or oil
100 g	4 oz	chopped mushrooms
100 g	4 oz	chopped lean ham
100 g	4 oz	tomatoes, skinned, deseeded, diced
		salt, pepper and rosemary
		fresh breadcrumbs

1 Cook kohlrabi in salted water, drain.
2 Cut a slice from the top of each and hollow out centres with a spoon.
3 Cook onion in butter without colour.
4 Add mushrooms and cook 2–3 mins.
5 Add ham, tomatoes and season.
6 Cook 2–3 mins, correct seasoning. Adjust consistency with breadcrumbs if necessary.
7 Stuff kohlrabis, replace lids and brush with butter or oil. Heat through in a hot oven and serve.

28   Buttered leeks   *4 portions*

600 g	1 ½ lb	leeks, trimmed and washed
35 g	1 ½ oz	butter or oil
		salt and mill pepper

1 Slice leeks and sweat in the butter until soft.
2 Add 1 tablespoon water or stock and season.
3 Cover pan with a lid, simmer for 5 mins and serve.

29   Leeks in cream or yoghurt   *4 portions*

600 g	1 ½ lb	leeks, trimmed and washed
35 g	1 ½ oz	butter or oil
		salt, mill pepper and grated nutmeg
60 ml	⅛ pt	double cream or natural yoghurt

1 Chop leeks and sweat in butter until soft.
2 Season, stir in the cream or yoghurt, simmer 2–3 mins and serve.

30   Mooli

Mooli or white radish – or rettiche as it is sometimes known – is a parsnip-shaped member of the radish family and is available all year round. Mooli does not have a hot taste like radishes but is slightly bitter and is pleasant to eat cooked as a vegetable. Mooli should have smooth flesh, white in appearance and be a regular shape.

Mooli has a high water content which can be reduced before cooking or serving raw by peeling and slicing, sprinkling with salt and leaving to stand for 30 mins. Otherwise, the preparation is to wash well and grate, shred or slice before adding to salads or cooking as a vegetable.

Mooli may be used as a substitute for turnips.

31   Okra

Okra are also known as gumbo or ladies' fingers. The flavour is slightly bitter and mild. Select pods that are firm, bright green and fresh looking.

Methods of cooking: cut off the conical cap at the stalk end, scrape the skin lightly, using a small knife, to remove any surface fuzz and the tips, then wash well. Okra can be served as a plain vegetable, tossed in butter or with tomato sauce and may be prepared in a similar fashion to a ratatouille. Okra are also used in soups, stews, curries, pilaf rice and fried as fritters.

Okra contain a high proportion of sticky glue-like carbohydrate which, when they are used in stews, gives body to the dish.

32   Stewed okra   *4 portions*

400 g	1 lb	okra
25 g	1 oz	butter or oil
100 g	4 oz	finely chopped onion
		1 clove of finely chopped garlic
400 g	1 lb	tomatoes, skinned, deseeded, diced
		salt and mill pepper

1 Top and tail okra, clean, wash and drain.
2 Melt butter in a thick-based pan, add onions and cook gently without colour for 5 mins.
3 Add garlic and tomatoes, cover with a lid and simmer for 5 mins.
4 Add okra, season, reduce heat and cook gently on top of stove or in oven until okra is tender, approx. 15–20 mins, and serve.

33   Palm hearts

Palm hearts are the tender young shoots or buds of palm trees and are generally available tinned or bottled in brine. Fresh palm hearts have a bitter flavour and need to be blanched before being used.

Methods of cooking: palm hearts can be boiled, steamed or braised and are served hot or cold, usually cut in halves lengthwise. When hot they are accompanied by a hollandaise-type of sauce or beurre blanc, when cold by mayonnaise or a herb-flavoured vinaigrette.

34   Stewed palm hearts   *4 portions*

		1 tablespn oil
50 g	2 oz	lean cooked ham
25 g	1 oz	finely chopped garlic

200 g	8 oz	tomatoes, skinned, deseeded, diced
		1 tablespn tomato purée
25 g	1 oz	chopped onion or chives
5 g	¼ oz	chopped parsley
		salt and pepper
400 g	1 lb	tinned palm hearts

1 Heat oil in a thick-bottomed pan, add ham and garlic and cook without colour for 2–3 mins.
2 Add tomatoes, tomato purée, onion, parsley and seasoning.
3 Simmer gently until of a thickened consistency.
4 Add the palm hearts, mix in, simmer 3–5 mins and serve.

35   Peas and mushrooms in cream or yoghurt   *4 portions*

200 g	8 oz	shelled peas
100 g	4 oz	sliced button mushrooms
		1 tablespn oil or butter
50 ml	2 fl oz	cream or natural yoghurt
		salt and pepper

1 Cook peas with a sprig of mint and drain.
2 Cook mushrooms in the oil, and add the peas.
3 Mix in cream or natural yoghurt, correct seasoning and serve.

36   Scorzonera

Scorzonera, also known as black-skinned salsify or oyster plant, has a white flesh when skinned, with a slight flavour of asparagus and oysters. Select salsify with fresh looking leaves at the top.

Methods of cooking: wash well, boil or steam in the skin, then peel using a potato peeler and immediately place in a blanc to prevent discoloration. Cut into suitable length pieces and serve plain, with butter, with cream or as for any cauliflower recipe. If peeling salsify raw, immediately place into cold water and lemon juice and cook in a blanc to prevent discoloration. Salsify requires approx. 20–30 minutes cooking; test by pressing a piece between the fingers, if cooked it will crush easily.

37   Salsify sautéed in butter   *Salsifis sautés au beurre*

4 portions

400 g	1 lb	salsify, peeled and cooked in a blanc
50 g	2 oz	butter
		salt and pepper
		chopped parsley

1 Cut salsify in 8 cm (3 in.) pieces, dry well.
2 Heat butter in a pan until foaming.
3 Add salsify and sauté until lightly brown.
4 Season, finish with chopped parsley and serve.

Note A little chopped garlic may be mixed with the parsley if desired.

38 Salsify with onions *Salsifis lyonnaise*

Proceed as for previous recipe, adding 100 g (4 oz) finely sliced, lightly browned onion.

39 Salsify fritters *Beignets de salsifis*

Mix 400 g (1 lb) cooked salsify in 2 tablespoons olive oil, salt, pepper, chopped parsley and lemon juice, and leave for 30–45 mins. Dip in a light batter, deep fry to a golden brown and serve.

40 Salsify with onion, tomato and garlic *Salsifis portugaise*

4 portions

400 g	1 lb	salsify	
50 g	2 oz	margarine or butter	
50 g	2 oz	chopped onions	
		1 crushed and chopped clove of garlic	
100 g	4 oz	tomatoes, skinned, deseeded, diced	
25 g	1 oz	tomato purée	portugaise sauce
250 ml	½ pt	white stock	
		seasoning	
		chopped parsley	

1 Wash and peel the salsify, cut into 5 cm (2 in.) lengths. Place immediately into acidulated water to prevent discoloration.
2 Place salsify into a boiling blanc or acidulated water with a little oil and simmer until tender, approx. 10–40 mins. Drain well.
3 Melt the margarine or butter, add the onion and garlic. Sweat without colour.
4 Add the tomatoes and tomato purée, cook for 5 mins.
5 Moisten with white stock, correct seasoning.
6 Place the cooked and well-drained salsify into the tomato sauce.
7 Serve in a suitable dish, sprinkled with chopped parsley.

41   **Spinach gratinated**   *Epinards au gratin*   *4 portions*

600 g	1 ½ lb	spinach, picked and washed
		salt and pepper
50 g	2 oz	butter or margarine
50 g	2 oz	grated cheese

1 Lightly cook the spinach, drain well and season.
2 Place in an ovenproof dish and sprinkle on the melted butter and grated cheese.
3 Gratinate in a hot oven or under the salamander.

42   **Shallow-fried spinach cakes**   *Subrics d'épinards*

4 portions

600 g	1 ½ lb	spinach, picked and washed
		salt, pepper and nutmeg
60 ml	⅛ pt	thick béchamel
		1 tablespn double cream
		2 egg yolks plus 1 egg
		clarified butter, margarine, or oil for frying

1 Lightly cook the spinach, dry well, season and coarsely chop.
2 Thoroughly mix over gently heat, adding béchamel, cream and yolks plus egg.
3 Lift the mixture out in tablespoons and shallow fry.
4 Colour on both sides, drain well and serve.

Note Alternatively, in place of béchamel, cream and yolks, the subrics can be passed through a light batter.
  A cream sauce may be offered separately.

43   **Spinach with cheese sauce and croûtons**   *Epinards á la Viroflay*   *4 portions*

1 Prepare a subrics mixtures as in previous recipe.
2 Add 50 g (2 oz) diced croûtons, fried in butter.
3 Shape the subrics but do not fry them.
4 Wrap the subrics in large blanched spinach leaves and place in a buttered ovenproof dish.
5 Coat with Mornay sauce, grated cheese and melted butter.
6 Gratinate in a hot oven or under the salamander and serve.

44   Leaf spinach with pine nuts and garlic   *4 portions*

```
400 g   1 lb   spinach
50 g    2 oz   pine nuts
               1 tablespn oil or butter
               1 garlic clove, chopped
               salt and pepper
```

1 Cook spinach for 2–3 mins and drain well.
2 Lightly brown pine nuts in oil, add garlic and sweat for 2 mins.
3 Add coarsely chopped spinach and heat through over a medium heat.
4 Correct seasoning and serve.

45   Spinach moulds   *Timbale d'épinards*   *4 portions*

```
50 g     2 oz    carrot, cooked
600 g    1 ½ lb  spinach
125 ml   ¼ pt    thick béchamel
                 2 eggs, separated
                 salt, pepper and nutmeg
```

1 Butter 4 dariole moulds and place in bottom of each a slice of fluted cooked carrot.
2 Line the moulds with blanched spinach leaves.
3 Prepare a dry spinach purée and heat it through thoroughly.
4 Mix in the béchamel and yolks, season and allow to cool.
5 Fold in the stiffly beaten whites and use to three-quarters fill the moulds.
6 Poach in a bain-marie in moderate oven (200°C, 400°F, Reg. 6) for approx. 15–20 mins.
7 Test by finger pressure to ensure that the moulds are cooked before turning out to serve.

46   Squash

There are many different varieties of squash, which is a relative of the pumpkin. Squash should be firm with a blemish-free skin; summer squash should have a more yielding skin than winter squash, which are allowed to harden before harvesting.

The most usual variety sold is the custard squash, which is best when eaten young and can be cooked in similar ways to courgettes – sliced and lightly boiled, stewed or fried with the skins on and served with butter. Winter squash have the skin removed before cooking and can then be cooked like marrow, e.g. stuffed.

47   Swiss chard

Swiss chard or seakale beet have large, ribbed, slightly curly leaves. The flavour is similar to spinach, although it is milder, and it can be prepared in the same way as any of the spinach recipes.

It can also be served *au gratin* and made into a savoury flan or quiche, using half lean cooked ham or bacon, flavoured with onion, garlic and chopped parsley.

48   Stuffed vegetables

Certain vegetables can be stuffed and served as a first course, as a vegetable course and as an accompaniment to a main course.

The majority of vegetables used for this purpose are the bland, gourd types, such as aubergines, courgettes, and cucumbers, in which case the stuffing should be delicately flavoured so as not to overpower the vegetable. Below are some of the more popular types of vegetable used for this purpose and the usual type of stuffing in each case. There is, however, considerable scope for variation and experimentation in any of the stuffings.

Artichoke bottoms: duxelle stuffing, cordon of thin demi-glace flavoured with tomato.
Aubergine: *egyptienne*—the cooked chopped flesh is mixed with cooked chopped onion, sliced tomatoes and chopped parsley.

au gratin—the cooked chopped flesh is mixed with duxelle, sprinkled with fresh breadcrumbs, grated cheese and gratinated. Served with a cordon of light tomato sauce.

à la provençale—the cooked chopped flesh is mixed with cooked chopped onion, garlic, tomato concassé, parsley, breadcrumbs and gratinated. Served with a cordon of light tomato sauce.

à la serbe—the cooked chopped flesh is mixed with diced or minced cooked mutton, cooked chopped onion, tomato concassé, cooked rice and chopped parsley. Served with a cordon of tomato sauce.
Mushrooms and **ceps**: duxelle stuffing.

stuffed ceps, forest style (Morilles à la forestière)—equal quantities of duxelle stuffing and sausagemeat.
Stuffed cabbage: veal stuffing and pilaff rice.
Cucumber: can be prepared in two ways—

    1 Peeled, cut into 2 cm (1 in.) pieces, the centres hollowed out with a parisienne spoon and then boiled, steamed or cooked in butter.

    2 The peeled whole cucumber is cut in halves lengthwise, the seed pocket scooped out and the cucumber cooked by boiling, steaming or in butter.

Suitable stuffings can be made from a base of duxelle, pilaff rice or chicken forcemeat, or any combination of these three.

To stuff the cucumber pieces, pipe the stuffing from a piping bag and complete the cooking in the oven. When the whole cucumber is stuffed, rejoin the two halves, wrap in pig's caul and muslin and braise.

Lettuce: stuff with two parts chicken forcemeat, one part duxelle and braise.

Turnips: peel the turnips, remove the centre almost to the root and blanch the turnips. Cook and purée the scooped-out centre and mix with an equal quantity of potato purée. Refill the cavities and gently cook the turnips in butter in the oven, basting frequently.

Turnips may also be stuffed with cooked spinach, chicory or rice.

Pimentos: pilaff rice, varied if required with other ingredients, e.g. mushrooms, tomatoes, ham, herbs.

Tomatoes: usually duxelle or pilaff rice.

à l'ancienne—duxelle stuffing with garlic and diced ham. Served with a cordon of demi-glace flavoured with tomato.

à la carmelite—chopped hard-boiled egg bound with thick béchamel, grated cheese and gratinated. Served with a cordon of light tomato sauce.

à la hussarde—scrambled egg, mushrooms and diced ham, sprinkled with breadcrumbs fried in butter.

à l'italienne—risotto with tomato concassé. Coat with thin tomato sauce.

à la provençale—cooked tomato concassé, chopped onion, garlic and parsley, bound with fresh breadcrumbs and gratinated. May be served hot or cold.

à la portugaise—pilaff rice in which has been cooked dice of tomato and red pimento. Cook gently in oven and sprinkle with chopped parsley.

49   Wild mushrooms

Ceps, morels, chanterelles and oyster mushrooms are four of the most popular of the wide variety of wild mushrooms that may be gathered.

Ceps are bun-shaped fungi with a smooth surface and a strong distinctive flavour. Ceps are also available dried and should be soaked in warm water for approx. 30 minutes before use. The soaking liquid should be used as it contains a good flavour.

Methods of cooking: ceps hold an amount of water and need to be sweated gently in oil or butter and then drained, utilising the liquid. Ceps may be used in soups, egg dishes, particularly omelets, fish, meat, game and poultry dishes. They may also be: sautéed in oil or butter with garlic and parsley and served as a vegetable; stuffed with chopped ham, cheese, tomato and parsley; or sliced, passed through batter and deep fried.

Morels appear in spring. They vary in colour from light to dark brown and have a meaty flavour. Morels are obtainable dried, and then require soaking for 10 minutes, are squeezed dry and used as required.

Methods of cooking: morels can be used in soups, egg dishes, meat, poultry and game dishes and as a vegetable, first course or as an accompaniment.

Chanterelles are common, trumpet-shaped and frilly. They are generally bright yellow with a delicate flavour, slightly resembling apricots, and are obtainable in summer and autumn. There are many varieties and they can be obtained dried, when they require about 25 minutes soaking in warm water before cooking.

Methods of cooking: because of their pleated gills, chanterelles must be carefully washed under running cold water then well dried. As they have a rubbery texture they require lengthy gentle cooking in butter or oil. They can be served with egg, chicken or veal dishes.

Oyster mushrooms are 'ear' shaped, grey or greyish brown in colour, and have an excellent flavour. They can be tough in texture and therefore need careful cooking.

Method of cooking: cook in butter or oil with parsley and garlic, or flour, egg and breadcrumb then deep fry.

50 Yams

Yams may be white or yellow, with a texture similar to potatoes. In certain parts of the world orange-fleshed sweet potatoes are known as yams, but the true yam is sweeter and moister than the sweet potato. However, they may both be prepared and cooked in the same way.

51 Fried yam cakes   *4 portions*

400 g	1 lb	yams
10 g	½ oz	butter
50 g	2 oz	onion
5 g	¼ oz	chopped parsley
		salt and pepper
		2 egg yolks
		oil

1 Wash, peel, wash and finely grate the yams.
2 Add the melted butter, finely chopped onion, parsley, salt and pepper.
3 Add the egg yolks, mix well, form into a roll and cut into an even number of cakes.
4 Neaten the shapes, using a little flour only if necessary, and shallow fry for 3–4 mins on each side, then drain and serve.

52 Yam soufflé

4 portions

400 g	1 lb	yams
50 g	2 oz	butter or margarine
125 ml	¼ pt	milk or cream
25 g	1 oz	grated parmesan cheese
		salt and pepper
		3 egg yolks
		4 egg whites

1 Wash, peel, wash and cut the yams into even-sized pieces.
2 Boil or steam until tender, drain well.
3 Purée the yams, return to a clean pan and dry out thoroughly over a gentle heat, stirring continuously with a wooden spoon.
4 Mix in the butter and then gradually the milk.
5 Mix in half the cheese, seasoning and the egg yolks.
6 Allow the mixture to cool, and butter and flour a soufflé dish.
7 Carefully fold in the stiffly beaten egg whites, and place mixture in soufflé dish.
8 Carefully smooth the surface, add remainder of cheese and bake at 220°C (425°F, Reg. 7) for approx. 20 mins. Serve immediately.

Potato dishes

Introduction

When using potatoes as a vegetable dish, for 4 portions, allow 400 g (1 lb) for new potatoes and 500 g (1 lb 4 oz) for old potatoes. The actual quantity required will vary according to the number of courses and how many other vegetables are served. As a garnish, allow approximately 50 g (2 oz) potatoes per head.

Traditional classical names must be used for traditional classical recipes and should not be given to variations or original recipes.

Potato combinations

Traditionally potatoes have been served as a vegetable in a separate dish; however, small new potatoes can give a pleasing appearance by being served with other vegetables.

Small young carrots, turnips and peas mixed with small potatoes, finished in butter and chopped mint bring both potatoes and vegetables together. Other additions could be button mushrooms, button onions and cauliflower florets. Lightly sautéing the vegetables to a golden colour lends variation to the presentation.

1   Bubble and squeak   *4 portions*

300 g	12 oz	potatoes (pureed)
200 g	8 oz	cabbage (cooked and chopped)
50 g	2 oz	margarine or butter
		salt and pepper

1 Mix and season the potatoes and cabbage and shape into potato cakes with a little flour.
2 Shallow fry in hot oil on both sides to colour and heat through.

Notes The proportion of cabbage to potato can vary according to taste.

As an alternative, cook all the mixture in a small frying pan and cut into portions.

Bubble and squeak can include any cooked vegetables, such as carrots, onions, Brussels sprouts etc.

This traditional British dish originated in many homes on a Monday in order to use up any left-over vegetables that had been served the previous day with the Sunday roast.

2   Duchess potato – variations

Additions to the basic duchess potato mixture can include chopped herbs, such as parsley or mint, tomato purée or a purée of peas, chopped nuts or truffle.

The mixture may be cylinder-shaped, round cake, ball-shaped, or piped in rounds or in nests. When piped like a nest, as for marquise potatoes, in place of tomatoes, any of the following could be used: peas, peas and mushrooms, purée of spinach, purée of carrots, macédoine of vegetables, and so on.

3   Fried croquette potatoes with ham   *Pommes croquettes au jambon*   *4 portions*

500 g	1 lb 4 oz	potatoes
25–50 g	1–2 oz	butter
		1 egg yolk
50 g	2 oz	chopped ham
		flour, eggwash and crumbs
		seasoning

1 Prepare a duchess potato mixture from the potatoes, butter and yolk.
2 Mix in the ham.
3 Mould into croquette shapes.
4 Flour, egg and crumb and deep fry. Drain well and serve.

4   Fried croquette potatoes with ham and vermicelli   *Pommes St Florentin*   *4 portions*

1 Prepare the potatoes as in the previous recipe.
2 Flour, egg wash and roll the potatoes in cooked vermicelli which has been broken into small pieces.
3 Mould into rectangular shapes and deep fry.

5   Potato cakes stuffed with spinach   *Pommes Elizabeth*   *4 portions*

125 ml	¼ pt	choux paste (without sugar), see recipe 28, page 275
400 g	1 lb	duchess potato mixture
400 g	1 lb	cooked leaf spinach

1 Combine the choux paste with the potato mixture.
2 Mould carefully into croquette shapes, stuff with well-drained, seasoned, cooked spinach by cutting a line in the top, opening out gently, laying the spinach in the opening then carefully remoulding.
3 Carefully place on to oiled greaseproof paper.
4 Allow to slide off the paper into hot deep fat and fry at 185°C/370°F until golden brown.
5 Drain well and serve.

6   Fried potato balls with almonds

1 Prepare the duchess potato mixture.
2 Shape into rounds the size of apricots.

3 Flour, egg wash and roll in sliced or nibbed almonds.
4 Deep fry to a golden colour, drain well and serve.

Note If chopped truffles are added to the mixture, the classic name is *pommes Berny*.

7 Baked jacket potatoes with cheese *Pommes gratinées*
4 portions

		4 large potatoes
100 g	4 oz	butter
		salt and pepper
100 g	4 oz	grated cheese

1 Bake the potatoes in their jackets.
2 When cooked, halve and scoop out the centre without damaging the skin.
3 Mash the potato flesh with butter, season and return to the skin.
4 Sprinkle with the grated cheese and gratinate.

Variation Baked jacket potatoes with ham and onion: proceed as above, adding 50 g (2 oz) cooked chopped onion and 50 g (2 oz) diced cooked ham at stage 3. Stage 4 is then optional.

8 Baked jacket potatoes with cream and chives *Pommes arlie*
4 portions

1 Proceed as for previous recipe, adding 50 g (2 oz) chopped chives to the mashed centres.
2 Replace potatoes in their skins, sprinkle with cream and grated cheese and gratinate.

9 Potato cakes with chives *Pommes Robert*   *4 portions*

		4 large potatoes
		2 egg yolks
50 g	2 oz	butter
50 g	2 oz	chopped chives
		salt and pepper

1 Bake the potatoes in their jackets.
2 Halve and remove the centres from the skins.
3 Mash with the yolks and butter.
4 Mix in the chopped chives and season.
5 Mould into round cakes 2 cm (1 inch) diameter.
6 Lightly flour and shallow fry to a golden colour on both sides.

10 Shallow-fried potato slices *Pommes sautées à cru*

1 Slice peeled raw potatoes into ¼ cm (⅛ inch) thick.
2 Wash, drain, dry and shallow fry to a golden colour.
3 Drain, season with salt and toss in butter prior to service.

11 Shallow-fried potatoes with artichokes

1 Proceed as for the previous recipe.
2 Shallow fry 100 g (4 oz) quartered cooked artichokes in butter.
3 Add to the potatoes, season and finish with chopped parsley.

Note When sliced truffles are added the dish is called *pommes Mireille.*

Variations to sauté potato dishes from raw or cooked potatoes can include mushrooms, lardons of bacon, shredded onions, button onions, ham, peppers etc. When a julienne of red peppers is added to potatoes sautéd from raw the dish is called *pommes Columbine.*

12 Fried diced potatoes with breadcrumbs *Pommes sablées*

1 Cut peeled potatoes into 1 cm (½ in.) dice.
2 Wash, drain and shallow fry until cooked and golden in colour.
3 Either add 100 g (2 oz) breadcrumbs for the last few minutes of cooking *or* shallow fry the breadcrumbs separately in butter or oil then add to the drained potatoes.
4 Season and serve.

13 Fried diced potatoes with garlic *Pommes bordelaise*

Proceed as for the previous recipe but without the breadcrumbs. Add two crushed chopped cloves of garlic to the potatoes and cook for a minute before draining. Season and serve.

14 Sauté potatoes with garlic   *Pommes provençale*

Cook the sauté potatoes and add two crushed chopped cloves of garlic just
before finishing the cooking. Drain, season and serve finished with
chopped parsley.

15 Braised potatoes with thyme and cheese
Pommes champignol   4 *portions*

500 g	1 lb 4 oz	potatoes
375 ml	¾ pt	white stock (approx)
		pinch of powdered thyme
50 g	2 oz	butter or margarine
		salt and pepper

1 Trim or cut the potatoes to an even size.
2 Place in a dish, half cover with the stock to which has been added the
  thyme.
3 Brush with melted butter and season.
4 Cook in a hot oven (230°C, 450°F, Reg. 8), brushing occasionally with
  melted butter.
5 When ready the potatoes should have absorbed the stock and be golden
  brown in colour and cooked through.

Note As thyme is a strong pungent herb, it should not be used in excess.

16 Potatoes baked in stock with cheese and garlic
Pommes savoyarde   4 *portions*

400 g	1 lb	potatoes, peeled
375 ml	¾ pt	stock
		1 egg
50 g	2 oz	grated cheese
		1 clove garlic, crushed and chopped
50 g	2 oz	butter or margarine

1 Thinly slice the potatoes.
2 Mix the stock, egg and grated cheese in a basin.
3 Butter an earthenware dish and add the potatoes, stock and garlic.
4 Sprinkle with more grated cheese and a little melted butter.
5 Bake in a moderate oven (190°C, 375°F, Reg. 5) until the potatoes are
  cooked and golden brown.

17 Potatoes cooked with button onions and tomatoes
Pommes bretonne   *4 portions*

400 g	1 lb	peeled potatoes
100 g	4 oz	button onions
		1 clove garlic
375 ml	¾ pt	stock approx
		salt and pepper
100 g	4 oz	tomatoes, skinned, deseeded, diced

1 Trim and dice the potatoes into 2 cm (1 in.) pieces.
2 Add to the peeled onions, crushed garlic and stock.
3 Season and cook gently in a suitable pan in the oven or on the stove until the potatoes are just cooked.
4 Add the tomatoes and cook for a few more minutes then serve.

18 Potatoes cooked in milk with cheese   *Pommes dauphinoise*
4 portions

500 g	1 lb 4 oz	potatoes
250 ml	½ pt	milk, approx.
		salt and pepper
50 g	2 oz	grated cheese

1 Slice the peeled potatoes ½ cm (¼ inch) thick.
2 Place in an ovenproof dish and just cover with milk.
3 Season, sprinkle with grated cheese and cook in a moderate oven (190°C, 375°F, Reg. 5) until the potatoes are cooked and golden brown.

19 Potato fritters

1 Slice peeled potatoes ½ cm (¼ in.) thick, drain well and pass through seasoned flour and frying batter.
2 Deep fry – not too quickly – so as to cook the potatoes and give a golden brown colour.
3 Drain well, season and serve.

20 Soufflé potatoes   *Pommes soufflées*

Success with this dish depends on the type of potato used and the care taken in the handling of the potato. A waxy type of potato is required and experimentation is needed to find one that is suitable.

1 Cut peeled potatoes into rectangles approx. 5 cm (2 in.) by 2½ cm (1 in.) and then into ¼ cm (⅛ in.) slices lengthwise.
2 Wash and dry on a cloth.
3 Fry a small number at a time in deep fat at 180°C/360°F.
4 Add each piece separately, stirring carefully with a spider.
5 Turn down the heat and allow to cook for about 5 mins.
6 Carefully lift out the soufflé potatoes with a spider and arrange on absorbent paper or a thick cloth.
7 When required, place into hot fat at 190°C/380°F.
8 Fry until the potatoes are golden brown and puff up, stir with a spider to ensure even colouring.
9 Drain, season and serve.

21 Sweet potatoes

Also known as boniato, sweet potatoes have a sticky texture; they are slightly aromatic and sweet. Small or medium-sized potatoes with firm, fresh-looking skins should be selected.

Sweet potatoes can be steamed, boiled or baked in their skins, with the centre removed and puréed or creamed. They can be made into vegetarian dishes with the addition of other ingredients, and they may also be fried or made into bread or sweet pudding.

22 Candied sweet potatoes   *4 portions*

		1 tablespn oil or butter
400 g	1 lb	sweet potatoes, in 1 cm (½ in.) dice
100 g	4 oz	chopped onion
		2 tablespns honey
		2 tablespns cider vinegar } mixed in a bowl
		¼ teaspn cinnamon
		salt

1 Heat the oil in a frying pan and add the potatoes.
2 Cook for 10 mins, stirring occasionally.
3 Add the onion and cook until brown.
4 Pour on the honey mixture, heat through, season and serve.

23 Swiss potato cakes *Rösti*

In Switzerland the potatoes for this dish would be grated on a rösti grater, however a grater which produces large flakes can be used. Each canton has its own variations, which include gruyère or emmental cheese, grated raw apple, chopped onion, chives and parsley. Cumin or nutmeg may also be used to flavour and the potato can be coated with cream and glazed.

50 g	2 oz	lardons of bacon
50 g	2 oz	chopped onion
50 g	2 oz	oil, butter or margarine
500 g	1 lb 4 oz	grated raw potatoes
		salt and pepper

1 Sweat the lardons and onions in the fat or oil in a frying pan.
2 Add the potatoes and mix well, season.
3 Press together and cook on both sides until cooked and golden brown.

15

Pastry, yeast goods and petits fours

Introduction

The objective of this chapter is to provide an extension to more basic pastry knowledge and some variations of both traditional and new concepts.

All baking times and temperatures stated are approximate, as a pastry cook learns through experience how raw materials bake differently in various types of ovens. When using forced air convection ovens it is often necessary to reduce the stated temperatures in accordance with manufacturers' recommendations. Also, certain ovens produce severe bottom heat and to counteract this the use of double baking sheets (one sheet on top of another) is necessary.

When using vanilla pods, infuse the pod in the heated milk for approx. 30 minutes, remove, rinse, dry and store for further use in a jar of castor sugar.

Hot sweets

1 Apple strudel

8 portions

200 g	8 oz	strong flour	
		pinch of salt	
		1 egg	paste
25 g	1 oz	butter, margarine or oil	
85 ml	3/16 pt	hot water	
1 kg	2 lb	cooking apples	
50 g	2 oz	breadcrumbs (white or brown)	
25 g	1 oz	butter, margarine or oil	
100 g	4 oz	brown sugar	
100 g	4 oz	sultanas	
100 g	4 oz	raisins	filling
50 g	2 oz	ground almonds	
50 g	2 oz	nibbed almonds	
		grated zest and juice of 1 lemon	
3 g	⅛ oz	mixed spice	
3 g	⅛ oz	ground cinnamon	

1 First, make the paste: sieve together flour and salt and make a well.
2 Place the egg, fat and water in the centre and work until it is a smooth dough.

3   Cover with a damp cloth and relax for 20 mins.
4   For the filling: peel and core apples. Cut into thin small slices and place in a basin.
5   Fry the breadcrumbs in the butter, margarine or oil.
6   Add to the apples and mix well with all the other ingredients.
7   Roll out the dough into a square ¼ cm (⅛ in.) thick, place on a cloth and brush with melted fat or oil.
8   Stretch the dough on the backs of the hands until it is very thin.
9   Spread the filling onto the paste to within 1 cm (½ in.) from the edge.
10   With the aid of a cloth, roll up tightly and seal the ends.
11   Place on a lightly greased baking sheet and brush with melted fat or oil.
12   Bake in a moderate oven (approx. 190°C, 375°F, Reg. 5) for 35–40 mins.
13   When baked, dust with icing sugar and serve as required.

Note Alternatively the strudel paste may be made with: 50% wholemeal and 50% strong flour, or 70% wholemeal and 30% strong flour. With the increased proportion of wholemeal flour a little more water is required to achieve a smooth elastic dough.

2   Cherry strudel

Proceed as for apple strudel, replacing the apples with stoned cherries – fresh, canned or frozen.

3   Cherry and apple strudel

Proceed as for apple strudel, but replace 50% of the apples with stoned cherries (fresh, canned or frozen).

4   Cherry Yorkshire   *Clafoutis des cerises*   *4 portions*

200 g	8 oz	black cherries	
50 g	2 oz	castor sugar	
60 g	2½ oz	strong flour	batter
		1 egg	
100 ml	4 fl oz	milk	

1   Stone the cherries; if using canned cherries, drain well.
2   Sprinkle with 25 g (1 oz) of sugar.
3   Liberally butter a china dish and place in the cherries.
4   Make the rest of the ingredients into a batter and use to cover the cherries.

5 Bake in a moderate oven (approx. 220°C, 425°F, Reg. 7) for 20–30 mins and serve.

Variations Other fruits can be used, e.g. apples, gooseberries, plums etc.

5 **French rice pudding** *Riz à la française*   *4 portions*

500 ml	1 pt	milk (whole or skimmed)
50 g	2 oz	short grain rice (white or brown)
		2 eggs, separated
50 g	2 oz	castor or unrefined sugar
25 g	1 oz	butter or margarine
		natural vanilla essence or pod (see p. 265)

1 Boil milk in a thick-bottomed saucepan, add rice and simmer until almost cooked.
2 Prepare the liaison by creaming together the egg yolks, sugar and the butter or margarine.
3 Add the liaison carefully by stirring in one-third of the milk with the rice. Add vanilla essence.
4 Return all to the main saucepan and stir on the side of the stove until the mixture thickens but *do not boil*. Remove from the stove.
5 Stiffly beat the egg whites and carefully fold into the cooked rice.
6 Three-quarters fill a buttered pie dish.
7 Place in a bain-marie of warm water, bake at approx. 200°C (400°F, Reg. 6) for 20–30 mins and serve.

Note Semolina, sago or tapioca may also be prepared in this way.

6 **Soufflé pudding** *Pouding soufflé*   *6 portions*

185 ml	⅜ pt	milk, whole or skimmed
25 g	1 oz	flour, white or wholemeal
25 g	1 oz	butter or margarine
25 g	1 oz	castor or unrefined sugar
		3 eggs, separated

1 Boil the milk in a sauteuse.
2 Combine the flour, butter and sugar.
3 Whisk into the milk and re-boil.
4 Remove from heat, add yolks one at a time, whisking continuously.
5 Stiffly beat the whites and carefully fold into the mixture.
6 Three-quarters fill buttered and sugared dariole moulds.
7 Place in a roasting tin, half full of water.

8 Bring to the boil and place in a hot oven (approx. 230°–250°C, 450°–500°F, Reg. 8–9) 12–15 mins.
9 Turn out on to a flat dish and serve with a suitable hot sauce, e.g. custard or sabayon sauce.

7   Royal soufflé pudding   *Soufflé pouding royale*   *6 portions*

1 Prepare a soufflé pudding mix as in the previous recipe, adding vanilla.
2 Liberally grease moulds and line with thin slices of jam swiss roll.
3 Add the soufflé pudding mix and cook as in the previous recipe.
4 Serve with apricot sauce flavoured with Marsala or sherry.

8   Soufflé pudding with cherries   *Pouding soufflé Montmorency*
6 portions

1 Prepare a vanilla soufflé pudding as in recipe 6.
2 Add fresh or preserved cherries macerated in kirsch.
3 Cook as in recipe 6.
4 Serve with raspberry or redcurrant sauce.

9   Vanilla soufflé   *Soufflé vanille*   *4 portions*

125 ml	¼ pt	milk
		natural vanilla or pod (see p. 265)
		4 eggs, separated
10 g	½ oz	flour
50 g	2 oz	castor sugar
10 g	½ oz	butter

1 Coat the inside of a soufflé case/dish with fresh butter (as thinly as possible).
2 Coat the butter in the soufflé case with castor sugar, tap out surplus.
3 Boil the milk and vanilla in a thick-bottomed pan.
4 Mix 2 egg yolks, the flour and sugar to a smooth consistency in a basin.
5 Add the boiling milk to the mixture, stir vigorously until completely mixed.
6 Return this mixture to a *clean* thick-bottomed pan and stir continuously with a wooden spoon over gentle heat until the mixture thickens, then remove from heat.
7 Allow to cool slightly.
8 Add 2 egg yolks and the butter, mix thoroughly.
9 Stiffly whip the 4 egg whites and *carefully* fold into the mixture, which should be just warm. (An extra egg white can be added for extra lightness.)

10 Place mixture into the prepared mould and level it off with a palette knife, do not allow it to come above the level of the soufflé case.
11 Place on a baking sheet and cook in a moderately hot oven, approx. 200°–230°C (400°–450°F, Reg. 6–8) until the soufflé is well risen and is firm to touch, approx. 15–20 min.
12 Remove carefully from oven, dredge with icing sugar and serve at once. A hot soufflé *cannot* be allowed to stand or it will sink.

10 Chocolate soufflé   *Soufflé au chocolat*   *4 portions*

1 Proceed as for vanilla soufflé, dissolving 50 g (2 oz) grated couverture or powdered chocolate in the milk.
2 If the mixture is found to be too stiff an extra beaten egg white may be added.

11 Chocolate and vanilla soufflé   *Soufflé arlequin*   *4 portions*

1 This is half vanilla, half chocolate.
2 The mixtures should be carefully placed side by side in the mould.

12 Grand Marnier soufflé   *Soufflé grand marnier*   *4 portions*

1 Proceed as for vanilla soufflé.
2 Before adding the beaten egg whites to the basic mixture add 15 ml (1 fluid oz) of Grand Marnier and 2–3 *drops* of cochineal in order to give a delicate pink colour to the mixture.

13 Soufflé with crystallized fruit   *Soufflé Rothschild*
4 portions

1 Prepare the basic soufflé flavoured with vanilla (recipe 9).
2 Cut into small dice 100–150 g (4–6 oz) crystallized fruits to 250 ml (½ pt) milk. Macerate in kirsch.
3 Add fruits to the panada (stage 8), then add the whites of egg.

14 Rum soufflé   *Soufflé jamaique*   *4 portions*

1 Add the grated rind of 1 or 2 oranges to 250 ml (½ pt) milk. Prepare a soufflé panada in the usual way (recipe 9).
2 Pour half the mixture into the soufflé dish and place in the centre a small dice of sponge fingers sprinkled with rum. Pour in remainder of soufflé mixture.

3 Place 3–4 diamonds of biscuit also sprinkled with rum on top.
4 Cook and finish as in recipe 9.

15   Soufflé with kirsch and anisette   *Soufflé Palmyre*   *4 portions*

1 Prepare a basic vanilla soufflé mixture, as in recipe 9.
2 Pour half the mixture into a well-buttered soufflé dish.
3 Place in the centre a small dice of sponge fingers sprinkled with kirsch
   and anisette. Pour the remainder of the soufflé mixture on top.
4 Place 3 or 4 diamonds of biscuit on top.
5 Cook and finish as in recipe 9.

Cold sweets

16   Charlotte russe

A charlotte russe is a vanilla bavarois (see opposite) set in a charlotte
mould which has been lined with finger biscuits (biscuits à la cuillère,
recipe 77, p. 299). The bottom of the charlotte mould should be lined with
fan shaped pieces of finger biscuit. If, in place of fan shaped biscuit, ½ cm
(¼ in) of red jelly is used, the charlotte is called charlotte moscovite.

1 Prepare and cook the finger biscuits.
2 Remove on to a cooling grid.
3 Prepare the bavarois.
4 While the bavarois is setting line the bottom of the charlotte mould by
   either method described below in point 5.
5 Trim sufficient biscuits into fan shaped pieces of a length half the
   diameter of the base of the mould and neatly arrange in the bottom of
   the mould round side down, *or* pour in sufficient red jelly for a
   thickness of ½ cm (¼ in.).
6 Neatly line the sides of the mould with trimmed finger biscuits, round
   sides facing outwards (if using a red jelly base, allow this to set first).
7 Pour the bavarois mixture into the lined mould at the last possible
   moment before setting point is reached.
8 Place the charlotte in the refrigerator to set.
9 To serve, trim off any ends of the biscuit which may project above the
   mould.
10 Carefully turn the charlotte out on to a serving dish (if red jelly base is
   used dip the bottom of the mould into boiling water for 2–3 seconds,
   wipe dry and turn out).
11 Decorate the charlotte with whipped sweetened cream (crème
   Chantilly).

Vanilla bavarois (6–8 portions)

10 g	½ oz	gelatine
		2 eggs, separated
50 g	2 oz	castor sugar
250 ml	½ pt	milk, whole or skimmed, flavoured with vanilla
250 ml	½ pt	whipping or double cream or non-dairy cream

 1 If using leaf gelatine, soak in cold water.
 2 Cream the yolks and sugar in a bowl until almost white.
 3 Whisk on the milk which has been brought to the boil, mix well.
 4 Clean the milk saucepan (which should be a thick-bottomed one) and return the mixture to it.
 5 Return to a low heat and stir continuously with a wooden spoon until the mixture coats the back of the spoon. The mixture must not boil.
 6 Remove from the heat, add the gelatine, stir until dissolved.
 7 Pass through a fine strainer into a clean bowl, leave in a cool place, stirring occasionally until almost setting point.
 8 Then fold in the lightly beaten cream.
 9 Fold in the stiffly beaten whites.
10 Pour the mixture into a mould (may be very lightly greased with oil).
11 Allow to set in the refrigerator.

17 Kirsch-flavoured peach charlotte   *Charlotte Montreuil*
4 portions

		Orange jelly
		Sponge fingers
250 ml	½ pt	vanilla bavarois (see above)
125 ml	¼ pt	peach purée
50 g	2 oz	diced peaches
		kirsch, to taste

1 Line the bottom of a charlotte mould with orange jelly.
2 Line with sponge fingers.
3 Fill with vanilla bavarois mixed with peach purée and a small dice of peaches, soaked in kirsch.

18 Harlequin charlotte   *Timbale arlequin*   *4 portions*

Glaze sponge fingers with white, pink and chocolate fondant. Allow to dry well. Line a suitable timbale mould with silicone paper and the glazed sponge fingers, alternating the colours. Fill centre with vanilla bavarois and allow to set. Turn out on a flat salver, decorate with crème Chantilly and serve.

19   Chocolate mousse

4 portions

```
100 g   4 oz   plain chocolate
25 g    1 oz   butter
               4 eggs, separated
100 g   4 oz   castor sugar
125 ml  ¼ pt   whipped cream
```

1 Break the chocolate into small pieces, place in a basin, stand in a bain-marie and allow to melt with the butter.
2 Whisk the egg yolks and sugar until almost white and thoroughly mix in the melted chocolate.
3 Carefully fold in the stiffly beaten egg whites, pour into a suitable dish or individual dishes and refrigerate until set.
4 Decorate with whipped cream and serve.

20   Chocolate and orange mousse

Add the lightly grated zest of 2 oranges.

21   Chocolate rum mousse

Add 1–2 tablespoons rum.

22   Chocolate brandy mousse

Add 1–2 tablespoons brandy.

23   Chocolate and almond mousse

Add 50 g (2 oz) lightly toasted sliced almonds.

24   Burned, caramelised or browned cream   *Creme brûlée*

4 portions

```
125 ml  ¼ pt   milk
125 ml  ¼ pt   double cream
               natural vanilla essence or pod (see p. 265)
               2 eggs
               1 yolk
25 g    1 oz   castor sugar
               demerara sugar
```

1 Warm the milk, cream and vanilla essence in a pan.
2 Mix the eggs, egg yolk and sugar in a basin and add the warm milk. Stir well and pass through a fine strainer.
3 Pour the cream into individual dishes and place them into a tray half-filled with warm water.
4 Place in the oven at approx. 160°C (325°F, Reg. 3) for about 30–40 mins, until set.
5 Sprinkle the tops with demerara sugar and glaze under the salamander to a golden brown.
6 Clean the dishes and serve.

Variations Sliced strawberries, raspberries or other fruits, e.g. peaches, apricots, may be placed in the bottom of the dish before adding the cream mixture or placed on top after the creams are caramelised.

25 Chestnut meringue nests *Mont blanc aux marrons*

4 portions

It is best to use canned marron glacé for this recipe.

1 Pass the chestnuts through a sieve and flavour with rum.
2 Dust individual savarin moulds with icing sugar. Place the chestnut purée in a forcing bag with a 1 cm (½ in.) plain tube and fill the moulds but do not press down.
3 Turn out onto individual rounds of meringue and fill the centres with crème Chantilly using a star tube. Sprinkle with chocolate shavings.

Note In place of meringue nests (vacherins) individual rounds of cooked sablé paste may be used.

26 Pot creams – vanilla, chocolate or coffee *Petits pots de crème*

4 portions

500 ml	1 pt	milk
		3 egg yolks
100 g	4 oz	castor sugar
		natural vanilla essence or pod (see p. 265)
		1 egg

Coffee flavour add approx. 25 g (1 oz) coffee essence
Chocolate flavour add approx. 25 g (1 oz) bitter chocolate and omit the whole egg

1 Warm the milk.
2 Mix together the egg yolks and sugar, add the warm milk and flavouring, then strain.
3 Pour into small ramekins, place in a bain-marie, cover with aluminium

foil and poach in the oven for 20–25 mins at approx. 150°C (300°F, Reg. 2) until set.
4 Allow to cool, clean round the moulds, chill and serve.

27   Cream beau rivage   *Crème beau rivage*   *6 portions*

25 g	1 oz	butter
50 g	2 oz	praline (recipe 82, p. 302)
500 ml	1 pt	milk
		4 eggs
50 g	2 oz	sugar
		vanilla essence
		6 vanilla cornets (recipe 79, p. 300)
250 ml	½ pt	cream

1 Liberally butter a 6-portion savarin mould.
2 Evenly coat the buttered mould with the praline.
3 Warm the milk.
4 Pour the warm milk on to the beaten eggs, sugar and vanilla and mix well.
5 Pass the mixture through a fine strainer into a basin.
6 Carefully pour the mixture into the savarin mould.
7 Place the mould into a bain-marie in a moderate oven (approx. 180°C, 350°F, Reg. 4) to cook and set approx. 30–40 min.
8 When cooked, remove from the oven, allow to cool, then place in the refrigerator.
9 To serve, turn the mould out carefully on to a suitable dish.
10 Fill the cornets with the whipped sweetened cream and pipe the remainder into the centre of the ring.
11 Neatly arrange the cornets on top of the cream, points to the centre.
12 Place a crystallised violet or rose in the centre of the cream in cornets.

28   Sugar-topped choux buns filled with rum-flavoured pastry cream on chocolate sauce   *Salambos à la marquise*
4 portions

125 ml	¼ pt	choux pastry
250 ml	½ pt	rum-flavoured pastry cream*
200 g	8 oz	cube sugar
60 ml	⅛ pt	water } hard crack sugar
		pinch of cream of tartar
250 ml	½ pt	chocolate sauce

*Pastry cream may be made in the traditional way or using skimmed milk, unrefined sugar and wholemeal flour.

1 Pipe 4 large choux buns approx. 4 cm (1½ in.) diameter using a 1 cm (½ in.) star tube on a lightly greased baking sheet.

2 Egg wash lightly and bake in a moderately hot oven (approx. 220°C, 425°F, Reg. 7) for approx. 20–25 mins.
3 When cooked, split and allow to cool and fill with rum-flavoured pastry cream.
4 Dip the tops in hard crack sugar.
5 Serve individually on plates on a layer of chocolate sauce.

Choux paste (Pâte à choux)

250 ml	½ pt	water
		pinch of sugar and salt
100 g	4 oz	butter, margarine or oil
125 g	5 oz	flour (strong)
		4 eggs (approx.)

1 Bring the water, sugar and fat to the boil in a saucepan.
2 Remove from heat.
3 Add the sieved flour and mix in with a wooden spoon.
4 Return to a moderate heat and stir continuously until the mixture leaves the sides of the pan.
5 Remove from the heat and allow to cool.
6 Gradually add the beaten eggs, mixing well.
7 The paste should be of dropping consistency.

Note 50%, 70% or 100% wholemeal flour may be used.

29 Sablé paste

		1 egg
75 g	3 oz	castor sugar
150 g	6 oz	butter or margarine
200 g	8 oz	soft flour
		pinch of salt
75 g	3 oz	ground almonds

1 Lightly cream egg and sugar without over-softening.
2 Lightly mix in butter, do not over-soften.
3 Incorporate sieved flour, salt and the ground almonds.
4 Mix lightly to a smooth paste.
5 Rest in refrigerator before use.

Note Alternatively: 50% wholemeal and 50% white flour may be used, or 70% wholemeal and 30% white flour.
  Sablé paste may be used for petits fours, pastries and as a base for other desserts.

30   **Strawberry cream biscuits**   *Sablé aux fraises*

4 portions

200 g	8 oz	sablé paste
200–300 g	8–12 oz	ripe strawberries, washed and sliced
125 ml	¼ pt	whipped cream
125 ml	¼ pt	strawberry sauce
		icing sugar

1 Pin out sablé paste, ¼ cm (⅛ in) thick.
2 Cut into 8 rounds, 8 cm (3 in.) diameter, and bake in a cool oven (approx. 160°C, 325°F, Reg. 3) until light golden brown.
3 When cooked, remove from baking sheet on to a cooling grid.
4 Place a layer of cream on to 4 biscuits, then a layer of strawberries, a second layer of cream and top with the remaining biscuits.
5 Dust with icing sugar and serve with the strawberry sauce.

31   **Raspberry cream biscuits**   *Sablé aux framboises*

4 portions

Substitute raspberries for strawberries, keeping the raspberries whole, and proceed as for strawberry cream biscuits.

Note If required, the fruit may be macerated (after slicing) in a little castor sugar and a suitable liqueur e.g. grand marnier, cointreau.

   These sweets can also be made up in two layers using three biscuits instead of two.

32   **Snow eggs**   *Oeufs à la neige*

4 portions

500 ml	1 pt	milk, whole or skimmed	poaching liquid
50 g	2 oz	castor or unrefined sugar	
		vanilla essence	
		4 egg whites	meringue
50 g	2 oz	castor sugar	
		milk from poaching	sauce anglaise
		4 egg yolks	
25 g	1 oz	castor or unrefined sugar	
50 g	2 oz	granulated or cube sugar	caramel
30 ml	1/16 pt	water	

1 Place milk, sugar and vanilla essence in a shallow pan and bring to boil. Draw to side of the stove and simmer.
2 Whisk egg whites stiffly, add sugar and make meringue.
3 Using two large spoons, drop balls of the meringue into the milk, poach for 3–4 mins, turn over and poach for another 3–4 mins. Drain on a cloth.

4 Make the milk up to 500 ml (1 pt) and use to prepare a sauce anglaise with the egg yolks and the sugar. Strain and stir until cold, on ice.
5 Place a little sauce anglaise in a glass bowl, or in individual dishes, and place the snow eggs on top.
6 Mask over with sauce anglaise and decorate with a criss cross of caramel sugar.

33 Strawberry mousse (1)   *4 portions*

400 g	1 lb	ripe strawberries, picked and washed
50 g	2 oz	icing sugar
		3 eggs, separated
100 g	4 oz	castor sugar
10 g	½ oz	gelatine (dissolved in a little water)
250 ml	½ pt	whipping cream

1 Retain 4 strawberries for decoration and purée the remainder with the icing sugar.
2 Whisk egg yolks and castor sugar until almost white.
3 Whisk in the strawberry purée and the gelatine and strain.
4 Fold in three-quarters of the whipped cream and the stiffly whisked egg whites.
5 Pour into a suitable serving bowl or individual bowls or glasses.
6 Refrigerate until set, then decorate with whipped cream and a strawberry and serve accompanied by a suitable biscuit, e.g. sablé, shortbread, palmier etc.

34 Strawberry and orange mouse

Proceed as above, adding the lightly grated zest and juice of 1–2 oranges. Also increase the gelatine by 5 g (¼ oz).

35 Raspberry mousse

Proceed as for recipe 33, subsituting raspberries for strawberries.

36 Strawberry mousse (2)

375 ml	¾ pt	strawberry pureé
125 ml	¼ pt	water
75 g	3 oz	castor sugar
	1 oz	soaked leaf gelatine
		juice of ½ lemon
250 ml	½ pt	whipped cream
		4 egg whites

1 Place the strawberry pureé into a suitable basin.
2 Boil the water with the sugar, then add the soaked gelatine and the lemon juice.
3 Whisk this syrup into the pureé.
4 When the mixture is on setting point, fold in the whipped cream and whipped egg whites and place into a suitable mould or individual moulds. Place in refrigerator to set.
5 When set, turn out on to suitable dish or individual plates, decorated with whipped cream and a fresh strawberry.

37   Summer pudding

400 g	1 lb	redcurrants, raspberries, blackcurrants (fully ripe)
150 g	6 oz	sugar
200 g	8 oz	thinly sliced white bread, crusts removed

1 Prepare and wash the fruits.
2 Boil the sugar in 125 ml (¼ pt) water until dissolved.
3 Add the fruit and simmer gently until cooked, allowing the fruits to retain their shape and not cook to a mush.
4 Line the bottom and sides of either: (a) a 750 ml (1½ pt) basin or 4 individual pudding basins; (b) a 4-portion charlotte mould or 4 individual moulds, with the bread, packing the slices tightly so that no spaces are left in between.
5 Add the completely cold fruit and cover with more slices of bread.
6 Place a flat dish or plate with a weight on top and refrigerate overnight.
7 Turn out on to a flat plate or dish and serve with cream, clotted cream, ice-cream or yoghurt.

Note Fully ripe, soft, stoned cherries can also be used.

38   Fruit terrine   *Terrine des fruits*   *4 portions*

		3 eggs	
85 g	3½ oz	castor sugar	} sponge
60 g	2½ oz	soft flour	
200 g	8 oz	soft butter	
200 g	8 oz	icing sugar	
150 g	6 oz	fine ground almonds	
60 ml	⅛ pt	cointreau	} filling
250 ml	10 fl oz	whipping cream	
		selection of fruit approx. 2 kiwi,	
		150 g (6 oz) strawberries, 100 g (4 oz) peaches	

1 Prepare the sponge by whisking the eggs and sugar to ribbon stage over a bain-marie of warm water.

2 Carefully fold in the sifted flour.
3 Pour into a prepared swiss roll tin lined with greasepaper and lightly greased.
4 Cook sponge in a hot oven (approx. 220°–230°C, 425°–450°F, Reg. 7–8) for approx. 4 mins. Turn out onto a wire rack and allow to cool.
5 When cold, cut a layer of sponge to line a suitable terrine approx. 8 cm (3 in.) deep and 15–20 cm (6–8 in.) wide.
6 Place the sponge in the deep freeze to harden for easier handling.
7 Prepare the filling by creaming the butter and the icing sugar on a machine until soft, light and white.
8 Add the ground almonds and the cointreau and mix well.
9 Carefully fold in the whipped cream taking care *not to over mix*.
10 Line a suitable terrine with greaseproof or silicone paper.
11 Arrange the layers of thin sponge in the bottom and sides.
12 Place a layer of the filling in the base, on top of the sponge, and arrange pieces of fruit over this.
13 Continue with the filling and the fruit to achieve approx. 3 layers. Finish with a thin layer of sponge.
14 Place the terrine in the refrigerator to set for approx. 3–4 hours before serving.
15 Turn out, remove paper and cut into approx. 1 cm (½ in.) slices.
16 Serve on individual plates with a cordon of fresh raspberry sauce.

39 English trifle
4 portions

500 ml	1 pt	milk
		1 vanilla pod or 2–3 drops natural vanilla essence
		2 eggs plus 2 egg yolks *or* 8 egg yolks
50 g	2 oz	castor sugar
200 g	8 oz	sponge cake
150 g	6 oz	raspberry or strawberry jam
60 ml	⅛ pt	medium or sweet sherry
250 ml	½ pt	double cream, whipped
50 g	2 oz	flaked, sliced or nibbed almonds (toasted)
		4 or 8 glacé cherries

1 Heat milk with vanilla pod, cover with a lid, then remove from heat and stand for 15 mins. Remove vanilla pod.
2 Thoroughly whisk eggs and sugar in a basin.
3 Boil the milk, add a quarter to the eggs whisking continuously.
4 Add remainder of the milk and clean the saucepan.
5 Return eggs and milk to the clean pan and cook over a gentle heat, stirring continuously with a wooden spoon, until the mixture thickens.
6 Immediately remove from the heat. Strain the mixture into a clean basin and allow to cool, stirring occasionally.
7 Spread sponge cake with jam, cut into small squares and place in a 4-portion trifle bowl or individual dishes.

8 Sprinkle on the sherry, allow to soak in.
9 Pour the custard over the sponge cake and allow to set.
10 Decorate with whipped cream, almonds and halves of cherries.

Notes 100 g (4 oz) lightly crushed macaroon biscuits can be added with the sponge cake.

If whipping cream is available, use this in place of double cream as more volume can be achieved.

A layer of fresh soft fruit e.g. raspberries or sliced strawberries, which may be macerated in a little sugar and cointreau or grand marnier, can be used in place of jam.

The egg custard can be given a chocolate flavour.

The final decoration can include angelica or chocolate – grated, in curls or in piped shapes.

40 **Viennese pudding** *Pouding à la viennoise* *4 portions*

200 g	8 oz	butter or margarine
100 g	4 oz	castor sugar
		1 egg
		5 egg yolks
100 g	4 oz	brown breadcrumbs
50 g	2 oz	melted couverture
10 g	½ oz	nibbed almonds
		grated rind of ½ lemon
25 g	1 oz	diced glacé fruits
		5 egg whites, stiffly beaten

1 Cream the fat and sugar together until light and white.
2 Gradually add the whole egg and the yolks, breadcrumbs, melted couverture, almonds, lemon rind and fruit.
3 Fold in the stiffly beaten whites.
4 Place in well-greased ramekin moulds, lined with brown breadcrumbs.
5 Cook in a bain-marie in the oven at approx. 425°F (220°C, Reg. 7) for 10–12 mins and serve immediately.

Gâteaux, flans and slices

41 **Baked cheesecake** *8 portions*

50 g	2 oz	margarine or butter
100 g	4 oz	castor sugar
50 g	2 oz	egg
		zest and juice of ½ lemon
		pinch of salt
25 g	1 oz	cornflour
300 g	12 oz	low-fat curd cheese
50 g	2 oz	washed sultanas

filling

75 g	3 oz	margarine or butter	
25 g	1 oz	castor sugar	
10 g	½ oz	water	paste
100 g	4 oz	soft flour	
25 g	1 oz	crushed digestive biscuits	
100 g	4 oz	margarine or butter	
50 g	2 oz	castor sugar	paste for lattice
50 g	2 oz	egg	
125 g	5 oz	soft flour	

1 Prepare the filling by creaming together the fat and sugar until light and creamy.
2 Beat in the egg and add the lemon juice and zest. Mix well.
3 Add the salt. Mix in the cornflour and curd cheese.
4 Fold in the sultanas.
5 For the paste, cream together the fat and sugar and add the water. Mix well.
6 Fold in the flour and crushed digestive biscuits. Relax paste for 10 mins.
7 Roll out paste to approx ½ cm (¼ in) thick into a circle and use to line a lightly greased 20 cm (8 in.) shallow baking tin.
8 Add the filling to come to the top of the tin.
9 Prepare the lattice by creaming together the fat and sugar, beating in the egg and carefully folding in the flour. Mix to a smooth paste.
10 Roll out the paste into a rectangle approx. ½ cm (¼ in.) thick and cut into 1 cm (½ in.) strips.
11 Egg wash the edge of the cheesecake, lay a lattice work over the top using strips.
12 Bake in a moderate oven (approx. 200°C, 400°F, Reg. 6) for about 30 mins.

42   Black cherry cheesecake

		3 eggs	
85 g	3½ oz	castor sugar	sponge
60 g	2½ oz	soft flour	
		6 egg yolks	
300 g	12 oz	castor sugar	
		zest of 1 orange	
		zest of 1 lemon	
400 g	1 lb	cream cheese	
25 g	1 oz	gelatine	
		3 egg whites	
75 g	3 oz	castor sugar	
750 ml	1½ pt	whipped cream	
		natural vanilla essence or pod	
		1 × 20 cm (8 in.) disc sweet pastry	
200 g	8 oz	black cherries	

1 Prepare the sponge in the normal way (recipe 38, stages 1–4) using a swiss roll tin.
2 Beat together the yolks, sugar and orange and lemon zest.
3 Mix the cream cheese until smooth.
4 Blend the egg mixture into the cheese.
5 Stir in the gelatine which has been soaked in cold water and melted, add while still warm.
6 Whisk the egg whites, adding 75 g (3 oz) castor sugar.
7 When the cheese mixture is on setting point, fold in the cream and egg whites and flavour with vanilla essence.
8 Line a 20 cm (8 in.) cake tin with a disc of cooked sweet pastry and line the sides with greaseproof paper.
9 Half-fill the mould with half the cheese mixture. Place on top a layer of well drained black cherries.
10 Cover with a second layer of cheese mixture and finish with a layer of thinly sliced genoise.
11 Allow to set in the refrigerator for 3 hours.
12 Turn out of the tin and remove the greaseproof paper. Dust the sponge with icing sugar and mark trellis fashion with a hot poker.

Variations Blackcurrants, strawberries, apricots, peaches and raspberries may also be used in place of black cherries.

43   Apple and custard flan   *Flan à l'alsacienne*

1 Line a flan ring with short paste and place on a baking sheet.
2 Half fill with sections of apple and sprinkle with brown sugar.
3 Cook at approx. 200°C (400°F, Reg. 6) for 20–25 mins.
4 Fill with a raw egg custard (see below) and carefully replace in the oven.
5 Cook at 190°C (275°F, Reg. 5) until custard is cooked and set.
6 Remove flan ring and allow to cool.
7 Dust with a mixture of icing sugar and cinnamon.

Note Other types of fruit may be used in the same way.

Raw egg custard

125 ml	¼ pt	milk
		1 egg
25 g	1 oz	castor sugar
		natural vanilla essence or pod (see p. 265)

Mix all ingredients together and use as required.

44   Apricot and almond cream flan   *Flan aux abricots danoise*

1 Line a flan ring with sweet paste and place on a baking sheet.
2 Spread the base with a thin layer of almond cream (frangipane) – see below.
3 Half-fill with well drained, cooked or compôte apricots.
4 Cover with almond cream.
5 Cook at approx. 190°C (375°F, Reg. 5) for 20–25 mins.
6 When cooked brush with hot apricot glaze and water icing.
7 Return to oven for 30 seconds to glaze.

Note Other fruits may be used in the same way.

Frangipane

100 g	4 oz	butter
100 g	4 oz	castor sugar
		2 eggs
100 g	4 oz	ground almonds
10 g	½ oz	flour

Cream the butter and sugar, gradually beat in the eggs. Mix in the almonds and flour, mix lightly.

45   Apple trellis flan   *Flan aux pommes grillés*

1 Line a flan ring with short paste or sugar pastry and place on a baking sheet.
2 Fill with apple purée.
3 Egg wash the top edge.
4 Cover the top with thin strips of pastry to form a trellis and egg wash.
5 Cook at approx. 200°C (400°F, Reg. 6) for approx. 25 mins.
6 When cooked, dust with icing sugar and glaze under a salamander.

46   Fruit and pastry cream flan   *Flan Bourdaloue*

1 Line a flan ring with sweet paste and place on a baking sheet.
2 Fill with desired fruit, e.g. apple, gooseberries, apricots etc. Sprinkle with sugar.
3 Cook at approx. 200°C (400°F, Reg. 6) for 20–25 mins.
4 Carefully mask fruit with hot pastry cream.
5 Sprinkle with crushed macaroons. Dust with icing sugar and glaze under a salamander.

Note This flan can also be cooked blind and filled with poached or tinned fruit and finished as above.

47   Fruit meringue torte   *8 portions*

110 g	4½ oz	butter or margarine
50 g	2 oz	castor sugar
10 g	½ oz	whole egg
100 g	4 oz	soft flour

} sweet paste

110 g	4½ oz	butter or margarine
75 g	3 oz	icing sugar
		1 egg
175 g	7 oz	soft flour
		natural vanilla essence or pod

} piped shortbread

100 g	4 oz	egg whites
200 g	8 oz	granulated sugar
60 ml	⅛ pt	water

} Italian meringue

125 g	5 oz	blackcurrants, strawberries or raspberries (frozen or fresh)

1 Prepare the sweet paste by creaming together the fat and sugar, beating in the egg and gradually working in the flour to a smooth paste – but do *not* over-work.
2 Prepare the piped biscuits in the same way as for sweet paste.
3 Roll out the sweet paste into a base approx. ½ cm (¼ in.) thick, 22 cm (9 in.) round.
4 Pipe the shortbread into the base, using a forcing bag and 1 cm (½ in.) star tube.
5 Bake together for about 20 mins at approx. 200°C (400°F, Reg. 6).
6 Meanwhile, prepare an Italian meringue—see page 302.
7 To assemble: coat the base with Italian meringue, add the soft fruit and completely decorate with more meringue. Dust with castor sugar and flash in a very hot oven for 2–3 mins.

48   Gâteau japonaise

		10 whites of egg
200 g	8 oz	ground almonds
400 g	1 lb	castor sugar
25 g	1 oz	cornflour
200 g	8 oz	praline buttercream (see p. 285)
50 g	2 oz	chocolate fondant

1 Beat the whites to full peak and whisk in 100 g (4 oz) of sugar.
2 Carefully fold in the almonds, sugar and cornflour, well sifted together.
3 Pipe the mixture on to baking sheets lined with rice paper or silicone paper in circles of about 20–22 cm (8–9 in.) diameter using a 1 cm (½ in.) plain tube.
4 Dust with icing sugar and cook in a very cool oven at approx. 140°–150°C (250°–275°F, Reg. 1–2) for approx. 1 hour, until a light biscuit colour and crisp.

5 Remove silicone paper or, if using rice paper, leave on the rounds but trim the edges. Allow to cool.
6 Trim all rounds to the same size with the aid of a suitable round flan ring, and pass the trimmings through a sieve.
7 Sandwich 2 or 4 rounds together with praline buttercream, the bottom layer flat surface up and the top layer also.
8 Spread the top and sides with praline buttercream.
9 Cover the top trellis fashion. Pipe a disc of chocolate fondant in the centre.

Boiled buttercream (praline flavour)

125 ml	¼ pt	eggs
50 g	2 oz	icing sugar
300 g	12 oz	granulated sugar or cube sugar
100 g	4 oz	water
50 g	2 oz	glucose
400 g	1 lb	unsalted butter

1 Beat eggs and icing sugar until ribbon stage (sponge).
2 Boil granulated or cube sugar with water and glucose to 118°C (245°F).
3 Gradually add the sugar at 118°C (245°F) to the eggs and icing sugar at ribbon stage, whisk continuously and allow to cool to 26°C (80°F).
4 Gradually add the unsalted butter, while continuing to whisk, until a smooth cream is obtained.
5 Mix with praline (recipe 82, page 302) to make praline buttercream as required.

49 Choux pastry ring with toffee almond cream
Gâteau Paris Brest   *4 portions*

125 ml	¼ pt	choux pastry (page 275)
50 g	2 oz	flaked almonds
250 ml	½ pt	crème Chantilly, flavoured with praline *or* use non-dairy creamer flavoured with praline
50 g	2 oz	icing sugar

1 Pipe out a large ring of choux pastry, using a 1 cm (½ in.) star tube.
2 Egg wash and decorate with flaked almonds.
3 Cook at approx. 220°C (425°F, Reg. 7) for about 25–30 mins.
4 Split through the ring crossways and allow to cool.
5 Fill with cream flavoured with praline.
6 Replace the top and dust with icing sugar.

Note Alternatively, the ring may be filled with soft fruit and ice-cream, e.g. strawberries, raspberries etc.

50   Gâteau St. Honoré

125 g	5 oz	puff or short pastry
125 ml	¼ pt	choux pastry (page 275)
150 g	6 oz	cube sugar
60 ml	⅛ pt	water
		pinch of cream of tartar
50 g	2 oz	glacé cherries
50 g	2 oz	angelica
250 ml	½ pt	crème St. Honoré or chibouste (see below)

(cube sugar, water, pinch of cream of tartar) } hard crack sugar.

1 Roll out the pastry ¼ cm (⅛ in.) thick and cut out a circle approx. 23 cm (9 in.) in diameter, place on a slightly greased baking sheet.
2 Prick with a fork and egg wash the edge and centre.
3 Pipe on a ring of choux paste, approx. ¾ cm (⅜ in.) from the edge of the pastry and pipe on a choux bun in the centre, using 1 cm (½ in.) plain tube.
4 On a separate baking sheet, pipe out approx. 16–20 small choux buns.
5 Egg wash the choux ring and buns and cook in a fairly hot oven (approx. 230°C, 450°F, Reg. 8) for about 20–25 mins.
6 Place the cube sugar, water and cream of tartar into a suitable saucepan and cook to hard crack 155°C (312°F).
7 Dip the buns in hard crack sugar and decorate alternately with half a glacé cherry on one and a diamond of angelica on the other. As they are dipped and decorated place on the large ring. Make sure the buns match those on either side and that there is an even number.
8 Fill the finished case with a rocher of crème St. Honoré or chibouste, forming a dome shape in the centre. The finished item may be decorated with spun sugar (page 303).

Note A *rocher* is a quenelle shape formed by taking a dessert or tablespoon of the mixture, dipping a second spoon in boiling water, drying it and using it whilst warm to remove the mixture from the first spoon.

Crème St. Honoré

200 g	8 oz	cube sugar
		3 eggs, separated
125 ml	¼ pt	milk, whole or skimmed
6 g	¼ oz	leaf gelatine, soaked and squeezed dry

1 Boil the sugar with a little water to soft ball stage, 118°C (245°F).
2 Whisk the egg whites, pour on the sugar as for Italienne meringue (see page 302).
3 Cook the egg yolks and milk as for sauce anglaise and add the gelatine.
4 Add to the meringue.

Crème chibouste

6 g	¼ oz	leaf gelatine
250 ml	½ pt	pastry cream (made from skimmed milk, unrefined sugar and wholemeal flour, or in the traditional way)
		5 egg whites
100 g	4 oz	castor sugar

1 Add the soaked gelatine to the hot pastry cream.
2 Make a meringue with the egg whites and sugar.
3 Fold in the pastry cream, taking care not to overmix, and use as required.

51 Lucerne fruit and pastry cream   *10 portions (approx.)*

		8 yolks of egg ⎫
250 g	10 oz	castor sugar
25 g	1 oz	cornflour ⎬ plain russe
700 ml	1¼ pt	milk
6 g	¼ oz	soaked gelatine ⎭
60 g	2½ oz	soft flour ⎫
35 g	3½ oz	castor sugar ⎬ sponge
		3 eggs ⎭
200 g	8 oz	diced, cooked apple, sprinkled with lemon juice ⎫
50 g	2 oz	seedless raisins, boiled, cooled and soaked in ⎬ filling
		25 g (1 oz) rum
250 g	10 oz	whipped cream ⎭

1 Make a plain russe: mix together the egg yolks, sugar and cornflour. Boil the milk, add to the egg yolks and continue to stir for 1 min. Bring back to the boil.
2 Add the soaked gelatine and strain through a fine chinois.
3 Make the sponge as recipe 38 (page 278) stages 1–4. Pour into a lined swiss roll tin and bake at 230°–250°C (450°–500°F, Reg. 8–9) for approx. 3–4 mins.
4 Allow sponge to cool and use to line a half pudding sleeve.
5 Prepare the filling: add the apple and raisins to the cream, and fold in carefully 100 g (4 oz) of plain russe on setting point.
6 Place this mixture into the prepared pudding sleeve lined with sponge.
7 Set in the refrigerator for 3–4 hours.
8 Turn out, dust with icing sugar and mark a trellis with hot pokers to caramelise the sugar.
9 Decorate with whipped cream along the top in a rope fashion. This may be served on individual plates with a suitable sauce, e.g. raspberry or orange, or whole on a sweet trolley.

Note Other fruits may also be used, e.g. pears, raspberries, strawberries, peaches, apricots, kiwis etc.

52 **Slices** *Tranches*

There are three ways of making a tranche:

a) The tranche mould can be lined the same as for a flan ring, the ingredients and methods for flans can be used.

b) Roll out short paste to ½ cm (¼ in.) thick and cut a strip the length of the baking sheet and 10 cm (4 in.) wide. Place on a greased baking sheet and dock. Egg wash both sides. Prepare 2 strips of puff paste ½ cm (¼ in.) thick and 1 cm (½ in.) wide. Place on the eggwashed sides. Notch along the edges with the back of a small knife and egg wash. Cook at approx. 220°C (425°F, Reg. 7) for approx. 20 mins. When cold spread centre with crème Chantilly or pastry cream. Arrange suitable fruits neatly on this e.g. strawberries, raspberries, grapes, bananas, kiwi or poached or tinned fruits. Glaze with a suitable glaze and decorate sides with crème Chantilly.

c) Roll out sweet paste ½ cm (¼ in.) thick and cut into a strip 12 cm (5 in.) wide and the length of a baking sheet. Place onto a greased baking sheet and egg wash the edges. Turn the edges in by 1 cm (½ in.), thumb up and decorate with pastry pincers. Cook at approx. 200°C (400°F, Reg. 6) for 15–20 mins.

53 **Parisian slice** *Tranche parisienne*

This is a mixed fruit slice, using method (b).

54 **Almond slice** *Tranche amande*

1 Prepare a slice using methods (c) or (a), but do not cook.
2 Spread the centre with raspberry jam.
3 Pipe frangipane (page 283) over the jam.
4 Sprinkle with flaked or filleted almonds.
5 Cook at approx. 200°C (400°F, Reg. 6) for about 20–25 mins.
6 Brush with hot apricot glaze and lemon water icing.

55 **Belgian slice**

1 Prepare a slice using method (a).
2 Spread the bottom with raspberry jam.
3 Two-thirds fill with frangipane (page 283).
4 Decorate with a trellis of thin strips of sweet paste and egg wash.
5 Cook at approx 200°C (400°F, Reg. 6) for 20–25 mins.
6 Brush with apricot glaze and lemon water icing.
7 Replace in oven for 30 seconds to set the glaze.

56   Viennese slice

200 g	8 oz	cooking apples	⎫
50 g	2 oz	mixed fruit	⎬ filling
25 g	1 oz	brown sugar	
		mixed spice and apricot jam to bind	⎭

1 Prepare a slice using method (a).
2 Prepare the filling by peeling, coring and dicing the apple (¼ cm, ⅛ in., dice) and mixing with the remainder of the ingredients.
3 Place the filling down the centre of the slice.
4 Decorate with a trellis of sweet paste and egg wash.
5 Cook at approx. 225°C (425°F, Reg. 7) about 15–20 mins.
6 Dust with icing sugar and glaze under a salamander.

Yeast goods

57   Brioche   *yield approx. 20*

125 ml	¼ pt	milk
25 g	1 oz	yeast
450 g	1 lb 2 oz	strong flour
25 g	1 oz	castor sugar
		pinch of salt
50 g	2 oz	butter or margarine
		4 eggs
2 g	1 dram	malt extract
		zest of lemon
150 g	6 oz	butter or margarine, softened

1 Warm the milk to 26°C (80°F), disperse the yeast in the milk, add a little flour and all of the sugar. Sprinkle a little flour on the surface.
2 Stand in a basin of warm water covered with a damp cloth for 15 mins to ferment.
3 Take the rest of the flour, salt and 50 g (2 oz) of butter or margarine, rub together well.
4 Make a well and add the eggs, malt, lemon zest and the ferment, when it has broken through the surface flour.
5 Mix to a smooth dough.
6 Place on a machine with a dough hook and add 150 g (6 oz) of softened butter or margarine on low speed.
7 When all the butter or margarine has been incorporated, turn out of the bowl, cover with a damp cloth and allow to prove in a warm place for approx. 1 hour.
8 Knock back the dough and place it in the refrigerator until ready for use.
9 Divide into approx. 50 g (2 oz) pieces, mould into brioche shape (i.e. small cottage loaf shapes) and place into deep individual fluted moulds which have been well greased.

10 Egg wash, prove and bake at approx. 230°C (450°F, Reg. 8) for approx. 10 mins.

58   Croissants

yield approx. 20-24

600 g	1 lb 8 oz	bread flour
100 g	4 oz	butter or margarine
125 ml	¼ pt	milk
125 ml	¼ pt	water
60 g	1½ oz	yeast
125 ml	¼ pt	egg
60 g	1½ oz	castor sugar
10 g	½ oz	salt
200 g	8 oz	butter, margarine or pastry margarine

1 Sieve the flour into a suitable basin and rub in the 100 g (4 oz) butter or margarine.
2 Warm the milk and water to 32°C (90°F) and disperse the yeast in the milk and water. Add to the flour and fat.
3 Blend in all the rest of the ingredients except the 200 g (8 oz) fat. Mix lightly but do not develop or toughen up the dough.
4 Rest for 10 mins. Keep covered with a damp cloth or polythene in order to prevent skinning.
5 Roll into the dough, as in making of puff pastry, the 200 g (8 oz) fat and give the dough 4 single turns, resting for 15–20 mins between turns.
6 When the fat is incorporated, roll out dough to about ½ cm (¼ in.) thick and 22 cm (9 in.) wide.
7 Cut down the middle of the dough lengthways. Place one strip on another and cut into triangles approx. 10 cm (4 in.) wide.
8 Roll each triangle up from the widest end, pulling and stretching into a crescent.
9 Egg wash and prove in a little steam for 15 mins. Then bake at approx. 230°C (450°F, Reg. 8) for 20–25 mins.

Note Double baking sheets may be required if the oven gives out a fierce bottom heat.

59   Danish pastry dough

yield approx. 10-12

300 g	12 oz	medium strength flour
3 g	⅛ oz	salt
35 g	1½ oz	margarine
100 g	4 oz	milk
30 g	1¼ oz	yeast
75 g	3 oz	egg
25 g	1 oz	castor sugar
200 g	8 oz	butter, margarine or pastry margarine

1 Sieve the flour and salt, rub in the 35 g (1½ oz) margarine.
2 Warm the milk to 26°C (80°F) and disperse the yeast in the milk. Add this to the flour.
3 Add the egg and sugar to make into a slack dough. Do *not* toughen by over-working.
4 Fold into the dough 200 g (8 oz) fat, giving it 2 single turns and 1 double turn. Rest for 10 mins between turns.
5 Work the pieces into desired shapes and egg wash. Prove in a little steam and bake as indicated in the following recipes.

Note Double baking sheets may be required if the oven gives out a fierce bottom heat.

60 Danish pastries with almond fruit filling 10–12 pastries

125 g	5 oz	raw marzipan		
25 g	1 oz	egg		
35 g	1½ oz	melted butter		
35 g	1½ oz	chopped apple		
50 g	2 oz	cake crumbs	}	almond fruit filling
50 g	2 oz	water		
30 g	1½ oz	glacé cherries		
30 g	1½ oz	currants		
30 g	1½ oz	sultanas		
		zest and juice of ½ orange		

1 Soften marzipan with egg and melted butter to a smooth paste.
2 Add all remaining ingredients and mix well.

Triangles
Roll out the dough ½ cm (¼ in.) thick, cut into 8 cm (3 in.) squares and place a small amount of almond fruit filling into the centre. Fold over, egg wash. Prove at 29–32°C (85–90°F) without steam. Bake at approx. 220°C (425°F, Reg. 7) for approx. 10 mins. Mask with hot apricot jam and lemon water icing, sprinkle with roasted flaked almonds.

Round buns
Roll out the dough into an oblong ½ cm (¼ in.) thick. Spread the surface thinly with almond fruit filling. Roll up as for swiss roll and cut into 1 cm (½ in.) pieces. Place on a lightly greased baking sheet with the cut side up, prove at 29–32°C (85–90°F) without steam. Bake at approx. 220°C (425°F, Reg. 7). Mask with hot apricot jam and water icing, sprinkle with roasted flaked almonds.

Crescents
Roll out dough ¼ cm (⅛ in.) thick and cut into 8 cm (3 in.) squares. Pipe almond fruit filling in the centre. Egg wash, fold over and press down.

Cut the edge with a knife, making incisions right through, approx. 1 cm (½ in.) apart. Prove at 29–32°C (85–90°F) without steam. Bake at approx. 220°C (425°F, Reg. 7).

61   Danish pastries with custard filling   *10–12 pastries*

500 ml	1 pt	milk
50 g	2 oz	eggs
60 g	2½ oz	castor sugar
40 g	1¾ oz	cornflour
		colour and flavour as desired

1 Boil the milk in a suitable saucepan.
2 Mix the eggs, sugar and cornflour together to a smooth paste.
3 When milk is boiling, add half to the egg, sugar and cornflour, mix well to a smooth consistency.
4 Return to the rest of the milk, bring back to the boil and add flavour and colour as desired.

Maultaschen
1 Roll out the dough ½ cm (¼ in.) thick and cut into 10 cm (4 in.) squares.
2 Egg wash and pipe in the centre of each a little lemon-flavoured custard filling (recipe above plus zest and juice of 1 lemon).
3 Bring the four corners to the centre, seal lightly, egg wash and place on a greased baking sheet.
4 Roll a strip of dough ¼ cm (⅛ in.) thick and cut 8 cm (3 in.) strips.
5 Press two strips on to each pastry, crosswise (these will help to retain the shape during cooking and proving).
6 Prove and cook at approx. 200–220°C (400–425°F, Reg. 6–7) for about 20 mins.
7 Brush with hot apricot glaze and warm thin fondant.

Croquante rolls
1 Roll out the dough as for Chelsea buns and egg wash the sides.
2 Spread with cold custard filling and sprinkle generously with fine croquante (see below).
3 Roll up and cut as for Chelsea buns, arrange in rows in a 2 cm (1 in.) deep tin. Egg wash the tops and prove.
4 Cook at approx. 200–220°C (400–425°F, Reg. 6–7) for approx. 20 mins.
5 Brush tops with hot apricot glaze and sprinkle with coarse croquante (see below).

Croquante
200 g	8 oz	granulated sugar
		juice of lemon *or* pinch of cream of tartar
150 g	6 oz	nibbed almonds

1 Place sugar and lemon juice or cream of tartar in a suitable pan and stir over a gentle heat until all the sugar has melted.
2 Cook until of a pale amber colour.
3 Warm the almonds, stir into the sugar and remove from the heat.
4 Turn out onto an oiled tray and allow to cool.
5 When set, crush into a fine powder with a rolling pin. Pass through a sieve to remove any large particles and crush and sieve these.

Envelopes
1 Roll out the dough ½ cm (¼ in.) thick and cut into 10 cm (4 in.) squares, and lightly egg wash.
2 Bring 2 opposite corners to the centre and seal.
3 Lay the pastries on a greased baking sheet, egg wash and prove.
4 Pipe custard filling in the 2 open ends and egg wash again.
5 Cook at approx. 200–220°C (400–425°F, Reg. 6–7) for approx. 20 mins and brush with hot apricot glaze.

Fruit rings
1 After giving the dough a second turn, sprinkle with washed chopped fruit then give the final turn. Relax.
2 Roll out ½ cm (¼ in.) thick, in a strip approx. 24 cm (10 in.) wide.
3 Cut into 2 cm (1 in.) wide pieces.
4 Twist each strip fairly tightly then form into a ring.
5 Lay onto a greased baking sheet, egg wash and prove.
6 Fill the centres with custard filling, sprinkle on a few split almonds and cook at approx. 200–220°C (400–425°F, Reg. 6–7) for approx. 20 mins and brush with hot apricot glaze.

Hazelnut custards
1 Roll out the dough ½ cm (¼ in) thick and cut into 7 cm (3 in.) strips.
2 Lay one strip on a greased baking sheet and egg wash the edges.
3 Spread with custard filling, cover with a strip of dough and egg wash.
4 Sprinkle well with chopped roasted hazelnuts, cover with a third strip of dough, seal and cut into portions. (Do not separate the pieces at this stage.)
5 Egg wash, prove and cook at approx. 200–220°C (400–425°F, Reg. 6–7) for. approx 20 mins.
6 Brush with hot apricot glaze and warm thin fondant then divide into portions.

62 Burgomeister rolls

1 Roll out the paste ½ cm (¼ in.) thick in a large rectangle.
2 Cut out as for croissants, making the triangles longer and narrower at the bases.
3 Egg wash lightly and pipe in the centre a little burgomeistermasse (see page 294).

4 Roll up the pastries from the base to the point and lay on a greased baking sheet. Do not curve them.
5 Egg wash, prove and cook at approx. 200–220°C (400–425°F, Reg. 6–7) for approx. 20 mins.
6 Brush with hot apricot glaze and warm thin fondant.

Burgomeistermasse

150 g	6 oz	castor sugar	
350 g	14 oz	butter or margarine	mix all ingredients but do not aerate
400 g	1 lb	raw marzipan	

63 Schnecken

1 Roll out dough ½ cm (¼ in.) thick in a large rectangle and egg wash the edges.
2 Spread with "copenhagenmasse" (see below) and roll up tightly.
3 Lightly egg wash the outside and roll in maw seeds.
4 Cut into individual pieces and lay them on a greased baking sheet with the closing of the seam underneath. (This will help keep them in shape.)
5 Egg wash, prove and cook at approx. 200–220°C (400–425°F, Reg. 6–7) for approx. 20 mins, then brush with hot apricot glaze.

Copenhagenmasse

300 g	12 oz	granulated sugar	
300 g	12 oz	butter or margarine	mix all ingredients together, rub down well
200 g	8 oz	raw marzipan	
50 g	2 oz	nibbed almonds	

Sweetmeats (petits fours) and biscuits
64 Cherry rolls   *yield approx. 40 pieces*

300 g	12 oz	soft flour
200 g	8 oz	butter or margarine
		natural vanilla essence or pod
100 g	4 oz	glacé cherries (chopped)
35 g	1½ oz	icing sugar

1 Sift the flour, cream the butter and icing sugar, add the flour and vanilla and mix lightly.
2 Fraiser* the paste and add the chopped glacé cherries.
3 Roll into a sausage shape, 2 cm (1 in.) diameter, and place into the refrigerator to harden.
4 When firm, cut into rounds 1½ cm (¾ in.) thick.
5 Place on to a lightly greased baking sheet and bake at approx. 200°C (400°F, Reg. 6) for 10–12 mins.

Fraiser means to rub or scrape down, using either a palette knife or the heel of the hand.

65 Chocolate caramel

yield: approx. 50–60 pieces

150 g	6 oz	glucose
200 g	8 oz	castor sugar
100 g	4 oz	plain chocolate
250 ml	½ pt	single cream

1 Boil together the glucose, sugar and chocolate with half the cream to 118°C (245°F).
2 Once this temperature has been reached add the remaining cream and bring back to 118°C (245°F).
3 Pour onto an oiled marble slab or onto a suitable oiled tray and cut into pieces while still warm.
4 Place into paper cases.

66 Chocolate fudge

yield: approx. 60–70 pieces

200 g	8 oz	granulated sugar ⎫
75 g	3 oz	glucose ⎬ syrup
60 ml	⅛ pt	water ⎭
25 g	1 oz	evaporated milk
200 g	8 oz	fondant
30 g	1¼ oz	butter, melted
250 g	10 oz	plain chocolate, melted
		vanilla essence

1 Place the granulated sugar, glucose and water into a thick-based bottomed pan, place on the stove and cook to 115°C (240°F).
2 Add the evaporated milk and again cook to 115°C (240°F).
3 Place into a machine bowl the fondant, melted butter and melted chocolate. Add a few drops of vanilla essence and mix for 1 min at low speed.
4 Add the sugar syrup at 115°C (240°F) and mix well.
5 Place onto a suitable lightly oiled tray and allow to set.
6 When set, cut into pieces and place into paper cases.

67 Coconut biscuits

yield: approx. 40

250 g	10 oz	butter or margarine
375 g	14 oz	castor sugar
		2 eggs
375 g	14 oz	soft flour
250 g	10 oz	desiccated coconut

1 Cream together the fat and sugar.
2 Add the eggs, one at a time, beating well between additions.

3 Sieve the flour and it and the coconut into the butter and sugar, mixing to form a dough.
4 Roll out to ½ cm (¼ in.) thick and cut out rounds using a small plain or fancy cutter, 2 cm (1 in.) diameter.
5 Place on a lightly greased baking sheet and bake at approx. 150°C (275°F, Reg. 2) for approx. 15 mins, until a light biscuit colour.

68   Coconut macaroons   *yield: approx. 30–40 pieces*

250 ml	½ pt	egg whites
75 g	3 oz	ground rice or semolina
625 g	1 lb 10 oz	granulated sugar
150 g	6 oz	fine coconut
150 g	6 oz	coarse coconut

1 Mix in a basin the egg whites, ground rice or semolina and the granulated sugar.
2 Add the fine and coarse coconut and mix well.
3 Heat over a bain marie of warm water to 48°C (120°F).
4 Place into a forcing bag with a 1 cm (½ in.) plain tube and pipe onto a baking sheet on rice paper to the required size, approx. 2 cm (1 in.) diameter.
5 Place half a glacé cherry on each one and bake at 180°C (350°F, Reg. 4) for approx. 15 mins.

69   Florentines   *yield: 70–80 pieces*

200 g	8 oz	butter
200 g	8 oz	castor sugar
50 g	2 oz	fresh cream
50 g	2 oz	chopped cherries
100 g	4 oz	cut mixed peel
75 g	3 oz	sultanas
200 g	8 oz	nibbed almonds
200 g	8 oz	flaked almonds
25 g	1 oz	soft flour
		chocolate couverture or baker's chocolate

1 Place the butter, sugar and cream in a saucepan and bring to the boil to 115°C (240°F).
2 Remove from heat and add all the remaining ingredients, except the chocolate. Allow to cool.
3 Prepare baking sheets, lined with silicone paper.
4 Spoon the mixture onto the lined baking sheets into rounds approx. 10 g (½ oz) in weight, not too close together.
5 Bake at approx. 200°C (400°F, Reg. 6) for 10–12 mins.

6 When cooked the florentines will spread over the baking sheet, bring back to form a neat round with a plain cutter as soon as they are removed from the oven.
7 Remove from baking sheets and allow to cool.
8 Coat the backs of each florentine with couverture or baker's chocolate and mark with a comb scraper.

70 Marshmallows

yield: approx. 50 pieces

600 g	1 lb 8 oz	granulated or cube sugar
		3 egg whites
35 g	1½ oz	leaf gelatine, soaked in cold water

1 Place sugar in a suitable saucepan with 125 ml (¼ pt) water and boil to soft ball stage 140°C (245°F).
2 When sugar is nearly ready whisk egg whites to a firm peak.
3 Pour in boiling sugar and continue to whisk.
4 Squeeze the water from the gelatine and add.
5 Add colour and flavour if desired.
6 Turn out onto a tray dusted with cornflour and dust with more cornflour.
7 Cut into sections and roll in a mixture of icing sugar and cornflour.

71 Nougat Montelimar

yield: 50–60 pieces

350 g	14 oz	granulated sugar
100 g	4 oz	water
100 g	4 oz	honey
100 g	4 oz	glucose
35 g	1½ oz	egg white
50 g	2 oz	glacé cherries
50 g	2 oz	pistachio nuts
25 g	1 oz	nibbed almonds
25 g	1 oz	flaked almonds or flaked hazelnuts

1 Place the sugar and water into a suitable pan, bring to the boil and cook to 107°C (225°F).
2 When the temperature has been reached, add the honey and glucose and cook to 137°C (280°F).
3 Meanwhile whisk the egg whites to full peak in a machine, then add the syrup at 137°C (280°F) slowly, while whisking on full speed.
4 Reduce speed, add the glacé cherries cut into quarters, chopped pistachio nuts, and the nibbed and flaked almonds.
5 Turn out onto a lightly oiled tray and mark into pieces while still warm.
6 When cold cut into pieces and place into paper cases to serve.

72   Piped ganache

yield: approx. 20–30 pieces

125 ml	¼ pt	single cream
225 g	9 oz	chocolate couverture, cut into pieces
		rum, to flavour

1 Bring the cream to the boil, remove from the stove and add the couverture.
2 Flavour with rum.
3 Stir to a piping consistency over a bain-marie of cold water.
4 Using a piping bag and ½ cm (¼ in) tube pipe ganache into small paper cases and decorate with crystallized violets or mimosa.

73   Turkish delight

yield: approx. 60–70 pieces

600 g	1 lb 8 oz	granulated or cube sugar
200 g	8 oz	glucose
		zest and juice of 4 lemons
750 ml	1 ¾ pt	water
		sherry or rose water (optional)
150 g	6 oz	cornflour

1 Boil together the sugar, glucose, lemon zest and juice with 625 ml (1¼ pt) water in a suitable saucepan.
2 Flavour with sherry or rose water.
3 Thicken with the cornflour diluted with 250 ml (½ pt) water.
4 Pour into shallow trays and allow to set, then cut into sections and roll in cornflour.

74   Truffles

yield: approx. 30

125 ml	¼ pt	single cream
225 g	9 oz	couverture, cut in small pieces
		rum to taste

1 Bring the cream to the boil, then remove from heat and stir in the couverture.
2 Flavour with rum and allow to set in a refrigerator.
3 Turn out onto a tray and dust with icing sugar.
4 Form into rolls, 1½ cm (¾ in) in diameter and cut into sections.
5 Roll onto a mixture of icing sugar and cocoa powder, or grated couverture, and place into paper cases.

75   Snowballs
yield: approx. 30–35

		4 egg whites
200 g	8 oz	castor sugar
200 g	8 oz	ground almonds
100 g	4 oz	nibbed almonds
50 g	2 oz	apricot jam
50 g	2 oz	icing sugar

1 Whisk egg whites to full peak.
2 Add approx 100 g (4 oz) castor sugar and whisk to a meringue.
3 Carefully fold in the rest of the castor sugar with the ground almonds into the meringue.
4 Prepare lightly greased and floured baking sheets, or baking sheets lined with silicone paper, and pipe the mixture into bulbs, with a forcing bag and ½ cm (¼ in.) plain tube.
5 Sprinkle with nibbed almonds and dredge lightly with icing sugar.
6 Bake at approx. 140°C (250°F, Reg. 1) for approx. 30 mins.
7 Remove from baking sheets, stick together in pairs with hot apricot jam and dredge lightly with icing sugar.

76   Viennese biscuits
yield: approx. 40

350 g	14 oz	butter or margarine
350 g	14 oz	castor sugar
		2 eggs
		2 drops natural vanilla essence
450 g	1 lb 2 oz	soft flour
		melted chocolate, to finish

1 Cream the butter and sugar in a basin until white and light.
2 Add the eggs, one at a time, and cream well.
3 Add the vanilla essence and then the flour carefully, by gradually incorporating into the butter, sugar and egg mixture.
4 Pipe onto lightly greased baking sheets, using a 1 cm (½ in.) star tube.
5 Allow to stand for 2 hours or longer if possible.
6 Cook at approx. 200°C (400°F, Reg 6) for approx. 15 mins and allow to cool.
7 To finish, dip the points into melted chocolate.

Miscellaneous

77   Sponge fingers   *Biscuits à la cuillère*
yield: approx. 32

		4 eggs, separated
100 g	4 oz	castor sugar
100 g	4 oz	flour

1 Cream the egg yolks and sugar in a bowl until creamy and almost white.
2 Whip the egg whites stiffly.
3 Add a little of the whites to the mixture and cut in.
4 Gradually add the sieved flour and remainder of the whites alternately, mixing as lightly as possible.
5 Place in a piping bag with 1 cm (½ in.) plain tube and pipe in 8 cm (3 in.) lengths on to baking sheets lined with greaseproof or silicone paper.
6 Sprinkle liberally with icing sugar. Rest for 15 min.
7 Bake in a moderately hot oven (approx. 200°–220°C, 425°–450°F, Reg. 6–7) approx. 10 min.
8 Remove from the oven, lift the paper on which the biscuits are piped and place upside down on the table.
9 Sprinkle liberally with water. This will assist the removal of the biscuits from the paper. (No water is needed if using silicone paper.)

78 Chocolate fudge sauce approx. 10–12 portions

250 ml	½ pt	water
60 ml	⅛ pt	golden syrup
150 g	6 oz	dark brown sugar
50 g	2 oz	granulated sugar
200 g	8 oz	dark cooking chocolate
350 g	14 oz	condensed milk
175 g	7 oz	evaporated milk
		vanilla essence

1 Place water in a suitable saucepan, add golden syrup, brown and white sugar, bring to boil and simmer for 3 mins.
2 Melt the chocolate carefully in a basin over a bain-marie of hot water.
3 Add the chocolate to the sugar and water mix. *Do not boil.*
4 Heat the condensed and evaporated milk gently in a saucepan over a low heat; when warmed to simmering point add to the chocolate mixture.
5 Finish with vanilla essence.

79 Cornets

150 g	6 oz	icing sugar
100 g	4 oz	butter
		natural vanilla essence
		4 egg whites
100 g	4 oz	soft flour

1 Lightly cream sugar and butter, add 3–4 drops of vanilla.
2 Add egg whites one by one mixing continuously, taking care not to allow the mixture to curdle.

3 Gently fold in the sifted flour and mix lightly.
4 Using a 3 mm (⅛ in.) plain tube, pipe out the mixture onto a lightly greased baking sheet into rounds approx. 2½ cm (1¼ in.) in diameter.
5 Bake in a hot oven (approx. 230°–250°C, 450°–500°F, Reg. 8–9) until the edges turn brown and the centre remains uncoloured.
6 Remove the tray from the oven.
7 Work quickly while the cornets are hot and twist them into a cornet shape using the point of a cream horn mould. (For a tight cornet shape it will be found best to set the pieces tightly inside the cream horn moulds and to leave them until set.)

80 Brandy snaps   *yield: approx. 10*

75 g	3 oz	margarine or butter
200 g	8 oz	castor sugar
200 g	8 oz	golden syrup
100 g	4 oz	plain flour
6 g	¼ oz	ground ginger

1 Cream the margarine and sugar until light and fluffy.
2 Add the golden syrup and cream well.
3 Gradually fold in the sieved flour and ground ginger.
4 Place mixture into a piping bag with a ½ cm (¼ in.) plain tube.
5 Pipe on to a silicone lined baking sheet into 1 cm (½ in.) diameter rounds.
6 Bake in a hot oven (approx. 220°C, 425°F, Reg. 7) for approx. 5 mins until golden brown on the edges.
7 Allow to cool until slightly firm. Roll round a suitable wooden rod and allow to cool until crisp.
8 Remove from rod and use as required.

Uses Brandy snaps can be offered as petits fours and pastries. The mixture can be shaped as required, e.g. tartlets, barquettes, and can be used as containers for sweets, e.g. filled with lemon syllabub, raspberries and cream etc.

81 Frangipane   *Crème frangipane*   *yield: 600 g–1 lb 8 oz approx.*

250 ml	½ pt	milk
		natural vanilla essence or pod (see p. 265)
		2 eggs
100 g	4 oz	castor sugar or brown sugar
25 g	1 oz	strong or wholemeal flour
100 g	4 oz	butter or margarine
100 g	4 oz	ground almonds
		1 tablespn rum

1 Boil the milk and vanilla in a saucepan.
2 In a basin, mix together the eggs, sugar and flour, whisk on the boiling milk, return to the boil, then allow to cool.
3 Cream the butter or margarine and mix in with the pastry cream, ground almonds and rum. Use as required – for filling gâteaux, hot sweets etc.

82 Praline

Praline is a basic preparation used for flavouring items such as gâteaux, soufflés, ice-creams and many other sweets.

100 g	4 oz	almonds } peeled
100 g	4 oz	hazelnuts }
60 ml	⅛ pt	water
200 g	8 oz	sugar

1 Lightly brown the almonds and hazelnuts in an oven.
2 Cook the water and sugar in a copper or thick-bottomed pan until the caramel stage is reached.
3 Remove the pan from the heat and mix in the nuts.
4 Turn out the mixture on to a lightly oiled marble slab.
5 Allow to become quite cold.
6 Crush to a coarse texture using a rolling pin and store in an airtight container.

83 Italian meringue *Meringue italienne*

200 g	8 oz	granulated sugar or cube sugar
60 ml	⅛ pt	water
		pinch of cream of tartar
		4 egg whites

1 Boil the sugar, water and cream of tartar to hard ball stage (121°C).
2 Beat the egg whites to full peak and while stiff, beating slowly, pour in the boiling sugar.
3 Use as required for fillings, covering certain gâteaux, tartlets etc.

84 Swiss meringue *Meringue suisse*

		4 egg whites
200 g	8 oz	icing sugar

1 Place the ingredients into a suitable bowl in a bain-marie and beat to ribbon stage.

2 When it stands its own weight, use as required for vacherins, petit fours and nests.

85 Spun sugar

1 Place 125 ml (¼ pt) water in a sugar boiler and add 400 g (1 lb) granulated sugar or lump sugar. Place on the stove and bring to the boil slowly.
2 When all the sugar crystals have melted, well wash round the sides.
3 The sugar solution should not boil until all the crystals have melted.
4 Then boil rapidly to 155°–158°C (312°–315°F) or hard crack stage.
5 Have ready 2 very clean broom sticks, lightly oiled, and hold over the edge of a table 2 cm (1 in.) apart. A baking sheet over the sticks will keep them in place.
6 When the sugar is ready, place the sugar boiler for a few seconds in iced water to stop the cooking. If the sugar has to be coloured, add colour now, do not stir in, but just tilt the sugar boiler to and fro.
7 Dip the sugar thrower in the sugar and allow excess sugar to fall off.
8 Swing over the sticks, the sugar will form fine threads.
9 When the spun sugar is thick enough, remove from sticks. Continue until all the sugar has been used.
10 To make a dome, line a coupe with the spun sugar, cut off excess sugar and remove from coupe.
11 Keep in a dry place, free from damp, moisture or steam.

Note Care should be taken when weighing the sugar to see that there is no flour or fat on scale pan. Spun sugar will not stay dry very long in damp weather, so it should not be prepared until the last possible moment.
   As an alternative to a sugar thrower, a sawn-off whisk or two forks may be used.

Glossary

A blanc	To keep white, without colour
A brun	To colour brown
Agnolini	Half-moon shaped pasta filled with ham, cheese or minced beef
Aiguillettes	Small strips of cooked meat, poultry or fish
Al dente	Pasta or vegetables slightly underdone so that there is some resistence to the bite
Attereaux	Cooked small pieces of food (meat, fish or vegetables) coated with a thick sauce, crumbed and deep fried
Ballottine	Boned stuffed leg of poultry
Bamboo shoots	The inner shoots of the bamboo plant, used extensively in Chinese cooking
Beurre blanc	Sauce of finely chopped shallots, white wine and melted butter
Blanc de volaille	White flesh of poultry, breast or wing (or suprême)
Baklava	Very sweet Greek pastry with nuts
Bitok	A type of hamburger
Brioche	Yeast dough, enriched with eggs
Burghul	Cracked wheat used in Middle Eastern cookery
Calvados	Apple brandy from Normandy
Cappelletti	Hat-shaped pasta, filled with ham, cheese or meat
Cassolettes	Individual dishes, ramekins in which foods are cooked or served
Ceps	(Cepes Fr) an edible mushroom
Cerviche	Fish marinaded in lime and lemon juice, of Spanish Peruvian origin
Chanterelle	Small yellow mushroom with a frilly edge
Chantilly cream	Whipped cream, flavoured with vanilla and sweetened
Chapati	Crisp wholemeal pancake
Chilli con carne	Hot Mexican beef and bean stew
Chop suey	A dish of Chinese/American origin
Chow mein	A Chinese dish
Chowder	Unpassed shellfish or sweetcorn soup from USA
Clafoutis	Fruit baked in batter

Colcannon	Irish dish containing cabbage and potato
Coulibiac	Russian fish pie
Coulis (Fr) Cullis (Eng)	A purée in liquid form, e.g. tomato, raspberry, used as a sauce
Couscous	Arabic dish made using a fine type of semolina
Craquelins	Small, filled, pancakes crumbed and deep fried
Crepinette	Thin pig's caul (membrane)
Croustarde	Baked pastry cases in or on which cooked foods are served
Cru	Raw, not cooked, or from the raw state, e.g. pommes sautées à crue
Crudités	Raw vegetables cut in bite-size pieces e.g. celery, carrot etc.
Curaçao	Liqueur made from bitter oranges. Originally from the West Indies
Dahl	Indian dish using lentils
Demi-glace	Refined brown sauce
Dock	Pierce pastry with numerous small holes
Dolcelatte	Italian blue cheese
Dolmades	Stuffed vine leaves
Drambuie	Whisky-based liqueur flavoured with honey and herbs
Dulse	Edible red seaweed
Dutch binje	A particular kind of potato
Duxelle	Chopped shallot and chopped mushrooms cooked together
En-croûte	Wrapped in pastry
En papillote	Oiled greaseproof paper or foil in which raw food is cooked in the oven
Filo paste	Very thin paste of Greek origin, usually purchased prepared
Fraiser	The action of scraping sweet paste to make smooth and to mix before use
Fricadelles	Chopped raw or cooked veal or beef steaks like hamburgers
Fritots	Savoury fritters of meat, fish or vegetables, battered and deep fried
Forcemeat	Savoury stuffings of meat or poultry
Fromage blanc	Fat-free, skimmed milk fresh cheese
Fruits de mer	Seafoods: shellfish, crustaceans and molluscs
Fumet	Concentrated essence of fish, meat or poultry
Galette	Small flat cake e.g. sweetcorn, potato
Ganache	Rich chocolate cream filling for gâteaux or petits fours
Garam masala	A mixture of spices
Gazpacho	Spanish cold soup of cucumber, tomato and garlic

Ghee	Clarified butter, used in Indian cooking
Gravlax	Swedish dish of raw salmon, marinaded with dill
Grenadins	Small thick larded slices of veal which are pot roasted
Haunch	E.g. of venison, the leg and rump (hip, buttock and thigh)
Hummus	Paste of chick peas and sesame seeds
Infuse	To extract flavour and aroma by covering an ingredient with liquid and allowing it to stand
Jus-lié	Thickened gravy made from veal stock
Kirsch	Distilled white spirit made from wild cherries, mainly from France and Switzerland
Liaison	A thickening of yolks and cream used to finish certain soups and sauces
Magret	Type of duck, menu term to describe breast of duck
Mange-tout	Type of pea (sugar pea), the pod of which is also eaten
Maw seeds	Type of seed similar to poppy seeds
Monté au beurre	The adding of small pieces of butter to thicken a reduced cooking liquid to make a sauce
Morels	Type of edible fungi, brown, irregular and cone shape
Mozzarella	Cheese originally made from the milk of water buffalo
Okra	Type of vegetable, also known as gumbo and ladies fingers
Oyster mushrooms	Ear-shaped, grey or greenish-brown wild mushroom
Paella	Spanish dish of rice with chicken, shellfish, herbs, etc.
Panada or panade	Thick base mixture, e.g. choux paste before eggs are added
Paw-paw	Tropical fruit
Pecorino	Ewe's milk cheese with peppercorns
Perdrix	Older pheasant suitable for braising
Pimentos	Green, red or yellow coloured vegetables, also known as peppers
Pitta bread	Type of Middle Eastern unleavened bread
Physallis	Cape gooseberry used for petits four
Plain russe	Mixture of milk, egg yolks and sugar, set with gelatine and cornflour

Pluche	Small spray, e.g. of chervil, used as a garnish
Praline	Sugar and nuts cooked to hard boil stage. Crushed and used for gâteaux and ice-cream
Quenelles	'Dumplings' of fish, poultry or game. Made by finely mincing the flesh, beating in egg white and cream and poaching
Quark	Salt-free soft cheese, made from semi-skimmed milk
Râble	Saddle, e.g. of hare, râble de lièvre
Rack of lamb	Best-end of lamb
Radicchio	A red-leaved type of lettuce
Ramekins	Small dishes for serving individual portions of food
Ravolini	Pasta, half the size of ravioli
Ricotta	Cheese made from the discarded whey of other cheeses
Saffron	Stamens from a species of crocus used for flavour and yellow colour
Sake	Japanese wine made from rice
Salmis	A brown stew of game
Sauternes	Sweet white wine from Bordeaux region of France
Scorzonera	Type of vegetable, also known as oyster plant
Sec	Dry, not sweet
Silicone paper	Paper to which foods do not stick
Socle	A base of rice, wax or ice on which to place cold buffet items
Sweet potato	Potato with a chestnut flavour
Tahini	Paste of sesame seed
Taramasalata	Greek dish made of cod's roe with garlic
Tofu	Soya bean curd
Tortellini	Pasta of hat shape, larger than cappelletti
Tortillas	Type of unleavened bread served with Mexican dishes
Tranche	A slice
Ve-tsin	Chinese flavouring with a monosodium glutamate base
Vesiga	The marrow of the spinal column of the sturgeon
Water chestnuts	A white, crunchy, sweet root vegetable, about the size of a walnut
Yam	Type of vegetable
Yoghurt	An easily digested fermented milk product

Index of dishes in French

Index